The Developmental Psychology
of Time

DEVELOPMENTAL PSYCHOLOGY SERIES

SERIES EDITOR
Harry Beilin

Developmental Psychology Program
City University of New York Graduate School
New York, New York

LYNN S. LIBEN. *Deaf Children: Developmental Perspectives*

JONAS LANGER. *The Origins of Logic: Six to Twelve Months*

GILBERTE PIERAUT-LE BONNIEC. *The Development of Modal Reasoning: Genesis of Necessity and Possibility Notions*

TIFFANY MARTINI FIELD, SUSAN GOLDBERG, DANIEL STERN, and ANITA MILLER SOSTEK. (Editors). *High-Risk Infants and Children: Adult and Peer Interactions*

BARRY GHOLSON. *The Cognitive-Developmental Basis of Human Learning: Studies in Hypothesis Testing*

ROBERT L. SELMAN. *The Growth of Interpersonal Understanding: Developmental and Clinical Analyses*

RAINER H. KLUWE and HANS SPADA. (Editors). *Developmental Models of Thinking*

HARBEN BOUTOURLINE YOUNG and LUCY RAU FERGUSON. *Puberty to Manhood in Italy and America*

SARAH L. FRIEDMAN and MARIAN SIGMAN. (Editors). *Preterm Birth and Psychological Development*
LYNN S. LIBEN, ARTHUR H. PATTERSON, and NORA NEWCOMBE. (Editors). *Spatial Representation and Behavior Across the Life Span: Theory and Application*

W. PATRICK DICKSON. (Editor). *Children's Oral Communication Skills*

EUGENE S. GOLLIN. (Editor). *Developmental Plasticity: Behavioral and Biological Aspects of Variations in Development*

GEORGE E. FORMAN. (Editor). *Action and Thought: From Sensorimotor Schemes to Symbolic Operations*

SIDNEY STRAUSS. (Editor). *U-Shaped Behavioral Growth*

WILLIAM J. FRIEDMAN. (Editor). *The Developmental Psychology of Time*

In Preparation

NANCY EISENBERG. (Editor). *The Development of Prosocial Behavior*

MICHAEL POTEGAL. (Editor). *Spatial Abilities: Development and Physiological Foundations*

The Developmental Psychology of Time

EDITED BY

William J. Friedman

Department of Psychology
Oberlin College
Oberlin, Ohio

1982

ACADEMIC PRESS

A Subsidiary of Harcourt Brace Jovanovich, Publishers

New York   London

Paris   San Diego   San Francisco   São Paulo   Sydney   Tokyo   Toronto

ACADEMIC PRESS, INC.
111 Fifth Avenue, New York, New York 10003

United Kingdom Edition published by
ACADEMIC PRESS, INC. (LONDON) LTD.
24/28 Oval Road, London NW1   7DX

Library of Congress Cataloging in Publication Data
Main entry under title:

The Developmental psychology of time.

   (Developmental psychology)
   Includes bibliographies and index.
   1. Time perception in children--Addresses, essays,
lectures. I. Friedman, William J. II. Series.
BF723.T6D48   155.4'13   81-22835
ISBN 0-12-268320-X   AACR2

PRINTED IN THE UNITED STATES OF AMERICA

82 83 84 85   9 8 7 6 5 4 3 2 1

Contents

3

Iris Levin

The Nature and Development of Time Concepts in Children: The Effect of Interfering Cues

4

Friedrich Wilkening

Children's Knowledge about Time, Distance, and Velocity Interrelations

5

Paul Fraisse

The Adaptation of the Child to Time

6

Lorraine Harner

Talking about the Past and Future

7

William J. Friedman

Conventional Time Concepts and Children's Structuring of Time

8

Merry Bullock
Rochel Gelman
Renée Baillargeon

The Development of Causal Reasoning

9

Nancy L. Stein
Christine G. Glenn

Children's Concept of Time:
The Development of a Story Schema

Contributors

Numbers in parentheses indicate the pages on which the authors' contributions begin.

RENÉE BAILLARGEON (209), Department of Psychology, University of Pennsylvania, Philadelphia, Pennsylvania 19174

MERRY BULLOCK (209), Department of Psychology, University of British Columbia, Vancouver, British Columbia, Canada V5T 1Y7

PAUL FRAISSE (113), Laboratoire de Psychologie Expérimentale, Université René Descartes, Paris (VIe), France

WILLIAM J. FRIEDMAN (1, 171), Department of Psychology, Oberlin College, Oberlin, Ohio 44074

ROCHEL GELMAN (209), Department of Psychology, University of Pennsylvania, Philadelphia, Pennsylvania 19174

CHRISTINE G. GLENN (255), Neurological Science Institute, Portland, Oregon

LORRAINE HARNER (141), School of Education, Brooklyn College, City University of New York, Brooklyn, New York 11210

IRIS LEVIN (47), School of Education, Tel-Aviv University, Ramat-Aviv, Israel

D. DEAN RICHARDS (13), Department of Psychology, Carnegie-Mellon University, Pittsburgh, Pennsylvania 15213

NANCY L. STEIN (255), Department of Education, University of Chicago, Chicago, Illinois 60637

FRIEDRICH WILKENING (87), Institut für Psychologie, Technische Universität Braunschweig, Braunschweig, Federal Republic of Germany

Preface

After a fairly steady rate of publications on children's time concepts over the past 50 years, the last several years have shown an intensification of research and a variety of new and important approaches to the topic. The purpose of this book is to collect the recent work and to provide a forum for the researchers to relate their work to the important issues in time concept development and cognitive development in general. It is the first book on the development of time concepts since Piaget's *The Child's Conception of Time* of 1946.

This volume reflects the influence that Piaget's work has had on the field and also the variety of alternative models and approaches that have been taken. Four of the chapters discuss duration and its relationship to the dimensions of space and speed, an issue of central concern in Piaget's book. Other chapters present research on the representation and construction of temporal order and succession, natural and conventional time, the past–present–future distinction, time and causality, and time perception. In each chapter, the authors discuss the conceptual domain, theoretical issues, and research in their area as well as presenting their own contributions.

The book should serve as an introduction to the research and theory in this important area of cognitive development as well as an indication of some of the promising areas for future research. It is likely to be of special value to students and researchers with interests in cognitive development and for those concerned with the educational or clinical implications of children's knowledge of time.

The title of this book is adapted from the title of Paul Fraisse's *The Psychology of Time* and is a tribute to that important work. I would like to express my gratitude to my family and to my colleagues at Oberlin for their support.

The Developmental Psychology
of Time

William J. Friedman

1̲2̲3̲4̲5̲6̲7̲8̲9̲

Introduction

Research on cognitive development has a necessary first step, often implicit, of staking out a conceptual domain. This is done from the adult point of view, and the topical boundaries reflect the researcher's epistemology, not the child's. Time, the topic of this book, is a concept that, for adults, has a broad domain and contestable borders. In order to capitalize on the most productive trends, we will worry little about problems of internal and external topical borders and devote attention to the natural terrain of recent research related to the development of time concepts. Both the variety and common features of the region can be illustrated by charting some of the topical, theoretical, and methodological features.

A TAXONOMY OF TEMPORAL PROBLEM SOLVING

It is not unusual in reading the older literature to come across developmental studies of "the time concept." The implied unity is appealing but illusory. One author's time concept is clock and calendar time, another's is relative duration, and a third's is historical sequence. Here, as in an earlier work (Friedman, 1978), I will stress that time concepts are heterogeneous. The classification scheme that

1

follows, summarizing the variety of aspects of time discussed in the other chapters, serves to make this point.

Judging Duration—Logically Sufficient Information

One of the areas that has received the most attention concerns inferences about the magnitude of temporal intervals. Understanding of duration is usually assessed by demonstrating one or two carefully controlled events and requiring the child to judge relative temporal extent. Studies vary in the dimensions that are controlled, but in each case information is present that logically constrains the magnitude of a duration or relative durations. Here the ability of interest is inferring duration from temporally relevant information.

RELATIVE DURATION GIVEN LOGICALLY SUFFICIENT SUCCESSION INFORMATION

If the beginning and ending of temporal interval A are contained within temporal interval B, then A must be briefer. If the two begin and end simultaneously, then they have the same duration. Jean Piaget believed that the ability to make these inferences was a key element in the mature time concept, and the developmental pattern has been studied by him (1969) as well as by a number of other researchers. Piaget's assessment procedure involved a series of linear motion problems in which position, speed, and distance were varied in addition to the logical succession cues. Similar position–speed–distance problems have been used in most of the subsequent research on relative duration. (See Chapters 2, 3, 4, and 5, this volume.

When position–speed–distance problems are used, however, more is demanded of the child than the ability to make temporal inferences. The child must also be able to extract and select the crucial temporal information from other task irrelevant, but often compelling, features such as end points or distance. The information selection demand may be regarded as a factor interfering with performance or as a test of an ancillary concept, knowing which dimensions effect relative duration. This issue is discussed in Chapters 2 and 3. In several of her studies, Levin has used tasks other than the standard position–speed–distance ones, and Richards has isolated inference demands from information extraction demands in one of his experiments.

DURATION IN RELATION TO DISTANCE AND SPEED

A faster moving object will cover a given distance in less time. The greater the time, the more distance an object of uniform speed will cover. Greater speed is required to cover more distance in a given amount of time. These relationships illustrate an important feature of duration: its interdependence on distance and speed in cases of moving objects. Children's knowledge of the relationships between duration, distance, and speed has been studied by a number of researchers and is discussed by Wilkening (Chapter 4).

OTHER LOGICAL INFERENCES ABOUT DURATION

If temporal interval A includes the intervals B and C, then A has a greater duration than either. If interval $X > Y$ and $Y > Z$, then $X > Z$. If A and B are successive intervals, then their relative duration can be established by comparing each to repeatable events of constant duration. These examples of inclusion, transitivity, and measurement of duration illustrate the variety of additional logical inferences that can be made about duration. Other than Piaget's work (1969), there has been little research on these abilities.

Judging Duration in the Absence of Logical Information

Many judgments about duration are made in situations in which measurement or other logical solutions are precluded. Consistent judgments in such contexts are the raw materials for studying the perception of duration. Two sorts of questions have been raised about the development of duration perception: questions about the *accuracy* of judgments and questions about the presence and nature of *illusions* (See Fraisse, Chapter 5 and Friedman, 1978). Fraisse discusses these topics in addition to age changes in the explanations that children offer for their judgments.

Representing Succession and Simultaneity

The ability to represent relations of succession and simultaneity between two events has been studied primarily in the context of children's understandings of temporal relational terms (e.g., Amidon & Carey, 1972; Clark, 1971; Coker, 1978; French & Brown, 1977; Friedman & Seely, 1976). Language comprehension and production methods are the predominant approaches used to assess the representation of priority (e.g., using the term *before*), posteriority (e.g., *after*), and simultaneity (e.g., *at the same time*) for simple events. Fraisse (Chapter 5) presents a second approach to the representation of succession, one in which children's abilities to exploit pictorial cues of succession or nonsuccession are explored. Finally, Piaget (1969, chapters 3 and 4) has investigated the influence of spatial cues on succession and simultaneity judgments using position–speed–distance problems.

Constructing and Drawing Inferences from the Temporal Order

Temporal order is an important feature of many event sequences, whether the events are observable or presented in narrative form. The ordering of event sequences with causal or other meaningful connections depends upon both understanding the connections and coordinating them to form a temporal series. Similarly, drawing causal inferences from an observed sequence often requires attending to the temporal order of the events. Children's abilities to recreate or draw inferences from temporal orders of more than two events have been investigated in the following ways.

CONSTRUCTION OR RECONSTRUCTION OF TEMPORAL ORDER

The research on temporal construction and reconstruction involves having children either order a series of sentences or pictures representing events, insert a missing element or recount a sequence verbally. The referent events have included both causal or other meaningful sequences as well as logically arbitrary sequences. Usually construction of the forward order is required, but in several experiments children must conceptualize the reversal of a sequence. Piaget (1969, chapter 1) and Bullock, Gelman, and Baillargeon (Chapter 8, this volume) have studied the ability to represent physical transformations using picture sequencing tasks. Brown (1976) and Stein and Glenn (Chapter 9, this volume) have investigated the construction or reconstruction of stories.

DRAWING INFERENCES FROM TEMPORAL ORDER

As Bullock *et al.* point out in Chapter 8, temporal order provides crucial information about probable causal relations between events. They have studied young children's uses of two types of temporal relations in their causal attributions. According to one principle, prior but not posterior events can causally influence a given outcome. By a second, weaker principle, preceding events that are more proximate to the outcome than others are more likely causes of the outcome.

Distinguishing Past, Present, and Future

Most of the types of problem solving discussed thus far involve temporal relations that are fixed and external to the subject. In contrast, the relationship between an event and the past–present–future distinction can change with the passage of time when considered from the subject's current point of view. Alternatively, from the point of view of another moment in time, a given event is fixed in the past, present, or future. In Chapter 6 Harner discusses the development of children's understandings of the past–present–future distinction, the nature of the present, and the influence of temporal vantage point. Lexical and morphemic coding of these relations are studied both by experiment and through the analysis of spontaneous speech samples.

Representing Natural and Conventional Periodicities and Orders

Knowledge of another type of temporal structure—natural and social cycles and series—also has been studied developmentally. In contrast to most other temporal relations that have been investigated, the elements of these systems are separated by long periods of time. The spans of time involved in days, weeks, and years, the frequent feature of recurrence, and the availability of conventional representations are all features that may influence the way in which children operate on temporal systems and regularities. The research on conventional and natural time includes assessing children's knowledge of time systems verbally and by card arrangment tasks (see Friedman, 1978). Identifying conventional elements, representing order and recurrence, and distinguishing conventional and natural temporal features are among the abilities discussed in Chapter 7.

Other Types of Problem Solving

A number of other aspects of time have received little attention or have not been studied. Fraisse (Chapter 5) reports several approaches to conditioning to duration in young children and a study of the ability to wait. Harner (Chapter 6) summarizes research on temporal perspective in adolescence and adulthood. Children's knowledge of historical succession and duration has been studied only intermittently (see Friedman, 1978) and has rarely been related to general cognitive developmental processes (Smith & Tomlinson, 1977). Finally, we have little understanding of how children adapt to what we might call *social time,* which would include context differences in the importance of keeping track of the time or being prompt, as well as other conventions such as knowing when it is too early or late in the day to telephone a friend.

THEORIES OF TIME CONCEPT DEVELOPMENT

Given the diverse aspects of time that have been studied, it should not be surprising that there is no comprehensive theory of time concept development. The usual candidate for this role, Piaget's model (1969), really only applies to a few of the types of problem solving discussed above. The remaining theoretical approaches are similarly restricted in their range of application, but, as a set, address a variety of issues.

Piaget's (1969) account of time concept development is discussed in several of the chapters in this volume and briefly summarized by him in his 1955 work. In his model children come to solve succession and relative duration problems only when they acquire operations that permit the logical structuring of temporal relations, usually at 8 or 9 years of age. Until this time children will be misled by nontemporal information, for example, speed, distance or end point in the position–speed–distance problems.

Both Richards (Chapter 2) and Wilkening (Chapter 4) discuss alternative ways of modeling changes in children's knowledge of duration. In Richard's and Siegler's model, solving position–speed–distance problems requires learning both the relatedness of duration and other dimensions and duration's unique properties. The relationships are understood by children of different ages in terms of different implicit rules. Children eventually adopt roles that unconfound dimensions that typically covary in everyday experience, such as distance and duration. This developmental progression is viewed as an example of Siegler's (1979, 1981) principle that cognitive development consists of the sequential acquisition of increasingly powerful rules.

Wilkening's model of children's knowledge of the relationship between the dimensions duration, distance, and speed is framed in terms of Anderson's (1980) information integration theory. According to Wilkening, even young children are able to extract and integrate information from any two of these dimensions to judge a third. However, the particular integration rules implicit in children's judgments change with development.

In Chapter 3 Levin offers a fourth account of the development of duration concepts. She argues that there is not one but several levels of understanding duration and that a basic understanding can be shown in children who cannot yet solve position–speed–distance problems. Since duration, under some circumstances, can be understood by even preschoolers, it cannot be a concept that derives from the coordination of speeds as Piaget argues. Another feature of Levin's account is that young children fail to judge duration in position–speed–

distance problems because task features (such as the salience of nontemporal cues) and memory demands prevent the extraction of the critical starting and stopping time information. She proposes a model of the influence of salience factors on children's duration judgments.

As the succeeding chapters show, the four models are not flatly contradictory but rather depend on somewhat different definitions of the duration concept and methodological criteria for its attainment. Which model or combination of models will be the most productive is difficult to determine at present.

In Chapter 8 Bullock, Gelman, and Baillargeon present an account of the development of causal understanding which, like Levin's model, emphasizes the commonalities between the reasoning of preschool children and adults. Bullock *et al.* believe that under suitable testing conditions young children can use the same basic causal principles in their judgments as adults. Most important for the issue of time concepts is the position that young children can extract and use information about temporal order in making causal attributions and can represent sequential events in simple transformation. The main developmental differences, according to the authors, are the breadth and flexibility with which children can apply causal principles.

Stein and Glenn (Chapter 9) present a similar perspective on the development of children's abilities to order the components of stories. They argue that 5-year-olds, like adults, possess general story schemata that can be used to generate or reconstruct particular stories. When developmental differences in performance occur, they are attributed to task complexity rather than logical deficits.

In Chapter 7 Friedman proposes a model of the representation of conventional time systems based on the distinction of several cognitive theories between verbal and image symbolic systems. In this particular model, systems like the days of the week or months of the year can be represented as an articulable list, a network of semantic associations, and in an image format. Flexible use of the third mode is thought to be a later developmental achievement than the use of the first two.

Much of the work discussed in this book and in the larger literature on the development of time concepts is best described as pretheoretical. In the topic areas that have not been extensively studied, researchers must often take an initial descriptive approach, investigating age differences in the understanding of important features of time. Once some of the main developmental changes and continuities in an area are known, it is possible to begin to study the nature of the underlying processes. Both the pretheoretical research and the studies guided by theories, however, share a commitment to the view that developmental analysis is an important source of information on the nature of temporal knowledge. This view is the most general of the methodological dimensions to be discussed next.

RESEARCH METHODS

One of the motives that lies behind cognitive developmental research is the desire to separate the elements of a complex sort of knowledge and, perhaps by following the course of development, see how they are assembled. Another motive is the need to understand the origins and lineage of a concept. Kant's question, Is the structure of time intuitive?, and Einstein's question, Is the notion of time built upon the notion of speed?, both imply developmental patterns that are, in principle, subject to experiment. These epistemological motives, along with a healthy interest in understanding the competence of children of various ages, have fueled a variety of empirical approaches.

In addition to questions about the developmental pattern, research on time concept development has been influenced by two sorts of *process* questions. The first concerns the knowledge or performance factors that explain the problem-solving ability of children of particular ages, and the second concerns the factors that account for developmental change. Several of the main methodological approaches to these pattern and process issues are presented below.

As a number of the chapters in this book illustrate, duration, which has received the most attention in recent research, also has been subject to the greatest methodological variation. Much of the recent work not only provides theoretical alternatives to Piaget's position, but raises important issues concerning criteria for attributing knowledge. Piaget's work (1969) included both distinctive tasks (e.g., position–distance–speed problems) and a method for differentiating stages based on a combination of judgments and explanations. Levin, Wilkening, and Richards all discuss alternative tasks or response criteria used for answering questions about children's knowledge of duration.

Levin's interest in basic understanding of duration led to a number of task simplifications. For example, in one study she compares the performance of young children on traditional position–distance–speed problems with that on "still time" problems in which distance and speed information cannot be confused with duration. This simplification approach provides information about the developmental pattern—the early coordination of succession and duration—that would not have been known from the complex tasks discussed.

Another kind of simplification is using response criteria that make fewer demands on the child than those used by Piaget. Several of the authors have used children's choice judgments in the paired duration problems (e.g., *"Which train took more time?"*) but have not required an explanation for the judgment. In the rule assessment approach used by Richards, patterns of choices accross problem types, not explanations, are the source of information about children's knowledge. The functional measurement technique used by Wilkening avoids both explanations and relative judgments by having children make direct estimates of dimensions like duration over a series of problems in which other dimensions are systematically varied. Both Wilkening and Richards rely on patterns of responses over problems rather than on explanations in individual problems. Bullock, Gelman, and Baillargeon use a similar approach in their research on children's causal understandings. Using criteria based on the consistency of predictions and judgments rather than articulated rules, they are able to show the use of normative causal principles even in preschool children.

Task simplification and minimizing response demands are also used for problems of temporal order. Harner, Friedman, and Bullock et al. discuss work in which spatial arrangements of cards supplant purely verbal representations of the order of events. The research by Fraisse and his colleagues (Chapter 5) using conditioning procedures to study time perception also can be described as task simplification when contrasted to the estimation, production, and reproduction measures typically used with older children and adults. These approaches are each designed to increase sensitivity to the early developmental pattern.

A second methodological approach—systematically varying task parameters—has been used to clarify the cognitive processes underlying children's performances. For many newly described phenomena in psychology, dispute centers around whether one particular process or strategy or another accounts for performance. Progress frequently takes the form not of excluding one strategy but of identifying task features that bias subjects toward a particular strategy. In the research presented in subsequent chapters, a range of variations of the position–distance–speed problems have shown the influence of spatial end point, distance, beginning versus end succession, and other task features on children's duration judgments. The potency of each of these factors, under at least some circumstances, suggests that any simple process model of children's understandings of duration will be of limited value. But collectively, task variations of this sort should eventually provide a clearer picture of what children of different ages know about duration (and its relationship to other dimensions) and how this knowledge can be applied across a range of conditions. Parametric task variation also has been used to address process questions in Fraisse's research on the role of personal activity and rate of change in duration judgments and in Friedman's work on conventional time problems. Finally, Harner's chapter suggests that the variety of language research methods—spontaneous speech samples, comprehension and production tasks, and children's judgments of the correctness of utterances—which typically vary across studies might productively be varied within studies to clarify the nature of children's competences.

A third method—training—has been used infrequently in research on children's time concepts but deserves greater attention. In Chapter 2 Richards describes a study in which groups of children are given specific training on encoding problem information or combining this information to determine the correct choice. When different groups respond differentially to training, as in this study, we have an important source of information about the competence of each group and some indication of the sorts of experiences that may normally lead to change.

A final approach to cognitive process questions is to study the relationship between temporal problem solving and other developmental achievements. Developmental synchronies and sequences may be an important source of information about the functional relationships that obtain between two abilities (Flavell & Wohwill, 1969). In Piaget's (1969) work the apparent synchrony between the achievement of operational time concepts and other concrete operations convinced him that common cognitive structures were involved. Other sequence issues are evident in Levin's (Chapter 3) discussion of the relationship between speed and duration concepts, in Richard's (Chapter 2) and Wilkening's (Chapter 4) studies of duration, speed, and distance, and in Friedman's (Chapter 7) study of temporal and spatial seriation.

The second process issue raised above is accounting for developmental change. Drawing on the evidence of age differences in performance, several of the authors have suggested general developmental trends, for example, increasing the breadth and flexibility of application of concepts or learning the relationships between different dimensions. But the methods used thus far have not been adequate for identifying the factors responsible for age changes. Both correlation and intervention studies will probably be required before we understand why time concepts develop.

CONCLUSION

The work reported in this volume illustrates the diverse aspects of temporality that children come to understand, and the variety of theoretical and methodological issues that confront students of this development. In spite of the complexity of temporal knowledge, research on various aspects of its development can play an important role in our understanding of the process of cognitive development. Many forms of temporal structure are not directly perceptible; the events that compose time's contents cannot be manipulated like objects and are fleeting in nature; and, anticipation of future events is an important part of the awareness of time. Each of these senses of time's abstractness poses a representational challenge for the child and theoretical challenges for the researcher.

REFERENCES

Amidon, A., & Carey, P. Why five-year-olds cannot understand before and after. *Journal of Verbal Learning and Verbal Behavior*, 1972, *11*, 417–423.

Anderson, N. H. Information integration theory in developmental psychology. In F. Wilkening, J. Becker, & T. Trabasso (Eds.), *Information integration by children*. Hillsdale, N.J.: Erlbaum, 1980.

Brown, A. L. The construction of temporal succession by preoperational children. In A. D. Pick (Ed.), *Minnesota Symposia on Child Psychology* (Vol. 10). Minneapolis: University of Minnesota Press, 1976.

Clark, E. V. On the acquisition of meaning of *before* and *after*. *Journal of Verbal Learning and Verbal Behavior*, 1971, *10*, 266–275.

Coker, P. L. Syntactic and semantic factors in the acquisition of *before* and *after*. *Journal of Child Language*, 1978, *5*, 261–277.

Flavell, J. H., & Wohlwill, J. F. Formal and functional aspects of cognitive development. In D. Elkind & J. N. Flavell (Eds.), *Studies in cognitive development, Essays in honor of Jean Piaget*. New York: Oxford University Press, 1969.

French, L. A., & Brown, A. L. Comprehension of *before* and *after* in logical and arbitrary sequences. *Journal of Child Language*, 1977, *4*, 247–256.

Friedman, W. J. Development of time concepts in children. In H. W. Reese & L. P. Lipsitt (Eds.), *Advances in child development and behavior* (Vol. 12). New York: Academic Press, 1978.

Friedman, W., & Seely, P. The child's acquisition of spatial and temporal word meanings. *Child Development*, 1976, *47*, 1103–1108.

Piaget, J. *The child's conception of time*. London: Routledge & Kegan Paul, 1969.

Siegler, R. S. *A rule assessment approach to cognitive development*. Paper presented at the meeting of the Society for Research in Child Development, San Francisco, March 1979.

Siegler, R. S. *Seven generalizations about cognitive development*. Paper presented at the meeting of the Society for Research in Child Development, Boston, April 1981.

Smith, R. N., & Tomlinson, P. The development of children's construction of historical duration: A new approach and some findings. *Educational Research*, 1977, *19*(3), 163–170.

Children's Time Concepts: Going the Distance

The origins and development of the time concept have long been a philosophical puzzle as well as a psychological one. Kant (1965) argues from a purely
logical basis that the perception of time must be intuitive:

> The concept of alteration, and with it the concept of motion, as alteration of place, is
> possible only through and in the representation of time; and that if this representation
> were not an a priori [inner] intuition, no concept, no matter what it might be, could
> render comprehensible the possibility of an alteration. . . . Only in time can two con-
> tradictorily opposed predicates mete [sic] in one and the same object, namely one after
> the other [1965, p. 76].

In contrast with Kant's support of an innate time concept, two other
viewpoints of the growth of the concept have emerged from the psychological
literature. These two theories could be termed the *logical deficiency theory* and
the *interfering factors theory*. Supporters of the logical deficiency theory suggest
that the child must construct the time concept by coordinating related dimensions
into an algebraic structure. Immature knowledge states are the result of logical
deficiencies in that structure. By contrast, supporters of the interfering factors
theory suggest that the child has an intuitive grasp of the time concept, but that he
must learn to separate that concept from highly salient interfering factors. Each

The Developmental Psychology of Time

of these approaches and the results of studies based upon them will be examined in this chapter. We will begin by considering the logical deficiency theory.

THE LOGICAL DEFICIENCY THEORY

The logical deficiency theory suggests that the child passes through a number of immature knowledge states on the way to adult mastery of the time concept. These immature knowledge states are presumed to reflect logical deficiencies in the algebraic structures with which the child organizes the world. The best known articulation of this point of view comes from the work of Piaget (1969).

Piaget suggested that an understanding of the time concept required the coordination of speed, time, and distance into the mathematical formula: time = distance/speed. He presented children with a linear time comparison task involving two small figures that could follow paths parallel to each other. The figures started at the same place and time, but one of the figures moved for more time while the other ran faster, went the longer distance, and ended up farther ahead. Piaget reported that very young children asserted that the figure that had run the longer distance also had run a longer time, and that it had stopped moving some time after the other figure. He suggested that this knowledge state, termed Stage I, resulted because the child confused temporal cues with a spatial cue, distance.

Piaget reported that children around the age of 6 enter Stage II. This knowledge state is marked by the separation of some but not all of the spatial and temporal cues. These children either answered correctly concerning which figure stopped after the other, but incorrectly picked the figure that was farther ahead as having run for the longer time; or correctly answered which figure had run for the longer time, but incorrectly indicated which figure had stopped after the other. Piaget suggested that these children understood either duration or temporal succession "intuitively" but, by virtue of being preoperational, were unable to coordinate the two concepts to restructure their understandings.

Around the ages of 7 or 8, the children attain concrete operations. At that point, Piaget believed, they are able to construct an algebraic representation coordinating all the necessary spatial–temporal relationships. Thus, they enter Stage III, representing final mastery of the concept.

Many of the details of Piaget's account are not exactly clear and the data supporting critical aspects of his theory are not always supplied. For example, Piaget provided no explanation as to why the Stage I child confused distance with duration, rather than some other spatial cue. In the problems Piaget used to illustrate Stage I reasoning, time, velocity, and end point are confounded. There is no way to tell from the child's incorrect answer whether he or she picked the particular figure because it traveled more distance, because it ended up farther ahead, or because it went faster. Although Piaget alluded to the possibility of separating these factors using different types of problems, he provided no evidence that he actually did so.

Lovell and Slater (1960) replicated and extended Piaget's work in temporal understanding. Rather than giving different time problems to different children, as Piaget had done, they showed a number of different problems to the same children. Although supporting Piaget's results in general, Lovell and Slater found that some time problems could be solved by very young children, while other problems were difficult even for 9-year-olds (the oldest children tested). Linear comparison problems (two dolls racing on parallel tracks) were especially difficult. Lovell and Slater attributed this discrepancy in difficulty to the mastery of some of the logical relationships between spatial and temporal cues before others.

THE INTERFERING FACTORS THEORY

In contrast with the logical deficiency theory, which emphasizes the immature logic of the child, the interfering factors theory emphasizes the aspects of time problems that compel children to err. In this view the child may possess the logic necessary to understand duration, but cannot reconcile his or her answers with the answers suggested by interfering spatial cues. We will examine several studies supportive of this view.

Berndt and Wood (1974) suggested that even young children have the ability to make correct time judgments, but that the salience of the spatial cues present in the problems interfered with this capability. They exposed children to two types of duration problems. The first involved two trains on parallel tracks. When the trains ran down the tracks, the train that went the longer time could go for either more or less distance. Two tones of different frequency, one for each train, were sounded when the corresponding train was in motion. In the second task, a long tunnel was used to cover the tracks so the trains could not be seen and only the tones provided duration information. Berndt and Wood found that when the trains were in the tunnel, most of the children gave the correct answers. However, when the trains were uncovered, most of these children changed their answers. They concluded that the children had a "primitive capacity" to understand time but the salience of the distance cue overwhelmed that capacity.

Berndt and Wood's results must be viewed with caution, however. Although children did utilize an appropriate time cue when it was the only cue present, they utilized other cues when they were available. It is possible that spatial cues were used to judge time because children thought these cues were more appropriate, or because the children found them easier to use, rather than because they found the spatial cues more salient. There is no indication that the children ever attempted to use the auditory time cues when distance, end point, and speed cues were available.

Levin (1977) presented children from ages 5 to 9 with three types of duration problems: still time (the sleeping time of two dolls); rotational time (the time of rotation of two dolls mounted on turntables); and linear time (the travel time of two cars moving along parallel linear tracks). These three types of problems varied in both the type and number of potentially interfering variables: Linear time problems had two interfering cues, distance and speed; rotational time had only one, speed; still time had none. Levin found that linear time problems were much more difficult than the other two types. She concluded that children's understandings of time depended upon the number of interfering dimensions.

Citing the success of even very young children on still time problems, Levin rejected Piaget's position that the time concepts of young children were undifferentiated from spatial concepts through a lack of logical understanding. Rather, she suggested: "The child's conceptions of time are basically temporal but are vulnerable to countersuggestions from various factors, including spatial variables [1977, p. 422]."

To strengthen her argument that *any* dimension (not just logically related dimensions) can interfere with time concepts, Levin (1979) compared children's performances on the rotational time task and a task involving the burning time of lights of different intensities. Although no logical relationship exists between light intensity and duration, intensity of light interfered with duration judgments in the same manner and to the same extent as speed. Levin suggested that the interfering variables of light intensity and speed acted through a process of equating dimensions (more on one scale = more on the other scale).

The three time tasks in Levin's first study (still time, rotational time, and linear time) differ not only in the number of potentially interfering dimensions, the identities of the dimensions also differ. The fact that one of the interfering variables in the linear time task is distance could be more important than how many potentially interfering variables are present in all. Furthermore, Levin has not demonstrated that speed and distance cues interfere with time judgments to an equal degree. Thus, there is no reason to believe that the difficulty of the three tasks should increase linearly with the addition of more potentially interfering factors.

Levin's second study, using the intensity of light as an interfering factor, makes an additional point. Even though young children appear to have an understanding of the time concept, it is an extremely fragile understanding—so fragile that the availability of virtually any other dimension can lead to the use of that dimension as a time cue, even if it is not directly related to the time concept.

In addition, although Levin succeeded in demonstrating that interfering variables need not be logically related to time, her work lacks a developmental dimension. Ample evidence is presented that children improve in performance on time tasks with age, but little is said about why they improve. The lack of an account of this developmental change is a serious weakness of the interfering variables theory.

In another variant of the interfering variables approach, Wilkening (1979) suggested that information processing capacity determined the child's ability to coordinate time and spatial variables. Children ranging from 5 to 20 were given three tasks. In the first, they were asked to determine how far across a footbridge a turtle, a guinea pig, and a cat would travel in a given time period. In the second task, each of the three animals was placed on the footbridge a given distance from the start and the child was asked to press a key to indicate the length of time each animal had traveled. The third task involved the child judging which of seven animals would arrive at a given point on the bridge in a set time period. Wilkening found that the strategy for combining the spatial and temporal dimensions varied for each task and across each age group. The third task was especially difficult. While children as young as 5 combined the dimensions multiplicatively on the first task, even adults used a less sophisticated additive rule on the third task. Wilkening concluded that the additional information presented by using seven animals rather than the three in the third task was a major determinant of the less-sophisticated strategies used on that task.

Wilkening's conclusion is weakly supported at best, however. The third task, in addition to involving the use of more animals, required the coordination of different variables than the others. In the first task, only the travel time was set, and the child was allowed to set his or her own speed values and determine distance values through the proportional relationship between speed and distance when time is held constant. In the second task, only the distance traveled by each animal was set, and the child was allowed to set his or her own speed values and determine travel times through the proportional relationship existing between time and speed when distance is held constant. In the third task, however, both time and distance were set, and the child had to coordinate the speeds of the animals with both travel times and distances. This task difference by itself could be responsible for the greater difficulty of the third task.

In addition, it is impossible to compare the information processing loads of the three tasks without first specifying how each task is to be performed. If the children are to consider each animal in isolation, increasing the number of animals should only increase total processing *time* across all judgments, not the processing *load* at any one time.

Both the logical deficiency and interfering factors theories disagree on the answers to three important questions:

1. How can we characterize the developmental sequence of knowledge states leading to an understanding of the time concept?

2. How do children progress from one knowledge state to the next?
3. What makes the time concept so difficult, and why do children fail to understand it much earlier in development?

One reason for this disagreement is that both the logical deficiency theory and the interfering factors theory fail to consider all of the aspects of the development of time-understanding simultaneously. The logical deficiency theorists focus on the characteristics of the problem solver to the exclusion of the demands required by the task. They leave unanswered the question of why children can solve some time problems but not others. Interfering factors theorists dwell on the demands of the time judgment task with little emphasis on the problem solver. They are vague at best about why older children can solve time problems that younger children cannot. A more balanced approach would seem beneficial—one that considers not just the demands of the task or the abilities of the problem solver, but also the interaction between the two. The conceptual relationships theory is designed with this purpose in mind.

THE CONCEPTUAL RELATIONSHIPS THEORY

The *conceptual relationships theory* suggests that complete understanding of a concept such as time requires two distinct types of knowledge: (*a*) knowledge of the relationships between the concept and other concepts, and (*b*) knowledge of the unique aspects of the concept. The former (*a*) consists of an understanding of the imperfect correlations between the concept and other concepts and a knowledge of the conditions under which those correlations are moderate, weak, and strong. The latter (*b*) constitutes the unique part of the concept, not related to or describable in terms of any other concept.

Developmental change under the conceptual relationships theory consists primarily of learning the relationships between the concept and related concepts. This learning process involves both separating similar concepts as well as linking dissimilar ones—in particular, establishing under exactly what conditions each relationship appears, under what conditions it disappears, and through what mechanisms it operates. Relationships are hypothesized to be established and refined through repeated association. Thus, we would expect relationships based upon frequently encountered associations to be grasped before relationships based on less frequently encountered associations.

A final aspect of the conceptual relationships theory deals with the link between the child's understanding of a concept and her performance. The child's performance on a given task would depend solely on the match between the conceptual relationships grasped by that child and the conceptual relationships presupposed by the task. Complete mastery of the concept could be attained only when every perfect and imperfect relationship with other concepts was completely understood. For most complex concepts, such a criterion of understanding is far too stringent. Few, indeed, are the cases when all the relationships between a concept and other concepts, and all the conditions under which these relationships apply, can be known. Hence, an understanding of the relationships to a level sufficient to utilize the concept under most conditions likely to be encountered must in most cases serve as the definition of mastery.

How does this theory of development relate to the time concept? Under the conceptual relationships theory, the time concept would consist of both the unique aspects of time—those aspects described by Kant as "intuitive"—as well as the relationships between time and distance, time and speed, time and the size of growing objects, and so forth. The development of the time concept would consist primarily of establishing those relationships and the conditions under which they were applicable. For example, distance and time are directly proportional, but only under uniform speed conditions. The child's performance on time problems would depend upon the match between the child's understanding and the relationships tapped by the problem. For example, a child who believes time and distance are always proportional would do well on problems where this relationship holds and poorly on problems that exploit the exceptions to this rule.

In order to investigate the merits of the conceptual relationships theory of development, it was necessary to choose a methodology consonant with the tenets of the theory. The rule-assessment method, described in the next section, was chosen for this purpose.

The Rule-Assessment Method

The rule-assessment methodology (Klahr and Siegler, 1978; Siegler, 1976; 1978a; 1978b; Siegler and Vago, 1978) makes two assumptions consonant with the conceptual relationships theory: that children understand concepts in the form of specific rules, and that these rules can be discriminated through the construction of carefully designed problem sets. The rule the child uses reflects an interaction between the characteristics of the task and the knowledge of the child. Thus, this methodology combines the task-specific nature of the interfering factors studies with the emphasis on the child's understanding present in the logical deficiency studies.

The first step Robert Siegler and I took in using the rule-assessment approach was to select a task involving time, speed, and distance, and to formulate models of rules that children might use to perform that task. In keeping with the tenets of the conceptual relationships theory, a comparative duration task similar to Piaget's moving figures task was chosen. This task was chosen for three reasons. First, it allows the examination of all three dimensions within a single framework. Second, it is a task with a large number of potentially interfering dimensions, allowing examination of how these variables interact together, as well as allowing us to push the child's understanding of the time, speed, and distance tasks to its limits. Finally, it is a task that is comprehensible to very young children, yet is challenging even for older children.

Children were shown two parallel train tracks with a locomotive on each track. The two locomotives could start from the same or different points, stop at the same or different points, and go for the same or different distances. They could start at the same or different times, stop at the same or different times, and go for the same or different amounts of time. Finally, the speed of the trains could be the same or different.

Several rule models were constructed based upon the physical and temporal dimensions upon which the problems varied. Children using an end-point rule would designate the train farther ahead as having gone for more time, more distance, or faster. If the trains stopped in the same place, they would be said to have traveled for the same amount of time, for the same distance, or at the same speed. Children using the time rule would base their answers on which train ran for more time. Those using the distance rule would base their answers on which train went the longer distance. Those using the speed rule would base their answers on which train went faster. These three rules represent the appropriate formulas for the time, distance, and speed concept problems, respectively. In addition to these rules, many other rule variants could also be detected by the rule-assessment methodology, including attempts to utilize other dimensions such as beginning point or ending time, as well as inappropriate use of the distance rule on the time task, the time rule on the distance task, and so on.

The second step in the rule-assessment methodology was to design problems that could determine when these or other rules were being used by children. The six problem types chosen for the initial assessment are illustrated in Table 2.1. These problem types were designed to allow discrimination among rules corresponding to the seven dimensions along which the trains could differ: time, speed, distance, end point, end time, beginning point, and beginning time, as well as many combination rules including those mentioned previously. The dimensions that were discriminated from time by each problem type (i.e., the dimensions which predict a different answer than the answer predicted by the appropriate rule for that concept) are listed with each problem type in Table 2.1. These problem types were also chosen to limit the difficulty of the task in several ways. Duration, distance, and average speed of the trains were never equal. Even adults experience difficulty judging whether two trains that did not start and stop at the same time traveled the same speed or the same amount of time (Fraisse, 1963). The trains also either started or stopped at the same time, again because research with adults indicates that they experience difficulty in judging duration

TABLE 2.1

Percentage of Correct Answers Predicted by Each Rule for Each Problem Type on Time, Distance, and Speed Concepts

	Problem type					
Problem diagram	1	2	3	4	5	6
Train A	0 —— 6	0 —— 9	0 — 9	0 — 6	0 — 6	0 — 5
Train B	*f*	*f*	*f*	*f*	*f*	*f*
	2 6	0 5	4 9	0 5	0 4	2 5

Dimensions discriminated from each concept

Time	Speed	Speed	Speed	Speed	Begin point	End point
	Begin point	End point	Distance	Distance	Begin time	End time
	End time	Begin time	Begin point	End point		
			End time	Begin time		
Distance	Speed	Speed	Time	Time	Begin point	End point
	Begin point	End point	End point	Begin point	Begin time	End time
	End time	Begin time	Begin time	Begin time		
		End time	End time			
Speed	Time	Time	Time	Time	Begin point	End point
	Distance	Distance	End point	Begin point	Begin time	End time
	Begin point	Begin point	Begin time	Begin time		
	End point	End point	End time	End time		
	Begin time	Begin time				
	End time	End time				

Predicted percentage correct for each concept

	1	2	3	4	5	6
Time End-point rule	100%	0%	100%	0%	100%	0%
Distance rule	100%	100%	0%	0%	100%	100%
Time rule	100%	100%	100%	100%	100%	100%
Distance End-point rule	100%	0%	0%	100%	100%	0%
Distance rule	100%	100%	100%	100%	100%	100%
Speed End-point rule	0%	0%	0%	100%	100%	0%
Speed rule	100%	100%	100%	100%	100%	100%

when neither starting nor stopping time are equal. (See Siegler and Richards, 1979, for further details concerning problem set construction).

The initial experiment was designed to answer the first question posed above: What is the developmental sequence of knowledge states that lead to an understanding of the time concept and the allied concepts of speed and distance? A broad range of ages was chosen for this initial assessment: 5-year-olds, 8-year-olds, 11-year-olds, and adults.

Experiment 1

METHOD

Participants were 12 kindergarteners, 12 third graders, 12 sixth graders, and 12 adults. One-half of the individuals in each age group were male and one-half were female.

Included among the materials were two HO-gauge locomotives (one red and one blue), two 3-m lengths of track, two transformers, and three Hunter timers. Two of the timers served as duration timers for each train. The third timer served as a delay timer; it could be used to impose a delay between the starting times of the two trains. Each locomotive had its own transformer, allowing independent control of speed. Through the combined control of speed and time, the distance traveled by the locomotives could also be controlled. Because this control was good but not perfect, on trials where identical stopping points were required, small pins were placed at the intended stopping points. The timers were set so that the power was shut off just prior to the train reaching the pins, allowing each train to coast gently to a stop against the pin and making their stops barely premature.

For each concept, the children were presented 24 items, 4 each of the six problem types shown in Table 2.1. The same 24 items were used in assessing all three concepts; all that differed was whether the child was asked about speed, distance, or time. The examples of each problem type were ordered within the problem set using a stratified random sampling procedure, so that one example of each problem type was among the first six problems, one was among the second six, and so on.

In the diagrams at the top of Table 2.1, the numbers refer to the starting and stopping times of each train (in seconds), and the lengths of the lines correspond to the relative distances traveled by each train. The train which traveled faster is indicated by the letter f. Immediately below each problem diagram, the cues that were discriminated from (pointed to a different answer than) the correct time, distance, and speed answers are listed.

The pattern of responses that would be generated by children following various rules for each concept can be seen at the bottom of Table 2.1. For example, children following an end-point rule on the time concept would solve 100% of problem types 1, 3, and 5 but err on types 2, 4, and 6. Children following the same rule on the distance concept would answer problem types 1, 4, and 5 correctly but err on problem types 2, 3, and 6. Similarly, distinct error patterns for each concept existed for the rules listed in the table as well as for many more rules not listed.

Problems were designed so that the two trains' travel times differed by at least 2 sec, their speeds by at least 6 cm/sec, and their distances by at least 13 cm.

The criteria for rule usage were basically the same as those followed in previous studies using the rule-assessment approach (Siegler, 1976; 1978a; 1978b; Siegler and Vago, 1978). To be classified as using a rule, at least 20 out of 24 of the child's responses had to be in accord with the predictions of that rule. The presence of three possible responses (Train A is greater, Train B is greater, they are equal) meant that the rules had to predict not only which items were solved correctly, but also the particular errors that would occur. This made it unlikely that a random responder would be classified as a rule user.

Each child was brought individually to a vacant classroom in his or her school on three different days in a 1-week period. Upon arrival the child was shown the trains and instructed that on that day he was to judge which train ran for the longer time, which train ran for more distance, or which train went faster. The entire problem set took 15–20 min. Order of presentation was counterbalanced across concepts, so that one-third of the children in each grade were assessed on speed first, one-third on distance first, and one-third on time first.

The procedure followed with adults differed in two ways. Groups of three to six people were shown the problems at the same time, and the adults recorded their own responses. Otherwise, the procedure was identical.

RESULTS

Distance Concept

Forty-one of the 48 subjects could be classified as using a rule on the distance concept problems. As shown in Table 2.2A, 19 used an end-point rule[1] and 22 used the distance rule. There was a definite relationship between rule usage and

[1]From this point on, the term *end-point rule* will be used to denote both the pure end-point rule described previously and a partial end-point rule where end point was used when end points were not equal and the end-time cue was utilized when end points were equal. In view of the fact that these rules both appear in the same age groups with almost equal frequency, and the fact that they differ only in the way they deal with exactly equal end points, the two rules will be discussed together for the purposes of this report.

D. Dean Richards

TABLE 2.2
Number of Children Using Each Rule

	Rule used				
	End point	Distance	Speed	Time	No rule
A. Distance concept					
5- and 6-year-olds	10	0	0	0	2
8- and 9-year-olds	6	3	0	0	3
11- and 12-year-olds	3	7	0	0	2
Adults	0	12	0	0	0
B. Speed concept					
5- and 6-year-olds	12	0	0	0	0
8- and 9-year-olds	1	0	4	0	7
11- and 12-year-olds	0	0	10	0	2
Adults	0	0	11	0	1
C. Time concept					
5- and 6-year-olds	10	0	1	0	1
8- and 9-year-olds	3	0	0	0	9
11- and 12-year-olds	0	5	0	2	5
Adults	0	0	0	11	1

age. Five-year-olds used end-point rules; most 8-year-olds used end-point rules but some used the distance rule; most 11-year-olds used the distance rule but some used the end-point rule; and adults all used the distance rule.

Speed Concept

Thirty-eight subjects met rule criteria on the speed concept problems. Thirteen used an end-point rule and 25 used the correct speed rule (Table 2.2B). Again there was a clear relationship between rule usage and age. Five-year-olds used end-point rules, a minority of 8-year-olds used the speed rule but most met no rule usage criteria, and older children and adults used the speed rule on this concept.

Time Concept

Thirty-two of the 48 subjects could be classified as using a rule to determine which train ran for more time. Thirteen used an end-point rule, and 13 used the correct time rule.[2] In addition, five 11-year-olds consistently indicated that the train that traveled the greater distance had gone for more time—the distance rule.

[2]One 5-year-old used the speed rule.

Once again there was a clear relationship between rules used and age. Five-year-olds used end-point rules, 8-year-olds seldom met any rule criteria, 11-year-olds most often used the distance rule or met no rule criteria, and adults used the time rule.

The consistency of reasoning on the three concepts was considerable among the 5-year-olds. Six of the 10 kindergarteners who met rule usage criteria on all three concepts used the same rule on all of them; all six children used end-point rules. Eleven-year-olds showed a different consistency: Three of the seven sixth graders who used the distance rule on distance problems also used it on time problems. Finally, adults were consistent in still another way: they possessed fully differentiated understandings of all three concepts, using the distance rule on the distance concept, the time rule on the time concept, and the speed rule on the speed concept.

As Table 2.2 illustrates, 16 subjects did not meet the criteria for usage of any detectable rule on the time concept. Examination of the error patterns of these subjects revealed a distinctly nonrandom pattern. Therefore, multiple regression analysis was performed on the number of errors made on each problem by these "no-rule" subjects. The use of multiple regression follows naturally from the use of rule analyses. Both methods predict the correct answer and error patterns of children utilizing different dimensions as predictors of their responses. However, while rule analyses are based on individual performances, multiple regression is a parametric technique that can be used on group data. Unlike the rule-assessment method, multiple regression analysis is not limited by any arbitrary cutoff point. Thus, spatial or temporal dimensions influencing error patterns can be detected even if they do not reach the level of strength required to meet rule usage criteria.

The regression analysis of the errors of the no-rule subjects was performed in the following manner. The number of errors made on each of the 24 test problems served as the dependent variable. The predictor variables were duration, speed, distance, end point, end time, beginning point, and beginning time. Except for the time variable itself, all predictors were treated as dichotomous (they either pointed toward the correct answer or toward a wrong answer). Since the time variable always pointed toward the correct answer, the absolute difference between the travel times of the trains served to represent the time variable in the analysis.

The results of the regression analysis showed 67% of the total variance could be accounted for solely by the distance variable's status. In general, errors occurred when the train that had gone for more time went for less distance. None of the other factors added as much as 5% to the variance accounted for by distance. Regression analyses of the error patterns of the time rule subjects revealed a similar result: the status of the distance variable was the best predictor of the difficulty of a duration judgment. This finding is consistent with the view that the no-rule subjects were attempting to use the time rule but were not very good at it because of a difficulty in separating the distance and time dimensions.

The use of regression analysis also allowed a comparison between the predictions of the conceptual relationships theory and the predictions of the interfering factors theory. If, as suggested by the interfering factors theorists, it is the perceptual salience of physical cues that causes them to interfere with time judgments, then we would expect problems in which these differences are greatest to be the most difficult. Therefore, a multiple regression analysis using the absolute differences in magnitude between these physical cues as predictor variables should result in a more accurate prediction of problem difficulty than the dichotomous regression previously performed. If, on the other hand, the interference of spatial variables is a conceptual problem, as suggested by the conceptual relationships theory, then the mere fact that the cues disagree with travel time should be as good or better as a predictor of errors.

To test this hypothesis, two additional multiple regressions were performed, each corresponding to a possible interpretation of the interfering factors theory. If the salience of interfering cues leads to more errors on problems where they point to a different answer, and to fewer errors on problems where they do not, then the absolute magnitude of differences between the two trains' speeds, distances, end points, and beginning points should have a positive effect when consonant with the time answer, and a negative effect when dissonant with it. Alternatively, if the salience of interfering cues leads to more errors on problems when they differ from time in their predictions but has no effect when consonant with it, then the magnitude of the differences should be important only when dissonant with time.

To test the former interpretation, the absolute differences in speed, distance, end point, beginning point, and time were used as predictor variables, with the differences taking on positive values when they concurred with the answer suggested by the time rule, and negative values when they did not concur. The latter interpretation was tested using the same values of each variable when they disagreed with a time-rule-based answer, but substituting a constant value for each when they supported the time-rule-based answer.

The results of these regressions did not support the interfering factors theory. Recall that simply treating distance as a dichotomous predictor pointing toward or away from the answer based on duration allowed us to account for 67% of the variance in the number of errors on the 24 items. By contrast, the distance variable could only account for 53% of the error variance when continuous positive and negative differences in magnitude of each variable were used as predictors. When only the magnitude differences in opposition to the time-rule answer were considered, distance could account for only 38% of the error variance. Thus, the perceptual salience of the distance, speed, end point, and beginning point cues was not a better predictor of children's errors than the mere fact of the opposition of these cues to a duration-based answer. This result does not support the view that the perceptual salience of spatial cues is what leads the children to err. The confusion between spatial and temporal dimensions appears to be a conceptual problem rather than a perceptual problem.

DISCUSSION

The main goal of this initial study was to determine the sequence of knowledge states leading to mastery of the concept of temporal duration. In agreement with Piaget, it was found that 5-year-olds relied primarily on end-point rules to judge which train ran for more time. Adults almost all used the appropriate time rule.

The transition period, however, was found to be somewhat more complicated than Piaget suggested. The direct predecessor of the time rule appeared to be knowledge states where the concept of time was partially understood but still confusable with distance. This was supported by the large number of distance rule users among the 11-year-olds, the age prior to mastery of the concept. The results of the regression analysis of errors by no rule subjects provided further evidence for this assertion. Finally, a third source of evidence was the decrement in performance on problem type 3, the only problem type solvable by the end-point rules but not by the distance rule. While 5-year-olds solved 71% of these problems, 11-year-olds solved only 27% of them.

Having determined the sequence of knowledge states leading to mastery of the duration concept, the second question was addressed: How do children progress from one knowledge state to the next? To what extent could we use the rule assessments to predict an ability to respond to different types of training? To address this question, Robert Siegler and I performed Experiment 2.

Experiment 2

Experiment 1 demonstrated that both 5- and 11-year-olds were utilizing a spatial dimension as a cue to which train ran for more time. However, there was an essential difference between the age groups: the 5-year-olds used end point to judge time, whereas the 11-year-olds' responses were swayed by distance. Experiment 2 was designed to test whether these assessments of existing knowledge could be used to predict the effects of different types of feedback training on 5 to 6 and 10 to 11-year-olds. The training involved four types of problems: problems that discriminated end point from time, problems that discriminated distance from time, problems that discriminated distance and end point from time, and problems that discriminated neither distance nor end point from time. Since 5-year-olds had been found to utilize end point to judge which train ran for more time, problems that discriminated end point from time were hypothesized to be appropriate training for these children. By contrast, problem types that did not discriminate end point from time (including those that discriminated distance from time) were hypothesized not to be effective training for these children. The reverse was expected of 11-year-olds: The problem types that discriminated distance from time were hypothesized to be appropriate training, while those that did not discriminate distance from time (including those that discriminated end point from time) were not expected to be effective training. The problem types discriminating both distance and end point from time were expected to occupy the unique position of being appropriate training for both age groups.

In order to insure that only the children in each age group who would be expected to benefit most from each type of training were included, a pretest was employed that was similar to the original rule-assessment test of Experiment 1. The pretest was used to select the 5- and 6-year-olds who most closely followed an end-point rule and the 10- and 11-year-olds who most closely followed the distance rule. The selected children of each age were divided into four groups to receive the different types of training. Following training, a posttest was administered.

METHOD

Forty kindergarteners and first graders, and 40 fifth and sixth graders participated in Experiment 2. The 80 children were selected on the basis of pretest performance, as will be described in this section. One-half of the children in each age group were boys and one-half were girls.

Materials were similar to those used in Experiment 1 but with some improvements: The Hunter timers were still used to control run time, but the control of each train's speed was exercised by a resistance box. The resistance box consisted of a number of resistors and a multiposition switch that could direct current through various combinations of those resistors, allowing individual control of the speeds each train would travel. This allowed more accurate control of the distance the trains would travel than had been previously possible. However, since this control was still not perfect, hidden solenoids were used to stop the trains on trials where the stopping points had to be identical. The trains stopped no more abruptly on these trials than on trials where the solenoids were not used.

The pretest included 17 items: two corresponding to each of problem types 2, 4, 5, and 6 in Table 2.3, and three corresponding to each of problem types 1, 3, and 7. The overrepresentation of problem types 1, 3, and 7 was due to their having the greatest power to discriminate end point, distance, and time from other dimensions and from each other. Since the objective was to assess the children's existing knowledge, no feedback was presented at any time on the pretest.

Two primary selection criteria were applied to performance on this pretest: that each child's answers diverge from the predictions for the time rule on at least

TABLE 2.3
Predicted Percentage of Correct Answers by Each Rule for Each Problem Type (Experiment 2)

Problem diagram	1	2	3	4	5	6	7
Train A	0 —— 6	0 —— 6	0 — 6	0 —— 6	0 —— 6	0 — 8	0 — 5
Train B	f	f	f	f	f	f	f
	0 3	0 2 0	4 3 6	0 4		0 5 3	5

Dimensions discriminated from time

Speed	Speed	Speed	Speed	Begin Point	End Point	Speed
Distance	End Point	Distance	Begin Point	Begin Time	Begin Time	Distance
Begin Point	Begin Time	Begin Point	End Time			End Point
End Point		End Point				End Time
Begin Time		Begin Time				

Predicted percentage correct

	1	2	3	4	5	6	7
End-point rule	0%	0%	0%	100%	100%	0%	0%
Distance rule	0%	100%	0%	100%	100%	100%	0%
Time rule	100%	100%	100%	100%	100%	100%	100%

25% of the trials, and that the rule said to characterize the child's performance fit the responses better than any known alternative rule. Among the children meeting these criteria, the 40 5- and 6-year-olds whose responses most closely approximated the ideal pattern for the end-point rule and the 40 10- and 11-year-olds whose responses most closely approximated the ideal pattern for the distance rule were chosen for participation in the feedback and posttest phases of the experiment. These children were assigned to one of the four training groups through the use of a matched random assignment procedure. The end-point rule users (5- and 6-year-olds) and the distance rule users (10- and 11-year-olds) were divided into groups of four according to the number of trials on which their responses matched the predictions of their rule (that is, on all 17 trials, on 16 of 17, and so on). The four children whose responses best fit their rule were randomly assigned to the groups, then the next best fitting four, and so on (ties were broken arbitrarily). This insured that for each rule, the four experimental groups would be comparable in terms of the children's initial adherence to the predicted pattern.

The four feedback problem sets were classified according to whether they discriminated distance and/or end-point cues from time. Examples of each of the four are shown in Table 2.4. The control set discriminated neither distance nor end-point cues from time; all three cues pointed to the same answer (Table

TABLE 2.4
Specific Response and Percentage of Correct Answers Predicted by Each Rule for Training Problems

Training group	Problem diagram[a]		End-point rule	Distance rule	Time rule
A. Control	0″ faster 6″				
	———		"A longer"	"A longer"	"A longer"
	3″ 6″		(100)	(100)	(100)
B. End-point discriminating	0″ faster 6″		"B longer"	"A longer"	"A longer"
	———		(0)	(100)	(100)
	3″ 6″				
C. Distance discriminating	0″ —— 6″		"A longer"	"B longer	"A longer"
	———		(100)	(0)	(100)
	0″ faster 3″				
D. End-point + distance discriminating	0″ 6″		"B longer"	"B longer"	"A longer"
	———		(0)	(0)	(100)
	0″ faster 3″				

[a] Each problem set consisted of several similar problem types that discriminated the dimensions of interest from time but varied in the discrimination of other spatial dimensions from time.

2.4A). The end-point discriminating set included two types of problems: 12 end-point discriminating items on which distance and time cues pointed to one answer and end point pointed to another (Table 2.4B), and 6 control items. The purpose of including these control items was to discourage children from inducing a rule "always choose the train that stops less far up the track." The distance discriminating set also included two types of problems: 12 items on which end-point and time cues led to the same answer and distance to a different one (Table 2.4C), and 6 control problems. Similarly, the distance and end-point discriminating set included 12 items on which neither end-point nor distance cues led to the same answer as the time cue (Table 2.4D), and 6 control items.

To facilitate the examination of learning effects, the problems in each training group were divided into the first, second, and last one-third of the feedback set. This resulted in four discriminating and two nondiscriminating problems in each block for the end-point, distance, and distance + end-point training groups, and 6 nondiscriminating problems in each block for the control group.

The posttest consisted of four instances of each of the seven problem types in

Table 2.4, for a total of 28 problems. Stratified random sampling was utilized to insure that one item from each problem type was present in the first set of seven problems, one in the second set, and so on.

The rule-assessment criterion utilized for the posttest was comparable to that followed in Experiment 1. To be classified as using a rule, the child had to answer at least 25 out of the 28 posttest problems in accordance with that rule.

During the pretest phase of the study, each child was brought individually to a vacant classroom within his or her school. Upon arrival the child was shown the trains and instructed to watch which train ran for more time or if the trains ran for the same amount of time. The pretest took less than 15 minutes per child.

Children who most closely adhered to the end-point and distance approaches continued on to the feedback sessions. They were brought to the room individually and instructed to again observe which train ran for more time. Following instructions, the 18 feedback problems were presented. After each answer the child was immediately informed if his answer was correct or incorrect, and was told the correct answer if he had been mistaken. The child was encouraged to review the problem for five seconds after each incorrect answer and to determine, if possible, where the error had occurred.

One week after the training session, the children were brought back one at a time for the posttest portion of the study. The 28 posttest problems were presented in the same manner as the pretest problems, with no feedback.

RESULTS

Pretest

The first question addressed was whether the assessment results of Experiment 1 would be replicated in the pretest portion of Experiment 2. Multiple regression analyses were performed on the number of errors made on each of the 17 items on the pretest by the entire group of 5- and 6-year-olds and 10- and 11-year-olds who were pretested. Total distance, average speed, end point, end time, beginning point, and beginning time served as dichotomous predictors, and the absolute difference between the travel times of the trains served as a continuous predictor factor.

Results were similar to those in Experiment 1. For kindergarteners and first graders, 88% of the variance was accounted for by end point, with no other factors adding as much as 5% to the error variance. Among the fifth and sixth graders, the distance variable's status accounted for 64% of the error variance. In addition, the end-time variable increased the total accountable variance to 85%. As in Experiment 1, then, the status of the end-point cue was the best predictor of errors by the 5- and 6-year-olds, and the status of the distance cue was the best predictor of errors by the older children.

The pretest answers of just the 80 children selected to participate in the training portion of the study were examined next. Among the 40 5- and 6-year-olds selected for the training portion of the study, the end-point factor accounted for 98% of the error variance. Among the 40 10- and 11-year-olds, the distance factor accounted for 90% of the variance.

Training

The first step was to examine the training data to determine if end-point discriminating problems were more effective for 5- and 6-year-olds, and if distance discriminating problems were more effective for 10- and 11-year-olds. To examine this, the percentage of correct answers given by children in each age and training group were tabulated separately for the discriminating and nondiscriminating problems. A 2 (age) × 2 (distance discriminating problems: present or absent) × 2 (end-point discriminating problems: present or absent) × 3 (trial block) × 2 (control versus discriminating problems) ANOVA on the percentage of correct responses revealed significant main effects for age, distance training, end-point training, and control versus discriminating problems. In addition, there were significant interactions among age and end-point training; trial block, age, and distance training; trial block and control versus discriminating problems; trial block, control versus discriminating problems, and distance training; trial block, control versus discriminating problems, and end-point training; trial block, control versus discriminating problems, age, and end-point training; and trial block, control versus discriminating problems, distance training, and end-point training. The presence of all of these significant first, second, and third order interactions suggested that the performance of children of each age and training group would best be examined individually. These results are graphically illustrated in Figure 2.1.

Control Training.   The percentage of correct answers for children in the control group is presented in Figure 2.1A. The performance of both 5- and 6-year-olds and 10- and 11-year-olds was consistently correct and did not change significantly across the three blocks. Neither children using end-point rules nor children following distance formulations had any trouble answering these problems correctly.

End-Point Training.   The performance of 10- and 11-year-olds (Figure 2.1B) was similarly high on the end-point training problems and did not change significantly across blocks for either discriminating or nondiscriminating problems. Performance on the end-point discriminating problems by the 5- and 6-year-olds was initially poor and then improved significantly. Instead of picking the train that stopped farther ahead, these children began choosing the train that went for

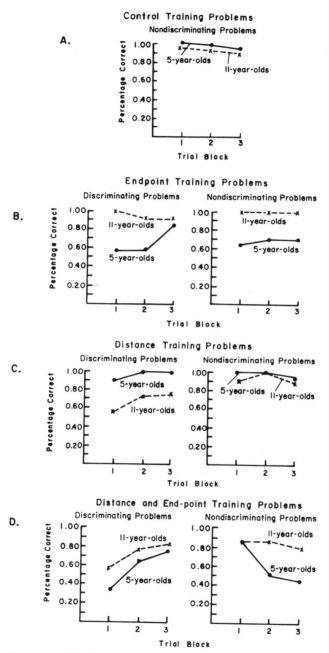

Figure 2.1. Percentage of discriminating and nondiscriminating problems solved by each age group in each training condition.

more time and more distance. The 5-year-olds' performance on the control problems was relatively constant throughout the session.

Distance Training.   The 5- and 6-year-olds' performance was consistently correct on all three blocks on both the discriminating and nondiscriminating problems within the distance training problem set (Figure 2.1C). The performance of the 10- and 11-year-olds was initially significantly poorer than that of the 5- and 6-year-olds on the distance discrimination problems. Despite significant improvement from the first to the third trial block, the performance of the 10- and 11-year-olds remained below that of the 5- and 6-year-olds. On control problems, the 10- and 11-year-olds were consistently correct.

Distance + End-Point Training.   On the distance + end-point discriminating problems (Figure 2.1D), both 5- and 6-year-olds and 10- and 11-year-olds initially made a great many errors. The number of correct answers by both groups increased significantly over trials. The situation was different in a surprising way on the nondiscriminating problems: The 10- and 11-year-olds showed no significant difference between performance on the third block and performance on the first block of the nondiscriminating problems. However, the 5- and 6-year-olds' performance decreased significantly from the first to the third block.

This finding suggests that older and younger children's improvements on the discriminating problems may come about for different reasons. The 10- and 11-year-olds responded to feedback by adopting a formulation that would allow them to get both types of problems correct. The time rule is virtually the only rule capable of this. By contrast, the drop in performance on nondiscriminating problems by the 5- and 6-year-olds indicated that they were not tending toward the time rule. An examination of the error patterns of these children during the third block of training provided an explanation for this result. Four of the 10 5- and 6-year-olds in the distance + end-point training group appeared to adopt a reverse end-point rule: that is, they consistently chose the train that stopped farther *behind* as having gone for more time. This rule did not appear in any of the other three training groups: children apparently resorted to it only when no alternative rule could be discovered.

Posttest

The effectiveness of different types of training on children of each age group was first examined using separate 7 (problem type) × 2 (distance training: present or absent) × 2 (end-point training: present or absent) analyses of variance of the number of correct posttest answers. Among the 5- and 6-year-olds, endpoint training exercised a significant effect, as did problem type. There was also a significant problem type by end point interaction. The two main effects reflected the fact that children who received end-point training performed better overall than children in the other groups, and that performance on problem types not discriminating end point and time was superior to performance on problem types discriminating end point from time. The interaction reflected the fact that children in the end-point training groups were more often correct than the children in the other two groups when responding to the end-point discriminating problems of the posttest.

Among the 10- and 11-year-olds, the significant effects were for problem type and the problem type by distance training interaction. The main effect of problem type reflected superior performance on problems not discriminating distance from time compared to problems discriminating distance from time. The problem type by distance training interaction reflected superior performance by the children who had received distance training on the distance discriminating problems but not on the nondiscriminating problems.

The results of the rule assessments on the posttest provided further evidence that the effectiveness of feedback was a function of both the child's initial knowledge and the type of problems to which he or she was exposed. In the control and distance training groups (Table 2.5), where end point was not discriminated from time, 14 of the 20 5- and 6-year-olds continued to use an end-point rule after feedback training. However, in the end-point training and distance + end-point training groups, where end point was discriminated from time, only 3 of the 20 5- and 6-year-olds continued to use the end-point rule after feedback.

The most powerful training effect among the 10- and 11-year-olds occurred in the number of children progressing to the time rule. Eleven of the 20 children in the distance + end point and the distance training groups, where distance was

TABLE 2.5
Rule Usage on Posttest

	Rule			
	End point	Distance	Time	None
5- and 6-year-olds				
Control	8	0	0	2
Distance	6	0	1	3
End point	3	0	1	6
Distance and end point	0	0	2	8
10- and 11-year-olds				
Control	0	4	2	4
End point	0	2	2	6
Distance	0	1	5	4
Distance and end point	0	1	6	3

discriminated from time, adopted this rule. Only 4 of the 20 children in the control and end-point training groups adopted it.

As in Experiment 1, some children did not meet any rule usage criterion, yet examination of their errors revealed a nonrandom pattern. This suggested that multiple regression analysis might again provide a useful indicator of the factors influencing the errors of these children. The same dichotomous predictor variables were used as before, with the number of errors on each posttest problem serving as the dependent variable.

The results of the analyses for the 10- and 11-year-olds indicated that regardless of training condition, the most difficult problems were those in which the train that went for more distance ran for less time. The regression analyses of the 5- and 6-year-olds' posttest errors presented a far more complex picture. For children in the control and distance training groups, where end point and time were not discriminated from each other, end point remained the best predictor of errors, as it had been before the feedback sessions. For children in the end-point training group, where feedback disconfirmed the end-point rule but left open the possibility of the distance rule, the best predictor of posttest errors was distance. However, in the distance + end-point training group, where both the end-point rule (which the 5- and 6-year-olds normally favored) and the distance rule (which they would normally follow next) were disconfirmed, no strong predictor of the children's numerous posttest errors emerged.

A closer examination of the individual responses revealed the reason for this: the four children who had adopted a reverse end point formulation during feedback training continued to be influenced by this rule, while the other six children adopted a different approach. This impression was confirmed by regression analysis using the posttest errors of the four children who had adopted a reverse end-point rule during feedback. End point accounted for 52% of the variance in the errors made by these children on the posttest. In addition, the coefficient of end point was negative, indicating that the hardest problems were those in which the train that went for more time stopped farther ahead of the other. A similar regression analysis of the remaining six children also resulted in end point being most significant predictor variable (28% of the variance). However, the coefficient of end point was positive for this group, indicating that the hardest problems were those in which the train that went for more time stopped farther behind the other.

DISCUSSION

The major goal of this experiment was to determine if rule assessments could be used to predict children's responses to different types of training. This proved to be the case: End-point discriminating problems were more effective training for 5- and 6-year-olds, while distance discriminating problems were more effective training for 10- and 11-year-olds. Feedback on problems that discriminated their favored rules from time seemed to be an effective method to encourage children to search for more accurate time rules.

Although feedback on problems discriminating a preferred cue from time was not sufficient to guarantee a child's success, it was sufficient to provoke the search for a new rule. When the 5- and 6-year-olds were given feedback on end-point discriminating problems, they turned their attention to the distance cue, the formulation favored by older children. However, when these children were given problems that discriminated end point (their favored cue) *and* distance (the cue they would normally come to use next) from time, they were not successful in discovering the time rule. Instead, two distinct groups of children emerged. One group tended to follow a reverse end-point rule during training and on the posttest, while the remaining children tended to follow the standard end-point rule. In this case, then, direct training of the concept was not as successful as training to the next state the child would normally acquire.

Ten- and 11-year-olds also had difficulties in their search for an effective time rule; although distance discriminating problems were much more effective in teaching the time rule to these children than the other forms of training, this form of training still allowed only 55% of the children to master the time rule. Two children in the distance training and distance + end-point training groups continued to use the distance rule even after training, and seven children fell in the no-rule group. Why did these 10- and 11-year-olds have so much difficulty learning the time rule after extensive feedback training with problems especially designed to fit their existing knowledge states? This question led to the next experiment.

Experiment 3A

In order to discover exactly why 10- and 11-year-olds had so much trouble mastering the time concept, Robert Siegler and I performed a task analysis of the time problems. To answer the question, "Which train ran for more time?" the child would have to perform two separate tasks. First, the child had to encode the relative beginning and ending times of the trains. Second, the child had to derive the correct answer from this information by making a logical inference. Difficulty in performing either the encoding task or the inference task could cause the child to make errors on these time problems. Finally, it was possible that both of these potential problems were present: that the children neigher encoded the information needed to solve the problems nor were able to draw the proper inference. Experiment 3A was designed to examine all of these possibilities.

METHOD

Sixteen children (eight fifth graders and eight sixth graders) participated in both the inference assessment and the encoding assessment portion of Experiment 3A.

Encoding Assessment

Nine different problem types were utilized in this experiment and the following one. This problem set consisted of problem types 1–5 from Experiment 2 plus four new problem types. These additions were prompted by the desire to increase the number of problem types discriminating each of the seven relevant dimensions (duration, speed, distance, end time, end point, beginning time, and beginning point) from each other.

The problem set was designed to assess the accuracy of beginning and end time encoding as well as rule usage on duration judgments. Three instances of each of the nine problem types were created. One of the three instances of each problem type was arbitrarily designated a duration problem, one a beginning time problem, and the remaining instance an end-time problem. The designations signaled whether the child would be asked about the travel times, the beginning times, or the end times of the trains. The 27 problems were presented in a stratified random order so that one of each of the problem types appeared among the first nine problems, one among the second nine, and one among the last nine. The following rule criterion was adopted: In order to be said to be using a rule on the time concept, the child was required to answer at least eight of the nine problems in the exact manner predicted by that rule.

Each child was brought individually to a vacant classroom as before. Upon arrival, the child was instructed to watch the trains and to be prepared to answer: (*a*) if the trains ran for the same amount of time or if one ran for more time, (*b*) if the trains started at the same time or if one started first, and (*c*) if the trains stopped at the same time or if one stopped last. The children were then shown the 27 problems and were asked one of the three questions after seeing each.

Inference Assessment

In order to test the inference-making abilities of these children, two inference problem types were developed. These two problem types corresponded to the two types of inferences that would correctly determine which train ran for more time. The two problem types were:

1. *The trains start at the same time. The blue (red) train stops last. Which train ran for more time, or did they run for the same amount of time?*

2. *The blue (red) train starts first. The trains stop at the same time. Which
train ran for more time, or did they run for the same amount of time?*

The children received the inference assessment test the day following the
encoding assessment test. They were given a sheet of paper with the two inference problems listed on it and were asked to read each problem aloud, to solve
each problem, and to record their answers.

RESULTS

Encoding Assessment

On the encoding assessment portion of this experiment the 16 children were
incorrect on 31% of the duration questions, 24% of the beginning time questions,
and 16% of the end-time questions. Only 5 of the 16 children were classified as
using the correct rule in judging which train ran for more time, only 5 could
answer correctly eight out of nine times which train started first, and only 10
could answer correctly eight out of nine times which train stopped last. The last
two of these results suggested that the children were experiencing difficulty
encoding the relative starting times and stopping times of the trains—the information necessary to answer which train ran for more time.

Inference Assessment

These children also experienced difficulty on the inference assessment test.
Recall that in this task, all of the information necessary to solve the time
problems—and only that information—was supplied to the children. Even so, the
10- and 11-year-olds were unable to utilize that information correctly on 25% of
the problems. Only 11 of the 16 children were correct on both problems.

DISCUSSION

In order to judge correctly which of the two trains ran for more time, children
would have to successfully accomplish two component tasks. First, they would
have to encode the relevant information—the relative beginning and end times of
the trains. Then, they would need to draw the appropriate inference from that
information. In Experiment 3A, children's abilities to perform each part of the
task were considered. Ten- and 11-year-olds were found to have difficulties both
in inference-making and encoding. These difficulties thus seem the plausible
causes of the 10- and 11-year-olds' poor responses to feedback training. In order
to further test this hypothesis, the next step was to train children in inference-

making and encoding and then to see if their time judgments improved as a consequence.

Experiment 3B

In order to conduct this experiment, instruction aimed at improving the inference-making and encoding abilities of 10- and 11-year-olds needed to be devised. One strategy hypothesized to aid encoding involved having the child say aloud at the beginning of each problem which train started first (or if they started at the same time) and having the child say aloud at the end of each problem which train stopped last (or if they stopped at the same time). The use of this encoding strategy would insure that the child paid attention to the beginning and end-time information. In addition, the strategy served as a memory aid, since the child would need only to remember what he had said to recall which train started first and which stopped last. Inference instruction involved briefly describing the two problem types to the child and providing him or her with explicit rules through which to determine which train ran for more time. A 2 (encoding instruction: present or absent) × 2 (inference instruction: present or absent) factorial design was employed. This resulted in four groups: a group receiving encoding instruction and inference instruction, a group receiving instruction only in encoding, a group receiving instruction only in inference-making, and a control group receiving no special instruction.

METHOD

Sixty-four children (32 fifth graders and 32 sixth graders) participated in Experiment 3B. The same 27 problems used to assess encoding in Experiment 3A served as stimuli for this study. Eight fifth graders and sixth graders were randomly assigned to each of the four instructional groups.

Each child was brought individually to a vacant classroom and given the same initial instructions given the encoding assessment group in Experiment 3A. Then, the children in the two encoding instruction groups were told to say out loud which train started first and which stopped last. The children in the two inference instruction groups were taught the two rules by which the beginning and end times of the trains could be combined to determine which train ran for more time. All children were then shown the 27 problems as in the encoding assessment portion of Experiment 3A.

RESULTS AND DISCUSSION

Separate 2 (encoding training: present or absent) × 2 (inference training: present or absent) ANOVAs were conducted for the duration, beginning time, and end-time problems. On the duration problems, there was a significant interaction between inference training and encoding training. Children who received both types of training made errors on only 5% of the duration problems, compared to 31% by the control group, 24% by the inference group, and 31% by the encoding group.

A similar pattern was presented by the number of children in each group who met the rule usage criterion for the duration problems. Fifteen children who received both encoding and inference training used the time rule, compared with five children in the control group, five in the inference training group, and four in the encoding training group.

The ANOVAs also revealed that verbal encoding instruction led to significant improvement in the accuracy of both beginning and end-time problems. However, verbal encoding by itself had no significant effect on the performance of duration problems. By contrast, inference training significantly improved performance on duration problems but did not significantly alter performance on beginning and end-time problems.

In sum, it appeared that both encoding and inference-making limitations were responsible for children's difficulty in separating time from spatial dimensions. When the children were taught how to remember the relevant dimensions as well as how to combine them to determine the outcome, they were consistently correct on both duration and encoding questions.

Finally, even though the problem set used in this experiment differed from that used in either Experiment 1 or Experiment 2, regression analyses of the duration errors made by each group in Experiment 3B resulted in the emergence of the same interfering factor. Sixty-four percent of the error variance of the control group, 84% of the error variance of the inference training group, and 77% of the error variance of the encoding training could be accounted for in terms of the status of the distance cue. Children in the inference and encoding training group made too few errors for reliable regression analysis.

GENERAL DISCUSSION

In the beginning of this chapter, three questions were posed. Experiments designed to address each question were presented. The first question, How can we characterize the developmental sequence of knowledge states leading to an understanding of the time concept? was addressed by Experiment 1. It was found that very young children predominantly confused time with end point, while many older children confused time with distance. In general, errors on time problems by subjects of all ages appeared to occur because of the confusion of time with spatial dimensions. Experiment 2 addressed the second question, How do children progress from one knowledge state to the next? The experiment demonstrated that one way children's understanding of the time concept might increase was through experience with problems that discriminated spatial dimensions from time. Such experience is believed to help the children more fully establish the relationships between those spatial dimensions and time and the conditions under which the relationships are valid.

The final experiment was designed to investigate the third question, What makes the time concept so difficult, and why don't children understand it earlier in development? To put the question another way, Why do children persist in utilizing the relationships between time and spatial dimensions as time cues instead of relying on purely temporal ones? Experiments 3A and 3B suggested two reasons for this (*a*) the children found it difficult to encode and remember the necessary temporal cues, and (*b*) the children had difficulty making the inference from these cues, which would determine which train ran for more time. Experiment 3A suggested that both of these difficulties existed. Experiment 3B found that when the children were trained in both encoding the proper cues and combining those cues to determine the outcome, they performed the duration comparison task at an adult level.

In the final section of this chapter, I would like to use the results of these three experiments to speculate about the answers of two difficult questions: (*a*) Why is the time concept so much more difficult then the speed and distance concepts? and (*b*) Why do children rely on end point and distance, rather than on other cues to judge time?

One answer to the first question can be found by comparing the task requirements of determining time, speed, and distance. The tasks appear to differ in three ways: in the type of material that must be held in memory, in the number of separate steps to the solution, and in the difficulty of each step. Speed perception requires only that the child observe whether the space between the trains narrows or lengthens when both trains are in motion. Distance perception requires that the child remember the beginning points of both trains. The child can then observe the clearly visible end points of the trains and compare the resulting distances. Time perception requires that both the relative beginning times and the relative end times of the trains be encoded and remembered, since neither is clearly visible as is end point.[3] In addition, the travel times of the trains cannot be compared by any method as simple as estimating which of two visible distances is longer. Instead, they must be compared by means of a logical inference. Experiment 3A has already demonstrated that this inference-making task is dif-

---

[3]This is not the only strategy that could be used. The problems employed in our experiments could also be solved by the simple strategy, "If at any time one train is moving and the other is still, the moving train will run for more time." This strategy is not obvious and its use requires the certain knowledge that the trains will always either start or stop at the same time as well as the ability to deduce this strategy from that knowledge. To my knowledge, in all the time studies run to date, no subject has ever spontaneously deduced this strategy.

ficult even for 11-year-olds. Thus, simply on the basis of the type of material that must be remembered, the number of steps to solution, and the difficulty of each step, we would predict that speed was easier to master than distance, and distance easier than time.

The second question, Why do children rely on end point and distance rather than time or some other cue? consists of two subparts: (*a*) Why are end point and distance easier to learn than time? and (*b*) Why are these particular cues used rather than other spatial or temporal cues? The results of the three experiments make tentative answers to these questions possible.

We have already considered reasons why distance might be easier to learn than time. Why might the end-point concept be easier to learn than the distance or time concepts? End point enjoys two major advantages in this duration task: recency and presence. In order to determine which train stopped ahead of the other, the child merely has to encode the positions of the two trains. This is made easier by the fact that end point (along with end time) is the final observable cue and is the only cue that remains clearly visible after the trains stop running. The method by which the children appear to determine distance, by contrast, requires several additional steps. It involves marking the beginning points of the trains (either physically or mentally), observing their end points, and estimating which of the resulting lines is longer. Because this distance comparison method includes the encoding of end point plus several additional tasks, we would predict that the end-point judgment task would be easier than the distance judgment task.

The next question concerns why end point and distance should be utilized by young children instead of alternative cues such as speed, beginning time, or ending time. For the answer to this question, we must examine the way time is utilized in normal discourse.

Time is correlated with many physical cues in the world. In the case of uniformly moving objects, travel time and distance traveled are directly proportional. Because of the power of this relationship, time is often described in terms of distance, and vice versa. The farther a given goal is from the child's home, the longer it takes to get there. The child knows that Uncle Louis's home is farther than Grandma's and also that it takes more time to reach. It is usually equally acceptable to answer the question, "How far away is it?" either by saying "3 miles" or "15 minutes." The powerful relationship between distance and time in everyday usage could be easily recognized and seized upon, and might prove to be very hard to ignore.

Of course, there are other concepts that are related to time in everyday discourse. These include speed, end point, and dozens of others such as the size of growing things. However, none of these are as closely identified with time as distance is, or are associated with time as frequently as distance is. For example, although speed and time are often linked in phrases such as "We must go faster to get there on time" or "We don't need to go fast, we have plenty of time," the terms are not used interchangeably, as distance and time are. The statement "We must go a long distance" implies we will also travel a long time. The statement "We must go at a rapid speed" implies nothing about the length of time we will be traveling.

Finally, one last piece of evidence of the special relationship between time and distance is found in the language itself. Both time and distance share the same descriptors, the terms *long* and *short*. This coincident usage of adjectives could only further the difficulty that the separation of the distance and time concepts poses for children.

Why do 5- and 6-year-olds use end point and not distance to determine travel time? The answer to this question might lie in these children's understanding of the distance concept. Recall that in Experiment 1 it was found that 5-year-olds equated distance with end point. Any attempt to utilize a distance rule in judging total time would appear from the experimenter's point of view to be a use of the end-point rule (cf. Acredolo and Schmid (1980), for a similar argument). Support for this view is provided by the fact that the use of the distance rule to make time judgments appears at the same age that the use of the end-point rule to make distance judgments ceases, at about age 8.

In the beginning of this chapter, I suggested that in the study of concepts in general, as well as the time concept in particular, it was necessary to consider not just the knowledge of the child or the characteristics of the task, but also the interaction between the two. In this chapter I have described three experiments that I believe come close to meeting these requirements.

It is through the study of the interaction between task and child that the myth of immaturity can best be appreciated. Children do not make silly or nonsensical errors on time problems. When viewed in the context of the physical world and the child's limited experience with that world, their errors often make a great deal of sense. It is no accident that many of Piaget's reasoning tasks portray exceptions to general rules—it is on those exceptions that differences between adults' thinking and children's thinking can be appreciated. Whether one attributes knowledge of a concept to a child when he or she first knows the general rule or when he or she knows all the exceptions can often make a difference of many years. The adoption of either point of view as the sole index of development seems extreme. The first associations between time and other dimensions must be formed at a very early age, yet even adults of advanced years probably do not know all of the correlations between time and real world events, or all of the conditions for taking advantage of these correlations. It is time to expand our definition of conceptual mastery to include not only the child's strategies for applying the concept, but also the likelihood of the success of those strategies in the world outside the laboratory. It is through consideration of both of these aspects that we stand the greatest chance of addressing not only the what or the how of conceptual development, but also the why.

REFERENCES

Acredolo, C., & Schmid, J. *The understanding of relative speeds, distances, and durations of movements.* Unpublished manuscript, 1980.

Berndt, T. J., & Wood, D. J. The development of time concepts through conflict based on a primitive duration capacity. *Child Development,* 1974, *45,* 825–828.

Fraisse, P. *The psychology of time.* New York: Harper & Row, 1963.

Hollander, M., & Wolfe, S. A. *Nonparametric statistical methods.* New York: Wiley, 1973.

Kant, I. *Critique of pure reason.* (Norman Smith, trans.) New York: St. Martin's Press, 1965.

Klahr, D., & Siegler, R. S. The representation of children's knowledge. In H. Reese and L. P. Lipsitt (Eds.), *Advances in child development* (Vol. 12). New York: Academic Press, 1978.

Levin, I. The development of time concepts in young children: Reasoning about duration. *Child Development,* 1977, *48,* 435–444.

Levin, I. Interference of time-related and unrelated cues with duration comparisons of young children: Analysis of Piaget's formulation of the relation of time and speed. *Child Development,* 1979, *50,* 469–477.

Lovell, K., & Slater, N. The growth of the concept of time: a comparative study. *Child Psychology and Psychiatry,* 1960, *1,* 179–190.

Piaget, J. *The child's conception of time.* (A. J. Pomerans, trans.) New York: Ballantine, 1969.

Piaget, J. *The child's conception of movement and speed.* (G. E. T. Holloway and M. J. Mackenzie, trans.) New York: Ballantine, 1970.

Siegler, R. S. Three aspects of cognitive development. *Cognitive Psychology,* 1976, *4,* 481–520.

Siegler, R. S. Cognition, instruction, development, and individual differences. In A. M. Lesgold, J. W. Pellegrino, S. Fokkema, & R. Glaser (Eds.), *Cognitive psychology and instruction.* New York: Plenum, 1978. (a)

Siegler, R. S. The origins of scientific reasoning. In R. S. Siegler (Ed.), *Children's thinking: What develops?* Hillsdale, N.J.: Erlbaum, 1978. (b)

Siegler, R. S., & Richards, D. D. Development of time, speed, and distance concepts. *Developmental Psychology,* 1979, *15,* 288–296.

Siegler, R. S., & Vago, S. The development of a proportionality concept: Judging relative fullness. *Journal of Experimental Child Psychology,* 1978, *25,* 371–395.

Weinreb, N., & Brainerd, C. J. A developmental study of Piaget's groupement model of the emergence of speed and time concepts. *Child Development,* 1975, *46,* 176–185.

Wilkening, F. *Integrating time, distance, and velocity information.* Paper presented at the meeting of the Society for Research in Child Development, San Francisco, 1979.

The Nature and Development of Time Concepts in Children: The Effects of Interfering Cues[1]

This chapter presents three studies carried out in collaboration with my colleagues on the nature and development of time concepts in young children. These studies were inspired by Piaget's theoretical framework. Therefore, our presentation will begin with a detailed analysis of Piaget's contributions, including the epistemological implications he derived from his findings, as well as a short review of replication studies performed by others in Western and non-Western cultures. We will present criticism concerning some of his basic assumptions that we investigated in our studies and will attempt a more satisfactory characterization of the time concepts of young children based on an integration of our findings and those of others.

We believe that three aspects of Piaget's theory deserve reconsideration in light of our studies: (*a*) the developmental sequence of various achievements in the understanding of time concepts; (*b*) the nature of difficulties that children encounter in dealing with time problems at different ages; and (*c*) the epistemological meaning of Piaget's findings. For the sake of brevity, procedural details as well as details of statistical methods and of results have been omitted

---

[1]This chapter is Working Paper Number 1 of the Tel-Aviv University Study Group on Human Development.

The Developmental Psychology of Time

from the description of our studies. The interested reader may refer to the original publications (Levin, 1977; Levin & Gilat, 1981; Levin, 1979); for further information on studies I, II, and III, respectively.

Our studies are part of a general trend in present day developmental psychology, namely the attempt to understand children's processing of information by using a wider variety of tasks than those used by Piaget and by undertaking a careful analysis of the difficulties that children encounter on different types of tasks. Following the description of our studies, we will present the facet model, which incorporates the salience factors we used to predict the relative difficulty of various problems in the different tasks employed in all three studies.

PIAGET'S "CYCLIC" MODEL OF DEVELOPMENT: THE CHILD, NEWTON, AND EINSTEIN

A General Outline: From the Child to Einstein

The development of time concepts in children is an interesting issue in its own right for developmental psychologists as well as for educators. For Piaget, the epistemologist, however, interest in this issue stems from a different source as well. He believes that the child's intuitive schemes of time, space, and speed are illustrations of the occurrence of partial isomorphism between children's intuitions and concepts in modern science (Piaget, 1950, 1957, 1964, 1971).

According to Piaget, the child's intuitive notions of time, space, and speed are in some ways more consistent with modern physics, particularly with Einstein's relativity theory, than are the physical concepts of adults. With development, however, the child gives up these intuitive notions in favor of concepts that are in line with Newton's mechanical theory of physics. For all practical daily purposes, Newtonian physics continues to provide adults with the only, absolute, comprehensive and self-evident logic of the physical world.

This state of affairs, though it implies a kind of "return to the primitive" by the modern physicist (Piaget, 1950, pp. 234–235), does not indicate any regression in cognitive development. On the contrary, children's acquisition of the Newtonian scheme marks a step forward in their understanding of the physical world, a step that is necessary for the subsequent construction of modern physics. Such a "cyclic" model of development is somewhat different than that proposed by Piaget in his explanation for the reoccurrence of parallel achievements at different cognitive stages and from the cycles that have recently become a focus of attention in theories of development (Bower, 1974, 1979; Strauss, in press). It differs in that the Einsteinian concept of time is achieved only with special training in physics and, thus, cannot be viewed as the natural end state of the development of the time concept. It may be, however, that this understanding will become in the future as widespread and self-evident for the adult as the knowledge that the earth is not flat.

The explanation provided by Piaget (1950, 1957, 1971) for the intriguing phenomenon of some commonalities between the intuitions of the young child and the concepts of the sophisticated modern physicist was further interpreted and elaborated by Capec (1971). Physical concepts, according to Piaget's general theory, develop with age through adaptations to, and assimilations of, the experience of physical objects (Piaget, 1970b, 1971). But this experience is limited by the very nature of our sensory systems to the macrophysical world of solid bodies. It does not include "the microphysical world of quanta and the world of fleeting galaxies [Capec, 1971, p. 65]." In this respect, daily human experience is limited to what Reichenbach calls "the world of middle dimensions." Newton's classical theory of physics, which was based on the macrophysical world, can only be applied to that framework. Hence, Piaget claims that infants and children are free from conceptions derived from the experience with solid bodies (such as the permanence of objects or the absolute nature of time and space) due to their limited sensorimotor experience. By gaining that experience, children begin to construct the Newtonian concepts of time, space, and speed that continue to serve them in daily adult life. The modern physicist, on the other hand, abandons Newtonian conceptions "because his experience *transcends* macroscopic experience [Capec, 1971, p. 70]."

Piaget attempted to provide empirical support for this proposed "cyclic" model of development by analyzing the developmental sequence of the concepts of duration and speed. His analysis is based on the difference between Newton's classical physics and Einstein's theory of relativity regarding the relationship between the concepts of time, space, and speed. "In classical mechanics speed is seen as a relationship between space and time. Space and time are the simple intuitions and speed is a relation between them. In the theory of relativity, however, speed is an absolute with a maximum. The maximum speed is the speed of light, and time and space are relative to it [Piaget, 1964, p. 40]."

Hence, in line with modern physics, speed would be seen as the intuitive notion from which time is derived and, therefore, should emerge earlier developmentally. In line with Newtonian physics, on the other hand, speed is derived from time and distance and, therefore, the concept of speed should be grasped later in development. Piaget's findings as to the developmental sequence of time, space, and speed concepts, as well as the implications of our studies in regard to his interpretation of his findings, will be dealt with in the last section of this chapter, "Implications of the Present Studies for the Validity of the Cyclic Model."

The Newtonian Scheme

In order to present Piaget's analysis of the development of time concepts, we will begin by briefly describing the Newtonian "picture of the physical world" which the child is claimed to acquire with development. According to this scheme, time is conceived as a *unitary* and *continuous* dimension, flowing at a *uniform* pace, along which *all events* can be ordered (Piaget, 1969, p. 272). The location of each event on the temporal dimension is unique and absolute so that it does not change under any transformation or perspective taking. Hence, the points on the temporal dimension, as well as the intervals between them, obey the same logicomathematical rules as those of space and number.

A case in point is transitivity of order relations between events: if A preceded B, and B preceded C, then it can be logically deduced that A occurred before C. This succession of events is also logically related to the quantification of the intervals between events. Following the above example, it can be further deduced that duration AC is longer than either duration AB or BC and, moreover, is equivalent to their sum.

Within the Newtonian scheme, time, space, and speed are functionally interrelated (speed = distance/time), but yet are conceived as distinct dimensions. Hence, it is by all means possible for two events to reach *different* points in space at the *same* point in time, or for events that entail *different* velocities to consume the *same* interval of time.

Stages Along the Road to the Newtonian Scheme:
From the Child to Newton

THE INTUITIVE CONCEPT OF TIME

Piaget analyzed the reconstruction of children's time concepts within the framework of three general stages: the intuitive; the articulated–intuitive or transitional; and the concrete operational.

According to Piaget (1969), the intuitive notions of time, space, and speed emerge at about 4–5 years of age, and are reconstructed stagewise until they reach the Newtonian logic at about the age of 9 years. The intuitive child does not distinguish between the abstract dimension of time and the events that occur during that time. Time at that stage acquires its meaning through movements, events, or actions. When two events entail different speeds, the child considers the pace of time of the faster event to be faster itself, as though the movement is its own clock. In the same vein, when two actions conclude with different amounts produced, the child attributes the longer duration to the event that accomplished more.

Thus, time is not conceived to be a unitary, continuous, or uniform dimension. Each event has its own time scale with its particular pace. This pace is not even homogeneous since it may be accelerated or decelerated, according to the speed of the movements concerned. Similarly, the arrest of a movement marks a stop in time, rendering time itself to be discontinuous.

The difficulty of the intuitive child in abstracting time from the events that fill it stems from the inability to take into account, or to coordinate, different velocities. Since the notion of speed is not clearly distinct from the pace of time, when two events flow at different speeds the child is unable to locate them along a unitary common time scale. Hence, he or she treats the two events or movements as a single action ignoring their speed differences. Thus, duration becomes directly related to the action's outcome or production.

Since intuitive children's images of time are action-centered, or movement-bound, they fail to infer the logical relations between the various time concepts of succession, simultaneity, and duration. For them, two events can start together and stop together but nevertheless last for different durations. Similarly, one of two events that started together can stop later but nontheless consume less time. Within this framework, transitivity of order relations does not exist when two or more events of different velocities are involved, and no objective unit of time is applied when points or intervals are temporally compared.

In Piaget's own words, intuitive time is a

> localized time in the double sense that it varies from one motion to the next, and that it is confused with the spatial order. It is . . . a time without velocities, or a time that is homogeneous only so long as all the velocities are uniform. As soon, however, as actions at different velocities are introduced, the terms "before" and "after" lose all meaning or else preserve their purely spatial sense . . . ; simultaneity is denied . . . ; the equality of two synchronous durations ceases to make sense . . . ; the colligation of durations can no longer be performed . . . —nor *a fortiori,* can the measurement of time. . . [Piaget, 1969, pp. 257–258].

FROM INTUITIVE TO NEWTONIAN CONCEPTS

The advancement from the intuitive notions of time, just analyzed, to the transitional notions of time of the articulated–intuitive stage evolves from the articulation of the concept of speed. Speed, in its intuitive stage, is reduced to experiences of overtaking or overreaching (Piaget, 1970a). Thus, if two bodies move on parallel paths, the one that overtakes the other or that stops farther down the path is judged by children to be moving faster. The limitation of the child's concept of speed becomes apparent when, for example, he or she misjudges the faster body to be the slower one since it stops running first and is then overtaken by its slower counterpart. Similarly, children are at a loss when asked to compare the speeds of two movements when overtaking is unseen. This may happen when the two bodies are seen to enter into, and exit from two parallel tunnels where the phase of overtaking is hidden.

This intuitive notion of speed, in contrast with the more advanced Newtonian concept (i.e., velocity = distance/time), does not imply the understanding of the concept of duration since it does not refer to an interval of time, but rather to order relations between events. In order to grasp the notion of "overtaking," children have only to understand that the body that was at one point in time behind its counterpart, is at another point in time in front of it. Hence, they have only to distinguish "before" and "after" in time from "before" and "after" in space in order to understand overtaking.

With awareness of speed differences of synchronous events, even though speed is deduced only from overtaking or overreaching, children become able to distinguish between the time in which the events took place and their products (e.g., distance covered, water level in a pool). In the case that events are composed of two movements on parallel paths, by taking speed differences into account, children are able to differentiate time from space. The distinction between time and space is, however, limited during this stage (the transitional stage) to either duration or succession. To elaborate, children may understand that the concept of duration is independent of the distance covered, but fail to distinguish "before" and "after" in time from "before" and "after" in space. Hence, when presented with two cars running synchronically at different speeds, and thus covering different distances, children might answer that the cars ran for the same duration (correct) but that one of them stopped later (incorrect). The opposite may occur as well: children may be aware of the distinction between time and space as far as succession points are concerned, and yet fail to apply this distinction for duration. In this case they would judge that the two cars stopped running at the same moment (correct), but still claim that one of the cars ran for more time (incorrect). The common characteristic of these two patterns of responses is that they reflect a lack of understanding of the logical relation between duration and succession. From the adult's point of view, both patterns of responses are not only partially wrong in light of the stimuli presented, but more importantly, they are logically inconsistent.

The third stage, that of concrete operations, is characterized by two major achievements. First, children come to understand the necessary logical relation between succession and duration. It becomes self-evident to them that if two events begin simultaneously and one event stops later, or if one event starts earlier than its counterpart and they stop simultaneously, the two events are, by necessity, of different durations, with the first to start or the last to end being of longer duration. Secondly, children become able to coordinate time, speed, and distance. They are not only aware of the relation between each pair of these concepts, but grasp their total interrelations. Hence, they are able to deal with these concepts within the general logicomathematical framework characteristic of the concrete-operational stage.

The theoretical scheme of the development of time concepts proposed by Piaget, and the procedures he developed in studies carried out in Geneva, have been applied to a number of non-Western populations: Arabic (Al-Fakhri, 1977; Za'rour & Khuri, 1977); American Indian (Dempsey, 1971); African (Bovet & Othenin-Girard, 1975); and Far Eastern (Mori, 1976). By and large, it was found that the development of time concepts among non-Western subjects followed the Piagetian stages, although with a possible lag of 2–4 years (Al-Fakhri, 1977; Bovet & Othenin-Girard, 1975; Dempsey, 1971; Za'rour & Khuri, 1977). However, the ecological validity of studies using the Piagetian paradigm in a cross-cultural context has been questioned recently (see reviews in, for example, Cole & Scribner, 1974; Dasen, 1977).

A CRITICAL ANALYSIS OF PIAGET'S CONCLUSIONS: THREE STUDIES

The following studies critically appraise two aspects of Piaget's approach to the child's development of time concepts: (a) the sequence in the development of various competences in dealing with time concepts, particularly the point in development at which children acquire the logical inferential relation of duration and succession; (b) the nature of difficulties that children face in comparing duration, particularly the effect of interfering cues.

Study I: The Early Ability to Infer Duration from Succession Points and Its Susceptibility to Disruption by Interfering Cues

INTRODUCTION

The purpose of the first study was to examine the point in development at which children grasp the inferential relations between succession (i.e., starting times and ending times) and duration so that they are able to infer the relative durations from differences in succession. Piaget claims that the child's understanding of these inferential relations emerges *only after* each of these concepts has been differentiated from its spatial meaning, that is, when "before" and "after" in time are clearly distinguished from "before" and "after" in space, and when duration is clearly differentiated from distance. Likewise, the understanding of the inferential relations between duration and succession are claimed to follow the child's understanding of the inverse relation of duration and speed (it takes less time if you go faster) as well as the direct relation of duration and distance (it takes a longer time to go farther). In other words, an understanding of the logical relations of succession and duration marks the end state of the construction of the concrete-operational time concepts.

This sequence in development was demonstrated by Piaget (1969) and gained further support from studies that applied variations of his testing procedures (e.g., Al-Fakhri, 1977; Berndt & Wood, 1974; Dempsey, 1971; Lovell & Slater, 1960; Mori, 1976; Siegler & Richards, 1979; Za'rour & Khuri, 1977). In all of these studies, children were presented with two parallel movements (e.g., running cars) that either started or stopped moving simultaneously. They were asked to compare the movements on different dimensions related to the temporal scheme (e.g., duration, speed, distance). The crucial dimension for the present analysis, however, is that of duration.

In line with Piaget's analysis, young children were found to judge duration according to the amount produced, attributing the longer duration to the movement that accomplished more. The ''amount produced'' can, in principle, take on different forms (e.g., a person's height, number of fruits on a tree, etc.), but in the aforementioned studies, it was most often presented simply as the distance covered by two moving vehicles. The judgment of duration as dependent on differences in either starting times or ending times appeared among upper-middle-class Americans (Siegler & Richards, 1979) as well as among children of non-Western cultures (Dempsey, 1971; Mori, 1976; Za'rour & Khuri, 1977) at about 12–13 years of age, which is an even later age than that indicated by Piaget's work (i.e., 9 years).

However, we argue that this well-established finding (that children up to 12–13 years of age do not infer relative durations from the order of beginning times and ending times) does not mean that they are unable to apply this inference under all conditions. Generally speaking, children (or for that matter adults) may fail to apply a logical or empirical rule to relevant problems for reasons other than the rule being unavailable to them. The failure to utilize a rule may stem from other cognitive, emotional, or motivational limitations, including limitations in processing the information entailed in the particular problem at hand (Flavell, 1977). Different types of limitations in processing information have already been discussed in the literature: deficient detection of, and sensitivity to, the information presented (e.g., Odom, 1978; West & Odom, 1979); limited working memory (e.g., Case, 1974; Norman & Lindsay, 1972; Pascual-Leone, 1970); and inefficient strategies such as impulsivity (e.g., Zelniker & Jeffrey, 1976), to mention but a few.

The failure of young children to correctly compare the duration of two movements may be related to the fact that in the stimulus displays used by Piaget and others, children were presented with a multitude of cues: speed, distance, overtaking, starting points on the track, stopping points on the track, starting times, and stopping times. It is proposed here that when children are required to compare the durations of two movements, even preschoolers understand the relation of each of these cues to duration (e.g., if you stop later you go for a longer time; if you go farther it takes you more time). However, they are unable to coordinate all the relations involved and, hence, they cannot come up with a conclusion such as: if you run farther it takes more time unless you run faster and stop earlier in which case you run for less time. Since young children find it difficult to take all of the cues into account, they are led to consider only some of the cues, probably those that are more salient in the display. Thus, they will tend to ignore stopping times and, to an even greater extent, starting times in favor of other cues such as distance.

This analysis seems to be supported by previous findings. Children of about 6–8 years of age have been found to be able to utilize the inverse relation of duration to speed, but to fail to consider this relation as dependent on the relative distances (Montangero, 1979). In the same vein, young children treat duration as directly related to distance, or at least to stopping points on the track (Siegler & Richards, 1979), but fail to grasp this relation as dependent on the relative speeds. Similarly, we believe that they may infer duration from stopping times, but fail to take starting times into consideration as well.

To conclude the present analysis, we suggest that children's failure to infer relative durations from starting times and stopping times does not necessarily stem from their inability to make such an inference—as may be deduced from Piaget's writings (1969)—but rather because they are distracted from making the inference by other, probably more salient, cues.

In order to provide support for the above analysis, the first study was designed to examine: (a) whether very young children infer relative durations from order of succession points (i.e., starting times and stopping times) when other competing cues are deleted from the display; and (b) whether their tendency to apply this inference is reduced with an increase in the number of additional, possibly interfering, cues.

METHOD

Children in nursery school, first, and third grades were asked to judge the relative durations of three types of time problems: (a) synchronous problems, in which the events to be compared started and stopped simultaneously; (b) beginning problems, in which the events started one after the other and stopped simultaneously; and (c) ending problems, in which the events started simultaneously and stopped one after the other. In each problem the children were asked to judge which of the two events was of a longer duration and to justify their judgment.

The problems were presented on three different tasks: *still time, rotational time,* and *linear time.* These tasks differed on the number and type of interfering cues involved. The still time task was presented by the sleeping time of two dolls which "fell asleep" and/or "woke up" simultaneously. The rotational time task added the cue of speed and was presented by the spinning time of two figures, each fixed to the center of its own turntable and spinning on its own axis. The two figures again started and/or stopped rotating simultaneously, but on this task they also either rotated at the same or at different speeds. The linear time task involved distance cues in addition to those of speed and was presented by the running time of two toy cars on parallel tracks. The cars again started and/or stopped running simultaneously, at the same or at different speeds, but in this task they also covered the same or different distances. Thus, the linear time task entailed at least two interfering cues (i.e., speed and distance), the rotational time task entailed one (i.e., speed), while the still time task entailed none.

Children's answers to each problem included two parts: a duration judgment and an explanation. The following three levels of stringency were used to define correct answers: (*a*) correct judgment of duration regardless of the child's explanation; (*b*) correct judgment of duration with a correct explanation, either partial or complete; (*c*) correct judgment of duration with a correct and complete explanation. An explanation was complete if it referred to both starting and ending times (e.g., *"The red doll slept longer because it went to sleep first and they both woke up together"*). A partial explanation included only the nonsimultaneous succession point while the other point was ignored (e.g., *"The red doll slept longer because it went to sleep first"*). For problems in which both the beginning and ending times were simultaneous, reference to either one was counted as a partial explanation.

RESULTS

Each child received nine scores for his or her level of performance based on the proportion of problems solved correctly according to the three levels of stringency on the three tasks. The means of the three age groups are presented in Table 3.1. Analyses indicated that performance on each of the three tasks differed significantly from the other two tasks and improved significantly with age for each of the three levels of stringency examined.

To examine children's explicit recognition of succession (the relative starting times or ending times) as a relevant factor in explaining duration, the explanations that they gave for their judgments about durations were analyzed, irrespective of whether the judgment or explanations were correct with regard to the problem presented. A child was considered to relate to succession as relevant to duration on a beginning problem, for example, when he explained the difference in duration by differing ending times (the red doll woke up first) rather than by

TABLE 3.1
Mean Duration Judgment Scores According to Task, Grade, and Level of Stringency ($N = 144$)

Tasks	Judgment			Judgment and partial or complete explanation			Judgment and complete explanation		
	Still	Rotational speed	Linear speed and distance	Still	Rotational speed	Linear speed and distance	Still	Rotational speed	Linear speed and distance
Grade									
Nursery	74	67	39	53	42	19	12	6	5
First	89	85	43	84	74	25	50	28	7
Third	92	86	59	87	78	40	60	37	21
Average	85	79	47	75	65	28	41	24	11

NOTE: Score range is 0-100.

the actually differing beginning times, or simply selected the wrong doll as the one that slept longer. Two scores were used to assess each child's treatment of succession. The first score was based on a nonexclusive criterion according to which a correct explanation could include, in addition to succession, other aspects of the display, such as distance; the second score was based on a criterion that was exclusive and stipulated that a correct explanation include only succession. Each score consisted of the proportions of problems out of the total that met the criterion. The means of these two scores are shown in Table 3.2.

It is evident that even very young children tended to explain their duration judgments in terms of the relative starting times and/or ending times. Both exclusive and inclusive explanations based on succession increased significantly with age and decreased significantly with the addition of interfering cues to the task. However, this finding requires qualification. While logical explanations for still and rotational time necessarily require reference to succession, this is not the case for linear time, as duration in linear time could be expressed in terms of the relation between distance and speed. It was possible to provide a logical explanation for duration without referring to succession at all (e.g., *"The two cars went the same time because the blue one went faster but it went farther"*). Moreover, even reference to only one of these cues would not necessarily constitute an illogical explanation (e.g., *"The green car took more time because it was slower,"* with the child failing to mention that he knows the distances were equal).

To conclude, in line with Piaget's work (1969) and with other studies (e.g., Lovell & Slater, 1960; Siegler & Richards, 1979), children of the ages sampled (4,6–9,6) did not perform well on the linear time task. However, when they were asked to compare the duration of two rotational movements (i.e., spatial cues deleted), the majority of first and third graders compared durations correctly

TABLE 3.2
Mean Inclusive and Exclusive Succession Explanation Scores According to Task and Grade
(N = 144)

	Inclusive scores			Exclusive scores		
Task	Still[a]	Rotational speed	Linear speed and distance	Still[a]	Rotational speed	Linear speed and distance
Grade						
Nursery	73	62	38	73	49	18
First	97	88	49	97	75	20
Third	98	90	61	98	67	23
Average	89	80	49	89	64	20

[a] This test included no systematic variation of irrelevant cues and thus only succession explanation was analyzed.

NOTE: Score range is 0–100.

and explained their judgments logically by referring to starting times and/or ending times. The same holds true to an even greater extent for stationary events (i.e., spatial and speed cues deleted). On the still time task a majority of nursery school children succeeded in comparing durations correctly, and when asked to justify their judgments tended to refer to starting times or ending times. However, only half of them could provide correct duration judgments and back up their judgments by a correct reference to a succession point.

DISCUSSION

The present study supports the conclusion that very young children—even preschoolers—are able to infer relative durations from the order of succession points. This ability, however, is undermined by the introduction of interfering cues. Furthermore, the ability to relate duration to succession does not develop only after duration and succession have been differentiated from their spatial meaning, as might have been deduced from Piaget's analysis, but rather much earlier in development. These findings not only change our view of the developmental sequence of the acquisition of time concepts, but may also indicate that duration, even for very young children, can have a temporal meaning as distinguished from a spatial meaning or one based on amount produced.

Within each age level sampled, children's levels of performance declined from still time to rotational time and further to linear time tasks. This finding seems to suggest that an increase in the number of interfering cues undermines performance level. Such a conclusion, though, cannot be unconditionally established from the present study since the number of interfering cues is confounded with the type of interfering cues. The linear time task, which was the most difficult one, entailed cues that were not present in the other two tasks that did not involve progression in space: starting points and stopping points on the track, overtaking, and distance covered. Hence, an alternative interpretation for the results of the present study is that the young child distinguishes time from speed better and ontogenetically earlier than time from space. At this point we can only hint at two possible explanations for the child's greater and longer lasting difficulty in differentiating time from space: first, a possibly greater salience of distance than of speed; and second, a greater conceptual similarity between duration and distance than between duration and speed. These explanations will be examined later.

The observation that when children are asked to compare events on one dimension (e.g., duration), they often compare them in terms of another dimension (e.g., speed, distance), is not a phenomenon restricted to the area of time concepts. The inability to clearly distinguish between dimensions is indeed one of the major and more thoroughly analyzed characteristics of children's cognition, frequently investigated within the framework of conservation studies. It seems to us, however, that there is a need for careful examination of the cognitive bases for the apparent lack of distinction between dimensions, found in children's comparison behavior in the laboratory. We propose to consider three types of bases:

(*a*) *Preexisting* confusion between the dimension that children are asked to judge and the other *specific dimensions* manipulated in the task at hand. Within the framework of time concepts, this confusion means, for example, that children who systematically judge relative durations according to relative distances thereby reveal that they understand ''time'' to mean, or to be directly related to, ''distance'' cues. In a less strict sense, it may reflect a lack of clear differentiation between the two dimensions and a tendency to process the cues of distance over those of duration. Several authors appear to adopt this view (Mori, 1976; Siegler & Richards, 1979).

(*b*) *Preexisting* confusion between the dimension that children are asked to refer to and a *general category* of dimensions, of which the specific dimensions manipulated in the task are but private cases. Piaget's analysis (as well as Lovell & Slater's, 1960) is consistent with this proposition. The child who systematically judges relative durations in accordance with relative distances reveals, according to Piaget, a preexisting confusion of ''time'' with ''amount produced.'' For children, time does not specifically mean ''distance,'' ''person's height,'' or ''amount of water in a jar.'' Instead, it means, or is confounded with, ''production,'' which is expressed in particular studies by ''distance,'' ''height,'' etc.

(*c*) The confusion is *elicited* by the structure of the task at hand, due to a preexisting tendency among children to *adopt* salient dimensions as being *directly related* to the dimension they are asked to refer to. If this is the case, children who judge time by distance do not necessarily reveal their preferred mode of dealing with time, a mode that is likely to appear in a natural setting. Their behavior is seen as an outcome of an interplay between the structure of the task that emphasizes a particular dimension (distance differences, for example) and their own tendency to assume such salient cues as being *directly related* to the dimension they are concerned with.

Study II: Broadening the Range of Cues that Interfere with Children's Duration Comparisons and the Problem of Additivity of Interference

INTRODUCTION

The study to be described examines two issues that were raised by Study I. The first was concerned with whether children's performances on duration comparisons decrease with an increase in the *number* of interfering cues, irrespective of cue type; and the second, with delineating the *range* of cue types that interfere with children's duration comparisons.

The expectation that an increase in the number of interfering cues should decrease level of performance is not self-evident. On the one hand, if children at a certain cognitive level are ready to adopt any salient quantitative dimension as relevant to the comparison at hand, why should they be led astray by two quantitative dimensions more than by a single very salient one? On the other hand, however, the vast difference in difficulty found in Study I between rotational time problems (which entailed one interfering cue) and linear time problems (which entailed at least two) raises the possibility that the extent of interference is affected by the number of interfering cues.

In order to examine the first problem, it was necessary to separate the effect of number from that of type of interfering cues. To accomplish this, two cues that could be manipulated independently were chosen. The events to be compared could differ either on one of the two cues or on both. Moreover, they could differ on both cues in the same direction (i.e., the same event being higher on both cues) or in different directions (i.e., one event being higher on one cue and lower on the other cue than its counterpart). Such an independence cannot be achieved by speed and distance cues for all types of time problems due to the interdependence among time, speed, and distance. For example, when two vehicles run for the *same time,* it is impossible for the same vehicle to run *faster* and to cover a *shorter* distance. Thus, for this reason, as well as for the sake of broadening the range of interfering cues examined, interfering cues other than speed and distance were used in the present study (i.e., light intensity and lamp size).

The second issue referred to the range of cue types that interfere with children's duration comparisons. According to Piaget, time is perceived and conceived by children only within the context of movement. To quote Piaget's opening sentence of his major work on time concepts, "The aim of this section is to set the development of the concept of time in the kinetic context outside which it can have no meaning [Piaget, 1969, p. 1]." Within this kinetic context, the child does not differentiate between the pace of time and the speed of the movement or activity concerned. Hence, he or she confuses time with the speed itself or—due to ignoring speed differences—with the amount produced. Most of the studies that borrowed Piaget's methodological paradigm of presenting children with duration comparisons of concrete, partially synchronous movements (e.g., Al-Fakhri, 1977; Berndt & Wood, 1974; Dempsey, 1971; Za'rour & Khuri, 1977) provided evidence that children tend to confuse duration with distance. Lovell and Slater (1960) and Dempsey (1971), by replicating Piaget's work in a more comprehensive way, showed duration to be confused with another spatial cue as well: water level in differently shaped beakers.

In most of these studies distance was, at least on some problems, confounded with speed since, in the task presented, the body that covered a longer distance moved faster. Hence, some of their results could have been alternatively interpreted to mean that children may have judged duration by velocity—attributing the longer duration to the faster moving body—rather than by distance.

Siegler and Richards (1979), by using well-selected variations of time problems and by analyzing the *pattern* of children's responses along these variations, could diagnose systematic rules according to which children responded to duration comparisons. In this way they were able to refine the previous conclusions by showing that at an early stage (5–8 years) children judge duration according to spatial stopping points, and only later (12 years) according to distance traveled. The authors were also able to distinguish between duration judgments made in terms of distance cues and those made in terms of speed. They found only one child out of a sizeable sample who erred by basing a duration judgment on speed.

Their conclusion, based on the linear time task, that time is almost never systematically confounded with speed, is put into question, however, by two earlier studies in which different tasks were utilized (Levin, 1977; Montangero, 1977). Both works included situations in which movements clearly differed in speed while distance cues were perceptually minimized. In Study I (Levin, 1977), distance cues were almost eliminated on the rotational time task which was composed of bodies spinning at different speeds on their own axes (though, of course, since the bodies have some volume, the points on their circumference could be preceived as going in circles and thus the faster body covering a longer distance). In Montangero's (1977) research, distance cues were substantially reduced on one of the tasks that applied a pendulumlike movement at different speeds in the form of shoe shining. In both studies, children who erred in their duration judgments were found to be biased by speed in the sense that they tended to attribute the longer duration to the faster moving body, and to explain their judgment in terms of speed. To conclude, this entire body of studies provides evidence that young children's duration judgments are confused with spatial cues, and when these cues are missing or reduced in salience, durations are confused with speed.

In Study II we investigated whether children tend to confuse duration with a wider range of cues than those implied by Piaget's analysis. Children were asked to compare the duration of two stationary events. Since no movement was involved in the display, the events did not differ on speed, point in space attained, or any other accumulative production, but, rather, they differed on quantitative cues that were chosen for being logically unrelated to time. In this study, children compared the durations of two lights the experimenter manipulated to be equal or different in brightness and/or in lamp size.

The expectation that children's judgments of duration would be affected by variations in arbitrary quantitative dimensions, such as those selected in the present study, was based on a general assumption having to do with children's comparison behavior. When asked to compare stimuli or events on a specific dimension (be it duration, liquid quantity, size, etc.) when the events differ on other salient quantitative dimensions as well, young children tend to adopt the other dimensions as being directly related to the one they are asked to refer to. The fact that children are ready to judge one dimension in accordance with another does not mean, however, that they usually or preferably treat these two dimensions interchangeably. It may, rather, indicate patterns of responses they are ready to adopt under specific conditions. Hence, children who have never thought of time as being related to lamp size (why should they?), when asked to compare the burning time of two different sized lamps (a really unusual demand), might nonetheless be led to consider size to be related to time. A confusion of time with brightness and lamp size would indicate that the confusions apparent in children's comparison behavior are elicited by the structure of the task at hand rather than being due to a preexisting confusion between dimensions. This, however, may be true in some, but not all, cases of confusions between dimensions and demonstrating a distinction between the two possibilities may prove to be difficult.

METHOD

Nursery school children and kindergarteners were asked to judge if two lights were lit for the same time, and if not, to decide which light was on for more time. Subsequently they were asked to justify their judgments. Three types of time problems were presented: synchronous problems, beginning problems, and ending problems.

The interfering cues of size and brightness were manipulated so that the lights could be equal on both size and brightness, different only on one of these two dimensions, or different on both. When differing on both, they either differed in the same direction (i.e., the same light being both bigger and brighter), or in different directions (i.e., one light being bigger, the other being brighter than its counterpart).

RESULTS

In line with Study I, children's answers to each problem were scored according to three levels of stringency: (a) correct judgment of duration, irrespective of explanation provided; (b) correct judgment of duration with correct explanation, either partial or complete; and (c) correct judgment of duration with correct and complete explanation.

Each child was assigned nine scores based on the proportion of problems solved correctly according to the three levels of stringency on three tasks. The first two tasks to be mentioned involved the manipulation of a single interfering cue while the third task involved two cues: (a) size task—including problems that were either equal or different on size (b) brightness task—including problems that were either equal or different on brightness; and (c) size and brightness task—including problems differing on both cues either in the same or in different directions.

The means of scores of the two age groups for the three tasks, according to the three levels of stringency, are presented in Table 3.3. Analyses indicated that performance improved significantly with age for each of the three levels of stringency. Performance did not differ significantly between the tasks for each of the three levels of stringency, with the single exception of a significant difference between the size task and the size and brightness task on judgments among nursery school children. The general lack of difference in performance between the three tasks seems to indicate no additivity of interference. Children tended to err on their duration judgments to the same extent whether the tasks included one

TABLE 3.3

Mean Duration Judgment Scores According to Task, Grade, and Level of Stringency ($N = 120$)

Task	Judgment			Judgment and partial or complete explanation			Judgment and complete explanation		
	Brightness	Size	Brightness and size	Brightness	Size	Brightness and size	Brightness	Size	Brightness and size
Grade									
Nursery	57	67	54	30	30	22	5	7	7
Kindergarten	74	74	74	57	52	57	22	24	25

NOTE: Score range is 0–100.

interfering cue (lamp size or brightness) or two interfering cues (lamp size and brightness).

While the comparison between tasks clearly supported the equivalence of the interfering effect of size and of brightness, it could not lead to a clearcut conclusion bearing on the question of their additivity of interference. The preceding analysis is limited in its implications because of several problems. First, the size and brightness task included problems in which the two interfering cues were manipulated either in the *same* or in *opposite* directions. The effect of additivity that may have raised the difficulty of problems in which the two cues differed in the same direction may have been clouded over by performance on the other kind of problems. Second, in the size task as well as in the brightness task, baseline problems, in which no interfering cue was manipulated, were included. No such problem was included in the size and brightness task, so that the three tasks were not directly comparable. Third, the analysis referred to correct responses, treating all types of errors together as one category, so that errors that were presumably related to the interfering cue (i.e., attributing longer duration to the bigger or brighter lamp) were not distinguished from errors presumably unrelated to the interfering cue (i.e., erroneously judging the durations to be equal).

Hence, a more refined analysis was conducted comparing the frequencies of error types on three types of problems: (*a*) problems differing only on size, (*b*) problems differing only on brightness, and (*c*) problems differing on size and brightness in the same direction. A comparison was drawn between the frequency of two error types on these problems: (*a*) "more is more time"—error of attributing the longer duration to the brighter light, to the bigger lamp, or to the lamp that was bigger and brighter; (*b*) "less is more time"—error of attributing the longer duration to the smaller lamp, to the dimmer light, or to the lamp that was both smaller and dimmer. Errors of claiming both durations to be equal were excluded from the present analysis. The findings indicated that children tended to erroneously attribute the longer duration significantly more often to the bigger than to the smaller light, to the brighter than to the dimmer light, and to the bigger and brighter than to the smaller and dimmer light—with these tendencies occurring with a similar frequency on the three tasks and in the two grade levels. No additivity of interference could be inferred due to similarity between tasks in the proportion of the two error types.

We had no definite expectation about children's comparison behavior for problems in which one event had a higher value on one interfering cue while the other was higher on the second interfering cue. On the one hand, if we assume that preschoolers are inclined to consider every salient quantitative dimension as being directly related to the comparison at hand, but that in other respects their logical deductions follow those of the adult, we could expect children to conclude that the two opposing interfering cues would cancel each other out. The child's logical deduction could sound like this *"One light burns longer since it is brighter, yet the other burns longer since it is bigger, so they must burn for the same duration.''*

On the other hand, this kind of logical deduction, sometimes referred to in the Piagetian literature as compensatory reversibility (Flavell, 1977, pp. 83–85), has been claimed by Piaget (Piaget & Inhelder, 1969) to emerge later, a number of years after preschool. This claim has been supported in studies on conservation (e.g., Gelman & Weinberg, 1972) and in the area of duration comparisons as well. Children who could compare the sleeping times of two dolls that differed only in the time of falling asleep or only in the time of waking up, were at a loss when the same doll both started sleeping and stopped sleeping earlier, so that it gained time at the beginning while the other doll gained time at the end. The ability to arrive at an "equal time" judgment that seems to call for compensatory reversibility was lacking even among most third graders (Levin, 1977).

An analysis was carried out of errors on problems that entailed the two interfering cues varying in opposite directions: that is, the brighter and smaller lamp was compared on duration to the dimmer and bigger lamp. Two types of errors were examined: (*a*) errors in which the longer duration was attributed to the brighter light in spite of the other light being bigger and (*b*) errors in which the longer duration was attributed to the bigger lamp in spite of the other light being brighter. It was found that errors in duration judgments in accordance with brightness (type *a*) occurred significantly more frequently than errors on duration judgments in accordance with size (type *b*). The discrepancy between the interfering effect of the two cues was found to decrease significantly with age.

DISCUSSION

The present study supports the conclusion that even quantitative cues that can hardly be conceived in terms of speed, distance reached, or any other accumulative production can also influence (to some extent) the duration comparisons of preschoolers. The lack of additivity of interference seems to indicate that the number of interfering cues per se does not affect the extent of interference. Hence, the lower level of performance found in Study I on the linear time task (which involved both speed and distance as interfering cues) than on the rotational time task (which involved only the interfering cue of speed) cannot be attributed to the simple factor of number of interfering cues. The possible effect of type of interfering cue on level of performance was investigated in the following study.

The finding that, under the condition of direct competition between the two interfering cues, children tend to judge duration in terms of difference in brightness more frequently than in terms of difference in lamp size can be explained within two theoretical frameworks, one perceptual and the other conceptual.

According to the perceptual salience explanation, children's greater confusion of duration with brightness may be due to the possibly greater salience of brightness differences than lamp size differences. The proposed difference in salience between these two cues may be a general phenomenon or may hold true only for certain value differences, including those utilized in the present study.

According to the conceptual explanation, on the other hand, the greater confusion of duration with brightness depends on the meaning that children attribute to time. It will be remembered that Piaget claimed that children tend to grasp time in terms of rate of activity or amount produced. It is possible that brightness conveys energy or work to the child more than does lamp size. If this is the case, the aforementioned result is an outcome of the interplay between the way that children conceive duration on the one hand, and the way they understand each of the two interfering dimensions on the other. This theoretical issue is to be dealt with in future research.

Study III: Equivalence of the Interfering Effect of Time-Related and Time-Unrelated Cues

INTRODUCTION

A major conclusion from Study II is that preschoolers tend to process salient, even arbitrary, quantitative dimensions as relevant to their duration comparisons. Thus, the particular cues they tend to adopt as relevant to time in structured laboratory comparisons are not necessarily cues that they habitually, preferably, or spontaneously confuse with their notion of time. To go one step further, this conclusion may also imply that the confusions that children exhibit of time with speed, or of duration with distance, are not necessarily preexisting confusions, but may rather be readily activated in an experimental context in which distance or speed differences are emphasized while the child's task is related to duration. If this is the case, then children would confuse duration with cues that, according to the adult's logic, are related to time (e.g., speed, distance) to the same extent as with cues logically unrelated to time (e.g., brightness, lamp size). If, however, these two types of confusions are based on a different mediational mechanism, then *perhaps* the confusion of duration with time-related cues would outdo the confusion of duration with time-unrelated cues.

Study III investigated the interfering effect of a time-related cue (i.e., rotational speed) with that of a time-unrelated cue (i.e., light brightness). Rotational speed was chosen rather than distance since when movements differ on distance, they in fact differ concurrently on other cues as well: starting points on the track, stopping points on the track, overtaking, as well as linear speed. Rotational speed, however, can be manipulated singly. Brightness was chosen rather than lamp size since it appeared to be the more potent interfering cue, albeit only under the condition of direct competition between the two interfering cues.

METHOD

Children of nursery school, kindergarten, and first grade were asked to compare the durations of two events that started and/or stopped simultaneously and to justify their judgments. Two types of events were presented, one differing on speed, the other differing on brightness. Speed differences were presented, as in Study I, by two figures rotation on their own axes. Brightness differences were presented, as in Study II, by two equal-sized lights burning at different intensities. Thus, the interfering effects of the two cues were compared only with tasks in which each of the cues was manipulated singly. Since brightness and lamp size were found in Study II to have a similar interfering effect when each was manipulated singly, while brightness interfered with duration comparisons to a greater extent than lamp size when both differed concurrently in opposite directions, the design of the present study is somewhat limited. Due to technical difficulties, we could not include a task presenting two lamps burning at different intensities and rotating at different speeds on their own axes.

RESULTS

Each child received six scores for his or her level of performance on the two tasks based on the proportion of problems solved correctly, corresponding to the three levels of stringency. The means of these scores were presented in Table 3.4.

Consistent with the results of Studies I and II, when the events to be compared on duration differed on a single interfering cue, the majority of kindergarteners succeeded in comparing durations correctly and most of the first graders could also explain their judgments by providing the logical reference to starting times and/or ending times. Performance improved significantly with age and did not differ significantly between the two tasks.

The crucial result was the similarity in the interfering effect of speed and brightness. Analysis of the frequency of different error types indicated that among children who erred on their duration judgments, the number of those choosing the faster rather than the slower figure was similar to the number of those choosing the brighter rather than the dimmer light. We should remember, however, that in line with our finding for brightness versus size, it is possible that speed could have overridden brightness had both interfering cues been presented in opposite directions. This possibility must await future research.

TABLE 3.4
Mean Duration Judgment Scores According to Task, Grade, and Level of Stringency ($N = 72$)

Task	Judgment		Judgment and partial or complete explanation		Judgment and complete explanation	
	Brightness	Rotational speed	Brightness	Rotational speed	Brightness	Rotational speed
Grade						
Nursery	66	62	27	26	3	0
Kindergarten	76	74	48	42	9	6
First	86	87	78	70	33	27
Average	76	74	51	46	15	11

NOTE: Score range is 0–100.

DISCUSSION

A major conclusion that may be suggested by the present study is that neither the direction of interference nor its extent depends on the logical relatedness of interfering cue to time, at least when the interfering cue is manipulated singly. However, in contrast with these findings stands the finding that duration comparisons of linear time problems are far more difficult than any of the other problems utilized in our studies. While brightness, lamp size, and rotational speed seem to lose their effectiveness in interfering with duration comparisons by first grade, distance cues continue to hamper duration comparisons of children as old as 9–12 years of age (e.g., Al-Fakhri, 1977; Dempsey, 1971; Lovell & Slater, 1960; Mori, 1976; Piaget, 1969; Siegler & Richards, 1979). The long-lasting confusion of duration with distance, and especially its dominance over the confusion of duration with speed, requires examination. Two explanations are suggested for this phenomenon, one in terms of perceptual salience, the other in terms of conceptual similarity.

For the perceptual salience explanation, if we assume that (*a*) more salient cues are more likely to be processed as relevant to a problem at hand (e.g., Odom, 1978) and that (*b*) spatial cues are more salient than speed, lamp size, or brightness, then we can provide an explanation in terms of perceptual salience for the phenomenon that children confuse time with space more than with the other cues. It could be that spatial cues, and especially stopping points along the track, are more salient than the other cues due to the fact that the stopping points remain visible at the crucial moment of judging duration, while the other cues (i.e., speed and brightness) vanish from sight. This argument does not apply, however, to lamp size since it remains visible too. According to this explanation, the relatively greater difficulty children have in differentiating time from space stems from the structure of the tasks involved, and could be changed by manipulating the relative salience of the various cues.

For the conceptual explanation, if we assume that (a) cues that are more similar conceptually in terms of their attributes, network of relations, or semantics, are more likely to be confused, and that (b) space and time are conceptually more similar than time and speed or than time and each of the other two arbitrary cues, then we can explain the higher confusion of time with space in terms of conceptual similarity.

Time and space, or more specifically, duration and distance, share an attribute not shared by the other cues. Both duration and distance accumulate or increase throughout the event concerned, while each of the other cues remains constant. In other words, duration and distance are built up with time, whereas rotational speed, lamp size, and brightness remain unchanged from beginning to end.

This explanation brings us back to Piaget's formulation of the child's concept of time. He claimed that time is conceived in terms of work done or production accomplished. While we now know that duration may be confused with other types of cues as well (e.g., lamp size), this last phenomenon may be based on a different mediational mechanism of "*any* more is more time," and be limited to lower levels of cognition—that of preschoolers. If accumulation with time is the attribute that makes distance so potent in its interference with duration, then duration should be confused to a similar extent with accumulative nonspatial cues as well (e.g., a lamp that increases in brightness with time versus a lamp that burns with the same brightness from beginning to end).

Facet Model of Salience Factors: Analysis of Task Equivalence in Studies I, II, and III

THE MODEL: SALIENCE FACTORS AND THEIR INTERACTION WITH VARIOUS TIME PROBLEMS

To examine the contention that similar cognitive processing is involved in duration comparisons of events that differ on *any* single interfering cue, irrespective of cue type, a facet model (Shye, 1978) for the analysis of time problems was applied in all three studies to each of the tasks involving a single interfering cue. This facet model was expected to predict the relative difficulty of different problems within each of the following tasks: (a) rotational speed task (Studies I and III); (b) brightness task (Studies II and III); and (c) lamp size task (Study II).

According to this facet model, the difficulty of duration comparisons depends on three aspects of the stimulus display: (a) the relevant cue for duration comparisons, that is, the temporal order of beginning times and ending times; (b) the irrelevant cue for duration comparisons, that is, the equality or inequality of the interfering cue (i.e., rotational speed, brightness, or lamp size); and (*c*) the relationship between the conclusions derived from the relevant and the irrelevant cues.

The prediction of relative difficulty of time problems is derived from two factors that were claimed to affect cue salience and a basic assumption pertaining to the three time problems. The first salience factor involves equality of cues: unequal cues are claimed to be more salient than cues held constant (e.g., Levin, Gilat & Zelniker, 1980; Zelniker, Oppenheimer & Renan, 1975). The second salience factor concerns the recency of cues: recent cues are claimed to be more salient than less recent cues (e.g., Fraisse & Vautrey, 1952; Levin, Gilat & Zelniker, 1980; Smedslund, 1966).

As for the basic assumption pertaining to the three time problems, it is assumed that on a problem involving one differing and one simultaneous succession point (i.e., beginning and end problems), the frequency of correct duration comparisons increases as a direct function of the relative salience of the differing versus the simultaneous succession point; while on a problem that involves two simultaneous succession points (i.e., synchronous problems), the relative salience of the two points has no effect on the frequency of correct duration comparisons. When applied to a *beginning* problem, this assumption leads to the expectation that the frequency of correct duration comparisons will increase with a rise in salience of *beginnings* versus *endings*. With regard to *end* problems, the frequency of correct duration comparisons is expected to increase with a rise in salience of *endings* over *beginnings*. Duration comparisons on *synchronous* problems, however, are not expected to be dependent on the relative salience of the two succession points since the ''same duration'' judgment may be based on either of the simultaneous points.

Performance on all three problem types is expected to decrease with the rise in salience of the irrelevant cue, that is, speed, brightness, or lamp size. In line with the aforementioned two salience factors (i.e., recency and equality) and the assumption pertaining to the three different time problems, the following three categories of hypotheses were generated:

1. Performance on end problems will be better than performance on beginning problems due to the fact that the differing succession point is more salient on end problems than on beginning problems because it is more recent. Performance on end problams will also be better than performance on synchronous problems due to the inequality (i.e., nonsimultaneity) of the end succession point on end problems. The relative difficulty of beginning problems and synchronous problems cannot be directly derived from the aforementioned assumptions. We will tentatively assign more difficulty to beginning problems since their simultaneous end points may interfere with correct duration comparisons while no such interfering effect is to be expected on synchronous problems. Thus, an increase in

difficulty is expected from end problems to synchronous problems and further to beginning problems. (For a more detailed explication of these hypotheses, see Levin, Gilat & Zelniker, 1980).

2. Performance on all types of time problems will be better when the events are equal on the interfering cue rather than unequal.

3. Duration comparisons will yield the highest number of correct responses when the conclusion derived from the order of succession is concordant with that derived from the interfering cue (e.g., one light stops burning after the other and also burns more brightly, which, for the child, means that it burns for a longer duration on both grounds). Duration comparisons will yield the lowest number of correct responses when conclusions are discordant (e.g., one light stops burning after the other, but the other light burns more brightly). Duration comparisons will bring about a medium number of correct responses when the conclusions are partially discordant (e.g., one light stops burning after the other, but both burn with the same brightness).

Following the Guttman procedure (Torgerson, 1963), the model is composed of three facets: one pertaining to the relevant cues, another to the irrelevant cues, and the third to the relationship between the two. Each facet has a range of low to high values indicating different levels of expected frequency of correct responses. Thus, each problem is described three-dimensionally by a profile composed of one value from each facet. The comparison between profiles describing different problems indicates the relative frequency with which they are expected to be solved correctly. The facets and their values are listed in Table 3.5.

APPLICATION OF THE MODEL FOR PROBLEM ANALYSIS:
PREDICTIONS AND RESULTS

The facet model was applied to the tasks that entailed a single interfering cue. Each of these tasks was composed of eight problems (which are listed below) grouped into three categories. For the rotational speed task the high and low values of the interfering cue designate the faster and slower moving figure, respectively; for the brightness task they note the brighter and dimmer light; whereas, for the size task they refer to the bigger and smaller lamp.

1. Synchronous Problem Types
   a. equal interfering cues
   b. unequal interfering cues
2. End-Problem Types
   a. equal interfering cues
   b. unequal interfering cues; the longer duration
      being higher on the interfering cue

TABLE 3.5
The Facet Model

Relevant Cue	Irrelevant Cue	Relation between Relevant and Irrelevant Cue
a_1 = simultaneous beginnings + disparate endings	b_1 = equal	c_1 = concordant
a_2 = simultaneous beginnings + simultaneous endings	b_2 = unequal	c_2 = partially discordant
a_3 = disparate beginnings + simultaneous endings		c_3 = completely discordant

NOTE: The order of increasing difficulty is 1, 2, 3.

    c. unequal interfering cues; the longer duration being lower on the interfering cue
3. Beginning Problem Types
    a. equal interfering cues
    b. unequal interfering cues; the longer duration being higher on the interfering cue
    c. unequal interfering cues; the longer duration being lower on the interfering cue

Figure 3.1 presents the problems' profiles according to the order of difficulty predicted by the facet model. In order to clarify the meaning of the profiles presented in Figure 3.1, let us analyze the profile of problem 3c (the lowermost in the figure). According to the above list, this is a beginning problem with unequal interfering cues with the longer duration being lower on the interfering cue. Since this is a beginning problem, it has disparate beginnings + simultaneous endings, and hence is assigned a_3 according to Table 3.5. Since the problem is unequal on the interfering cue, it is further assigned b_2. Because the longer duration on this problem is lower on the interfering cue (slower, dimmer, or smaller), it is also assigned c_3. The position of this problem's profile in Figure 3.1 indicates the expectation that it will be the most difficult problem. Arrows run from problem 3b, 3a, 2c, and 1b to problem 3c since the latter is predicted to be more difficult than each of the former problems. The expectation for its greater difficulty over problem 3b, for example, is based on facet $c(c_3 > c_1)$. Arrows do not connect problems whose difficulty cannot be ordered by the model. For example problem 3b is not connected to problem 3a since, on the one hand, problem 3b might have been expected to be more difficult due to facet $b(b_2$

$> b_1$), while on the other hand problem 3a could be expected to be more difficult due to facet $c(c_2 > c_1)$.

Figure 3.2 presents the problems according to the aforementioned order of difficulty, giving the percentage of children who solved each problem correctly. In spite of the fact that the tasks presented entail different types of interfering cues, one logically related to time (i.e., speed), one possibly related by the children to work energy (i.e., brightness), and one presumably unrelated to both (i.e., lamp size), the problems included in these tasks were found to be ordered in difficulty in accordance with the same facet model, with rare exceptions. This result seems to be robust since the data were obtained by different experimenters, in different studies, with children who came from neighborhoods of somewhat different socioeconomic levels (though most were from middle- to upper middle-class). Furthermore, the frequencies for each grade level, taken separately, followed the same pattern, with almost no exceptions. This was also true for the third grade in Study I, which was omitted from Figure 3.2 for the sake of comparability in terms of age level with the other studies.

The predicted order of difficulty of the different problems within each task was further supported by analyzing the *individual* patterns of incorrect versus correct judgments for each child, within each task, through the use of the Guttman Scalogram Analysis. Since the model could not predict the complete order among all the problems (e.g., no order is predicted for problems 1a, 2a, and 2b; see Figure 3.1), all the possible complete scales were built, resulting in eight partially overlapping scales. The mean coefficient of scalability for the scales on each of the five tasks, presented in Figure 3.2, was found to be above the criterion level for perfect scalability (Torgerson, 1963, p. 328). Thus, the same model was shown to be applicable to different tasks entailing a single interfering cue, thereby supporting the equivalence between them in terms of information processing.

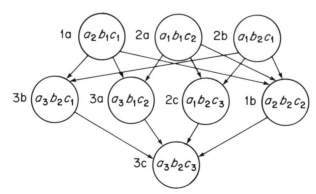

Figure 3.1. Problem profiles arranged according to predicted order of difficulty. Arrows run from easier to harder problems.

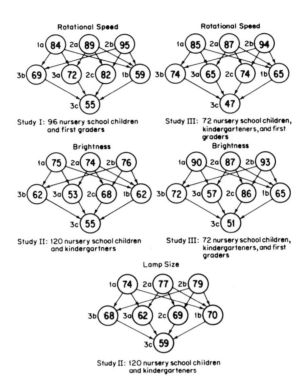

Figure 3.2. Problems arranged according to predicted order of difficulty, with the percentage of correct judgments.

GENERAL CONCLUSIONS

The Present Studies within the Framework of Current Issues and Methodology in Cognitive Development

The present studies seem to follow the line of research that appeared in the late sixties that was involved in simplifying Piagetian tasks in order to disentangle the various factors determining children's levels of performance. The assumption behind this line of research is that children's logic is more advanced, and that their knowledge of the physical or social world is richer than might have been deduced from their performances on the traditional Piagetian tasks. Hence, it is assumed that if (*a*) too great a load on their memory was eliminated; (*b*) the salience of cues that distract their attention decreased; (*c*) verbal misunderstandings removed; etc., children should be able to reveal their cognitive repertoire in more comprehensive form.

This line of inquiry has been applied in various areas, including conservation (Gelman, 1972; Mehler & Bever, 1967), spatial decentration (Hughes, 1975, reviewed by Donaldson, 1978), transitivity (Bryant, 1974) class inclusion (Markman & Seibert, 1976), and control of variables (Case, 1974), to mention but a few. We have applied it to the area of the development of time concepts, which had remained until recently in quite a deserted corner.

Early replications of Piaget's studies (e.g., Dodwell, 1960; Lovell, 1959; Lovell & Slater, 1960) seem to have been based on the assumption that the only operational definition of a *competence* proposed by Piaget (e.g., number conservation, having a concrete-operational concept of time) is the task he had invented to examine it or, at most, some minor variation of this task. It is now believed by many that the Piagetian tasks used confound informational processing limitations of the child with the logical inferential ability that the task was intended to examine. To overcome this objection, studies were designed that attempted to distinguish between the "core competence" and all the other "extraneous factors" that play a part in the child's performance on the Piagetian task but that do not belong to this core competence according to his own theoretical analysis. It should be fully understood, however, that no task, no matter how simple, can be claimed to exclude *all* extraneous information processing limitations. In fact, doubts may be raised as to whether the simplified tasks do, indeed, capture the competence, as defined by Piaget, in its entirety. (The interested reader may refer to Larsen (1977) for a harsh, but illuminating, criticism of this appraoch.)

Our definition of understanding time concepts follows *some* of the criteria that could be extracted from Piaget's analysis, but not all of them. Hence, we will refer to it as a *basic* understanding of the concept of time, rather than a comprehensive one. A *basic* understanding of the concept of time was defined in the present studies as "the ability to infer relative durations from differences in either starting times or in ending times, under the condition of no interfering cues being involved." This criterion of understanding time concepts is more lenient than Piaget's criteria or than that applied in subsequent studies in two different ways: first, the definition does not include the ability to ignore interfering cues; and second, it does not entail the ability to back up the correct judgment by a logical explanation.

The utility of this definition is that it draws attention to early intuitions that very young children have, even in nursery school, about time concepts, instead of emphasizing their total inability to compare durations in highly complex contexts. However, this definition does not seem to us any better or worse, more or less accurate, than traditional, more stringent criteria.

Both types of criteria—the lenient and the stringent ones—are arbitrary in the sense that neither may be claimed to screen out those children that have a comprehensive, full-blown, "end state" understanding of time concepts from those that do not. This is obviously the case with the lenient criterion, but is also true for the stringent one. This point is most easily illustrated with the concept of speed. Children who correctly compare speeds in the traditional Piagetian tasks (Piaget, 1970a) and, thus, according to Piaget's criterion, are claimed to understand the concept of speed, may easily fail on more complex tasks. This claim is supported by comparing the findings of different studies. While most adolescents and adults correctly compared speeds on Piagetianlike linear movement tasks (Siegler & Richards, 1979; Za'rour & Khuri, 1977), many adolescents failed on speed comparisons of two superimposed movements (Crèpault, 1979) and even quite a few adults failed the task of comparing speeds of circular movements (Ehri & Muzio, 1974) or of infering speeds from information given on duration and distance (Wilkening, 1981). While we cannot provide an example based on studies with regard to the concept of duration, it almost sounds like a truism that it is possible to devise such a complicated task of duration comparisons that quite a few of those screened as "having" the concept of duration by the regular Piagetian task would fail in that complicated task.

The conclusion, then, is that different competences, including those of "having a certain concept" such as speed, time, weight, etc., can be tested by various tasks, some of which may be ordered according to their level of difficulty. Acquiring a concept is a multistepped, gradual process and the form it takes can be highlighted via at least two complementary methods: by comparing performances of differnet children of different age groups on the same task, as well as by comparing the performance of the same child on different tasks that entail different sources of difficulty. These, in fact, were the methods utilized in the present studies.

The Developmental Sequence of Acquisition of Time Concepts: A Tentative Integration of the Present Studies with the Literature

The findings we obtained enabled us to support two interrelated contentions that refer to the developmental timing of time concepts. First, the application of different types of simplified tasks provided evidence for the gradual nature of the development of these concepts. Second, the present results seem to indicate that the development is not continuous or even, in that it includes various competencies that are acquired at different age levels.

While the basic understanding of time concepts appears among preschoolers, a comprehensive understanding is acquired only by adolescents, adults, or perhaps never, if we include the Einsteinian concept of time. The basic understanding of time concepts has been the focus of our studies. We have found that from preschool on, children evidence the ability to *infer* relative durations from starting times or ending times. Inevitably, this ability includes the prerequisite ability to *compare* starting times and ending times themselves—a competence that has been found to be acquired even earlier (Levin, Israeli & Darom, 1978).

Inferring relative duration from succession points is *the* suitable strategy in comparing durations, irrespective of the complexity of the display (e.g., still time and linear time tasks). However, children who are able to infer durations from starting times and ending times in simple contexts (e.g., still time) were observed not to carry out this strategy or to add other misleading considerations to it under interfering conditions. When the events to be compared on durations differ on quantitative cues other than duration, children's errors were mostly in the direction of attributing the longer duration to the event having the higher value on the interfering cue.

The interfering cue, however, does not replace the relevant cues of the order of starting times and ending times in the children's considerations. It only *adds* a misleading consideration that under particular conditions, to be specified later, leads to errors in duration comparisons. The conclusion that young children continue to take the relevant cue into account, even when interfering cues are involved in the display, is based on two findings. First, it was the rare child who compared the durations on every problem exclusively according to the interfering cue. Second, duration judgments were far more often explained in terms of starting times and ending times than in terms of the interfering cue (Levin & Gilat 1981).

In order to understand the mechanism of interference, we attempted to analyze the effect of three factors on the extent of interference: type, number, and salience of interfering cues. Three types of misleading cues were manipulated—speed, brightness, and lamp size. Speed was selected to represent cues that are logically related to time, whereas brightness and lamp size were chosen to represent cues that are not. By and large, the various cues examined were found to have the same interfering effect on duration comparisons when each was manipulated singly. It was concluded that the extent of interference apparent among preschoolers does not depend on the logical relation of the interfering cue to time. This conclusion implies that the interference does not reflect conceptual confusions between only specific cues and duration, but rather a general tendency to adopt *any* salient cue as relevant to the comparison at hand. Preschoolers and young school children seem to assume that "*any* more is more time."

Two findings, however, point to the conclusion that interfering mechanisms other than "*any* more is more time" are also involved in children's duration comparisons. First, brightness was found to interfere with duration comparisons to a greater extent than lamp size when both were manipulated in opposite directions (e.g., one light being brighter, the other being bigger with synchronous durations). This finding brings us to tentatively conclude that competition between cues leads the child to an additional consideration of "*which* more is more time." Brightness may be selected due to the child's conception that it conveys more "work" or "energy" than does size, and hence sees it as being more time related.

Secondly, while the tasks that included the aforementioned cues posed no difficulty for 7-year-olds, the linear time task continued to be difficult up to 12–13 years of age. The linear time task differs from the other tasks examined by the number of cues involved as well as by their type. If the crucial difference between the tasks is due to the type of interfering cue, then we can conclude that spatial cues, particularly distance, are especially prone to confustion with duration. It should be noted that any movement is a simultaneous change of position in space and in time. Thus duration and distance may be two dimensions that are difficult to disentangle either conceptually, perceptually, or both. It is interesting to note that even adults were found to perceptually confuse duration with distance in situations where both cues were presented and the subjects were required to estimate either durations or distances (Cohen, 1967).

Extent of interference was not found to be affected by the *number* of interfering cues. Two cues—brightness and lamp size—when manipulated concordantly, hampered duration comparisons to the same extent as each of them manipulated singly. The conclusion that the number of misleading cues is of no effect may, however, be restricted to certain types of cues only (e.g., time-unrelated cues) or to a small range of number of cues (e.g., two versus one). More studies are needed to examine these questions.

Analysis of the effect of cue *salience* was performed through the use of a facet model. The salience factors incorporated into the model were recency and inequality, with recent cues assumed to be more salient than less recent cues and unequal cues to be more salient than equal cues. The model successfully predicted the relative difficulty of different time problems on the basis of the salience of the interfering cues, the salience of the relevant cues (i.e., succession points), and the concordance between the interfering and the relevant cues. It was found that a problem became more difficult when the salience of the interfering cue was increased and the salience of the relevant cue was decreased.

This analysis points to the conclusion that perceptual properties of the display that affect the relative salience of the various cues entailed have an effect on problem difficulty. Studies incorporating various cue manipulations could be carried out within this framework and enhance our understanding of the interfering mechanism. One such study focused on salience factors related to similarity between successive problems (Levin, Gilat & Zelniker, 1980).

Duration comparisons, by their very nature, can logically be based on two types of relevant cues: (*a*) temporal cues—the order of starting times and ending times; and (*b*) speed and production cues, which were often presented in studies in the form of speed and distance. Until now our discussion has dealt with the ability to infer relative durations from starting times or ending times. By integrating our analysis with those of other studies that utilized more complex tasks as well, we come to the conclusion that at a very young age, probably in preschool, children exhibit the knowledge that time is directly related to distance and is inversely related to speed (e.g., Fraisse & Vautrey, 1952; Levin, 1977; Montangero, 1979; Wilkening, 1981). The ability to integrate both cues so as to infer duration from the relation of distance to speed is, however, achieved later, at about 10 years of age (Wilkening, 1981). However, even at this age children still fail to clearly distinguish between duration and distance (and perhaps also speed), or to selectively attend to the temporal cues of starting time and stopping time and to ignore other cues presented in the stimulus display (e.g., Levin, 1977; Lovell & Slater, 1960; Siegler & Richards, 1979). The ability to separate the "informational" temporal cues and to ignore the spatial ones—the most suitable strategy for comparing durations—is a very late achievement, one that is not apparent even among 12-year-olds, though it is exhibited by adults.

Implications of the Present Studies for the Validity of the Cyclic Model

Piaget found his claim of partial isomorphism between children's intuitive notions of time, space, and speed on the one hand, and the concepts of modern physics on the other, to be empirically supported by the sequence in development of the intuitive notions of speed versus that of time and of distance.

According to Piaget's analysis, within the framework of Newtonian physics, the concept of speed is derived from that of duration and distance; whereas within relativity theory, speed is the basic concept while time and distance are relative to it. Since the young child is free from Newtonian conceptions, his or her intuitive notion of speed, according to implications derived from modern physics, should be the more basic or fundamental of the three concepts, and hence is expected to develop before the intuitive notions of time and distance (Piaget, 1957, 1964, 1970a, 1971).

Piaget (1970a) provided evidence that the child's intuitive notion of speed is not derived from that of duration and distance. When asked to compare the speeds of two vehicles running on parallel tracks, intuitive children judged speed in terms of overtaking or overreaching. Thus, without grasping either the interval of time (i.e., duration) or the interval of space (i.e., distance) they succeeded in correctly comparing speeds in many contexts, though not in all. They failed, for example, when the faster vehicle stopped running first and subsequently was overtaken by the slower one. In that case children misjudged the slower vehicle to be the faster one, due to their reliance on the cue of overtaking.

The intuitive notion of speed, while not being based on either distance or duration, is based, according to Piaget, on the intuitive notions of spatial and of temporal orders. To understand overtaking means to note that the spatial order of the vehicles has changed from one point in time to the next. In the same vein, in order to grasp overreaching, the child has to note the temporal order of stopping times at the same spatial point.

The intuitive notion of duration, however, is based according to Piaget, on that of speed and distance. In Piaget's own words: "Psychologically, time itself appears as a relation (between space traveled and speed or between the work accomplished and power. . . .), that is, as a coordination of speeds. . . [Piaget, 1971, pp. 111–112]," and again "Speed is therefore initially independent of duration. On the other hand, any duration supposes at any age a speed component. . . [Ibid., pp. 14–15]." To conclude, according to this analysis, the child first grasps the order relations in time and space, thereafter acquires the intuitive notion of speed, and only subsequently grasps that of the interval of time and space.

Piaget's empirical claim as to the sequence of speed and time was neatly confirmed by Siegler and Richards (1979) who compared the relative difficulty of the three concepts—duration, speed, and distance—in a methodologically careful design. They presented trains running on parallel tracks, and asked children and adults to compare the runs on durations, on speeds, and on distances covered. Not only did they find correct comparison judgments for speed at an earlier age than for duration, but also that the incorrect judgments of younger age groups were based on more advanced rules for speed than for duration. Thus, the conclusion was supported that the concept of duration lags in its development behind that of speed throughout a wide age range, perhaps from preschool to adulthood.

This conclusion, however, needs reconsideration in light of the present studies. The intuitive notion of speed may indeed seem to emerge earlier in development than that of duration, when the understanding of these concepts is diagnosed with linear movements. On that type of task, the understanding of duration as related to starting times and ending times appears only at adolescence. However, we have shown that children infer duration from starting or ending times even in preschool, when no interfering cues are involved in the display, and in first grade when a single interfering cue was involved. Hence, the intuitive notion of duration as an interval emerges at approximately the same age level (i.e., preschool) as the intuitive notion of speed. Moreover, just as the intuition of speed does not imply an understanding of duration, the opposite is also true. Duration as inferred from succession points does not necessarily depend on the understanding of speed. Both intuitions—of duration and of speed—emerge in preschool and imply some understanding of temporal and/or spatial order relations (see also Levin, Israeli & Darom, 1978).

Our claim that speed does not emerge earlier in development than duration goes even farther than this. We would like to argue that not only is this developmental sequence refuted for the intuitive notions of speed and duration, but also that the concrete-operational concept of speed does not precede that of duration. The child who understands speed on the concrete-operational level basically grasps speed within the Newtonian framework, that is, as the relation of distance to duration. Hence, it is *logically* impossible for a child to understand speed at this level, while not understanding either distance or duration. In Flavell and Wohlwill's (1969) terminology, at the concrete-operational level, speed is implicatively mediated by both distance and duration and hence should follow them in development.

Why then, were speeds more successfully compared by younger subjects than were durations in Siegler and Richard's (1979) study? Our interpretation is that the children who succeeded in comparing speeds in spite of their failure in comparing durations utilized a different strategy for comparing speeds than that of relating to distance per time. For instance, they could have identified the faster train by direct perception of motion, an intuitive strategy already mentioned by Piaget (1970a) and called by Kuhn (1977) "perceptual blurriness." According to this interpretation, children may succeed in comparing speeds on Siegler and Richard's linear time task, while not understanding the concept completely in its Newtonian meaning.

This interpretation is supported somewhat by the fact that children succeeded in comparing speeds on a linear time task at about 11-12 years of age (Siegler & Richards, 1979), while even quite a few college students incorrectly compared the speeds of circular movements (Ehri & Muzio, 1974), a task that presumably calls for a more complicated strategy for correct speed comparisons.

The claim that speed is a more complex concept than duration was further supported by a study utilizing Anderson's (1980) technique of functional measurement (Wilkening, 1981). This technique, which was devised in order to extract the integrating rules that subjects use in inferring values on one dimension from values on other dimensions, was applied by Wilkening to duration, speed, and distance. While children as young as 10 years of age were found to succeed in inferring duration according to the normative rule of dividing distance by speed, even college students failed to correctly infer speed by dividing distance by duration. Thus, although the correct performance on the two concepts—speed and duration—entailed the same integrating rule (i.e., division), it was found to be applied earlier in development for duration than for speed.

Support for the cyclic model of development seems to be weak from other points of view as well. First, since time and space are claimed to be relative to speed within the framework of relativity theory, then speed should be expected to emerge in development not only before duration but also before distance. This expectation was rarely mentioned by Piaget, and more importantly, was not supported by empirical findings. Siegler and Richards (1979) have shown that on the linear time task, speed and distance emerged more or less concurrently and earlier in development than duration. Wilkening (1981), using the functional measurement methodology, has shown that distance was correctly inferred earlier than duration, which was correctly inferred earlier than speed, a finding that was partly interpreted by him in terms of the type of integrating rules called for and partly in terms of memory load.

Moreover, within the framework of relativity theory, not only is an interval of time dependent on speed, but also order relations in time, including simultaneity, are dependent on the relative speed. Thus, if we take the cyclic model seriously, we should have expected the notion of speed to emerge earlier than that of temporal order. According to Piaget's empirical analyses, however, the opposite occurs since the intuitive notion of speed involves that of temporal order. The conclusion we may draw at present is that the cyclic model does not seem to hold water.

SUMMARY

The studies presented in this chapter were stimulated on the one hand by Piaget's analysis of the development of time concepts, and on the other hand by the theoretical approach entailed in simplification studies analyzing the development of various concepts and logical operations. By using different tasks with various degrees of complexity, we could show that (a) very young children, nursery school children, or kindergarteners, are able to infer relative durations from differences in starting times or ending times, and that (b) this inferential ability is hampered by interfering cues. Interference, up to the first grade, could be created by different salient cues either logically related or logically unrelated to time. Young children's comparison behavior seems to reflect an assumption on their part that "*any* more is more time."

Four conclusions were drawn from our studies, concerning the factors affecting the extent of interference. Extent of interference was found to be dependent on the *salience of the interfering cue* as well as on the *salience of the relevant cues* of starting times and ending times. It was, however, not found to be dependent on the *type of interfering cue,* that is, on its logical relation to time or on the *number of interfering cues* involved in the display. These negative conclusions should be accepted with some reservations, which were presented in detail in the section "The Developmental Sequence of Acquisition of Time Concepts."

The present studies focus on difficulties in duration comparisons that children encounter up to the first grade only. It is, however, a well-established finding that up to adolescence children still fail on the linear time task, which entails a *series* of *time-related* cues. Of particular importance may be the spatial cues involved in this task: starting places, stopping places, distance, and overtaking. More work is needed to disentangle the various competences called for in this task and their sequential development.

Taken in its entirety, the present studies reflect the gradual nature of the development of time concepts and the various types of difficulties encountered at different ages. The studies also imply that the concept of duration, in its basic form, does not stem from the concept of speed. Hence, the developmental sequence of the concepts of duration and speed does not seem to be more consistent either with the Newtonian or the Einsteinian physical framework.

ACKNOWLEDGMENTS

Thanks are extended to Tamar Globerson, Lynn T. Goldsmith, Rachel Karniol, Sophie Kav-Venaki, Asher Koriat, Sidney Strauss and Tamar Zelniker for their helpful reactions and illuminating suggestions. Roberta Goldstein's editorial touch is apparent throughout the chapter, and is appreciated.

REFERENCES

Al-Fakhri, S. The development of the concept of speed among Iraqi children. In P. R. Dasen (Ed.), *Piagetian psychology: cross cultural contributions.* New York: Gardner Press, 1977.

Anderson, N. H. Information integration theory in developmental psychology. In F. Wilkening, J. Becker, & T. Trabasso (Eds.), *Information integration of children.* Hillsdale, N.J.: Erlbaum, 1980, pp. 1–45.

Berndt, T. J., & Wood, D. J. The development of time concepts through conflict based on primitive duration capacity. *Child Development,* 1974, *45,* 825–828.

Bovet, M. C., & Othenin-Girard, C. Etude Piagetienne de quelque notions spatio-temporelles dans un milieu Africain. *International Journal of Psychology,* 1975, *10,* 1–17.

Bower, T. G. R. Repetition in human development. *Merrill-Palmer Quarterly,* 1974, *20,* 303–318.

Bower, T. G. R. *Human Development.* San Francisco: Freeman, 1979.

Bryant, P. *Perception and understanding in young children, an experimental approach.* London: Methuen, 1974.

Capec, M. *Bergson and modern physics,* chap. 8: Bergson, Reichenbach and Piaget. In *Boston Studies in the philosophy of science* (Vol. VII). Dodrecht-Holland: D. Reidel, 1971.

Case, R. Structures and strictures: Some functional limitations on the course of cognitive growth. *Cognitive Psychology,* 1974, *6,* 544–573.

Cohen, J. *Psychological time in health and disease.* Springfield, Ill.: Charles Thomas, 1967, pp. 40–57.

Cole, M., & Scribner, S. *Culture and thought: a psychological introduction.* New York: Wiley, 1974.

Crèpault, J. Influence du repérage sur la durée étude génétique des inférences cinématiques. *L'Année Psychologique,* 1979, *79,* 43–64.

Dasen, P. R. (Ed.), *Piagetian psychology: cross-cultural contributions.* New York: Gardner Press, 1977.

Dempsey, A. Time conservation across cultures. *International Journal of Psychology,* 1971, *6,* 115–120.

Dodwell, P. C. Children's understanding of number and related concepts. *Canadian Journal of Psychology,* 1960, *14,* 191–205.

Donaldson, M. *Children's minds*. London: Croom Helm, 1978.

Ehri, L. C., & Muzio, I. M. Cognitive style and reasoning about speed. *Journal of Educational Psychology*, 1974, *66*, 569-571.

Flavell, J. H. *Cognitive development*. Englewood Cliffs, N.J.: Prentice-Hall, 1977.

Flavell, J. H., & Wohlwill, J. F. Formal and functional aspects of cognitive development. In D. Elkind & J. H. Flavell (Eds.), *Studies in Cognitive Development*. New York: Oxford University Press, 1969.

Fraisse, P., & Vautrey, P. La perception de l'espace, de la vitesse et du temps chez l'enfant de 5 ans. II: Le temp, *Enfance*, 1952, *1*, 102-119.

Gelman, R. The nature and development of early number concepts. In H. Reese (Ed.), *Advances in child development and behavior* (Vol. 7). New York: Academic Press, 1972.

Gelman, R., & Weinberg, D. H. The relationship between liquid conservation and compensation. *Child Development*, 1972, *43*, 371-383.

Hughes, M. *Egocentrism in pre-school*. Unpublished doctoral dissertation, Edinburgh University, 1975.

Kuhn, T. S. *The essentail tension*. Chicago: University of Chicago Press, 1977, chap. 10: A function for thought experiments.

Larsen, G. Y. Methodology in developmental psychology: An examination of research on Piagetian theory. *Child Development*, 1977, *48*, 1160-1166.

Levin, I. The development of time concepts in young children: Reasoning about duration. *Child Development*, 1977, *48*, 435-444.

Levin, I. Interference of time-related and unrelated cues with duration comparisons of young children: Analysis of Piaget's formulation of the relation of time and speed. *Child Development*, 1979, *50*, 469-477.

Levin, I. & Gilat, I. A developmental analysis of early time concepts: The equivalence and additivity of the effect of interfering cues on duration comparisons of preschoolers. Manuscript, 1981.

Levin, I., Gilat, I., & Zelniker, T. The role of cue salience in the development of time concepts: Duration comparisons in young children. *Developmental Psychology*, 1980, *16*, 661-671.

Levin, I., Israeli, E., & Darom, E. The development of time concepts in young children: The relation between duration and succession. *Child Development*, 1978, *49*, 755-764.

Lovell, K. A follow-up study of some aspects of the work of Piaget and Inhelder on the child's conception of space. *British Journal of Educational Psychology*, 1959, *29*, 104-117.

Lovell, K., & Slater, N. The growth of the concept of time: A comparative study. *Child Psychology and Psychiatry*, 1960, *1*, 179-190.

Markman, E. M., & Seibert, J. Classes and collections: Internal organization and resulting holistic properties. *Cognitive Psychology*, 1976, *8*, 561-577.

Mehler, J., & Bever, T. G. Cognitive capacity of very young children. *Science*, 1967, *158*, 141-142.

Montangero, J. *La notion de duree chez l'enfant de 5 a 9 ans*. Paris: Presses Universitaires de France, 1977.

Montangero, J. Les relations du temp, de la vitesse et de l'espace parcouru chez le jeune enfant. *L'Annee Psychologique*, 1979, *79*, 23-42.

Mori, I. A cross cultural study on children's conception of speed and duration: A comparison between Japanese and Thai children. *Japanese Psychological Research*, 1976, *18*, 105-112.

Odom, R. D. A perceptual-salience account of décalage relations and developmental change. In L. S. Siegel & C. J. Brainerd (Eds.), *Alternatives to Piaget: Critical essays on the theory*. New York: Academic Press, 1978.

Pascual-Leone, J. A. Mathematical model for the transition rule in Piaget's developmental stages. *Acta Psychologica*, 1970, *32*, 301-345.

Piaget, J. *L'introduction a l'epistemologie genetique* (Vol. 2) Paris: Presse Universitaire France, 1950.

Piaget, J. The child and modern physics. *Scientific American,* 1957, *196,* 45–61.

Piaget, J. Relations between the notions of time and speed in children. In R. E. Riffle & V. N. Rockcastle (Eds.), *Piaget rediscovered.* A report of the conference on Cognitive Studies and Curriculum Development, Cornell University, March 1964.

Piaget, J. *The child's conception of time.* London: Routledge & Kegan Paul, 1969.

Piaget, J. *The child's conception of movement and speed.* London: Routledge & Kegan Paul, 1970. (a)

Piaget, J. Piaget's theory. In P. H. Mussen (Ed.), *Carmichael's manual of child psychology,* New York: Wiley, 1970. (b)

Piaget, J. *Psychology and epistemology.* New York: Orion Press Grossman, 1971.

Piaget, J. Intellectual evolution from adolescence to adulthood. *Human Development,* 1972, *15,* 1–12.

Piaget, J., & Inhelder, B. *The psychology of the child.* New York: Basic Books, 1969.

Shye, S. (Ed.). *Theory construction and data analysis in the behavioral sciences.* San Francisco: Jossey-Bass, 1978.

Siegler, R. S., & Richards, D. D. The development of time, speed and distance concepts. *Developmental Psychology,* 1979, *15,* 288–298.

Smedslund, J. Concrete reasoning: A study of intellectual development. *Scandinavian Journal of Psychology,* 1966, *7,* 164–167.

Strauss, S. Ancestral and descendant behaviors: The case of U-shaped behavior growth. In T. G. Bever (Ed.), *Dips and drops in development and learning.* Hillsdale, N.J.: Erlbaum, in press.

Torgerson, W. S. *Theory and methods of scaling.* New York: Wiley, 1963.

West, R. L., & Odom, R. D. Effects of perceptual training on the salience of information in a recall problem. *Child Development,* 1979, *50,* 1261–1264.

Wilkening, F. Integrating velocity, time, and distance information: A developmental study. *Cognitive Psychology,* 1981, in press.

Za'rour, G. I., & Khuri, G. A. The development of the concept of speed by Jordanian school children in Amman. In P. R. Dasen (Ed.), *Piagetian psychology: Cross-cultural contributions.* New York: Gardner Press, 1977.

Zelniker, T., & Jeffrey, W. E. Reflective and impulsive children: Strategies of information processing underlying differences in problem solving. *Monographs of the Society for Research in Child Development,* 1976, (serial No. 168).

Zelniker, T., Oppenheimer, L., & Renan, A. Effects of dimensional salience and salience of variability on problem solving: A developmental analysis. *Developmental Psychology,* 1975, *11,* 334–341.

Children's Knowledge about Time, Distance, and Velocity Interrelations

INTRODUCTION

Many situations in everyday life require children to integrate information about time, distance, and velocity. Consider, for example, a little girl who must decide if she can cross the street safely before an oncoming car. Or consider a boy who wants to get peanuts from the next drugstore before the TV movie starts. How fast will he have to walk? Or will he have to take his bicycle? Or will he have to ask his mother to drive him there in her car?

In each case, values on two dimensions are given, and a value on the third dimension has to be inferred, implicitly or explicitly. The little girl has to consider the car's velocity and distance in order to estimate the point in time when the car will cross her path. The boy has to consider time (until the movie starts) and distance (to the drugstore) in order to estimate the velocity with which he must go. Valid inferences in these situations require that the information given be integrated according to a reasonable rule. What are the rules that underly children's judgments of time, distance, and velocity? And what do children know about the relations that exist between these variables?

Surprisingly little research has been carried out to answer these questions. Of the few studies that have dealt with children's understanding of all three

The Developmental Psychology of Time

variables of the time–distance–velocity set, only some have explicitly investigated children's knowledge of the relations that exist between the variables.
However, these studies have been restricted to nonmetric relations. Being in a
Piagetian tradition, these investigators have asked, for example, Does a child
know that "more time" means "more distance" or that "less velocity" means
"more time"?

It is obvious that such knowledge is hardly sufficient for coping with the kinds
of everyday life situations mentioned. First, these situations typically do not
involve comparisons between pairs of time, distance, or velocity information.
Second, the knowledge of a "more is more" or a "more is less" rule does not
necessarily imply that the child knows the exact form of the metric relation that
exists between the physical variables. Finally, these nonmetric responses about
two-by-two relations say nothing about the way in which children combine
information on two dimensions to predict a value on the third.

What is needed, therefore, is information on how children integrate time,
distance, and velocity information in nonchoice situations, on what they know
about the metric relations existing between these dimensions, and on how this
knowledge develops. This chapter describes two experiments that are a first
attempt to investigate these questions. Information integration theory serves as
the conceptual framework, and techniques of functional measurement (Anderson, 1981) as the methodological tool. To put the experiments into perspective,
an overview of previous studies follows.

PREVIOUS RESEARCH

Studying Concepts without Studying Relations

Almost all previous studies on children's cognition of time, distance, and
velocity have been conducted within a Piagetian framework emphasizing logical
operations. Accordingly, this research has concentrated on the acquisition and
development of concepts. Since "logical" concepts are usually characterized in
terms of their relevant features and also in terms of the relations that exist
between those features (e.g., Bourne, Dominowski & Loftus, 1979), one would
expect the previous studies to have investigated children's knowledge of the
relations that exist between the dimensions. However, this has not been the case,
as the following analysis will show.

In the logical–operational paradigm for the assessment of time, distance, and
velocity concepts (e.g., Piaget, 1946/1969, 1946/1970; Siegler & Richards,
1979), two objects, for example, two trains, travel on parallel tracks for different
times, over different distances, or at different speeds. The child's task is to watch
the trains and to tell which one, if either, went for a longer time, over a longer
distance, or at a faster speed. If the child correctly identifies the train that

traveled for the longer time, she is said to have mastered the concept of time. Likewise, if she correctly identifies the train that traveled over the longer distance, she is said to have mastered the concept of distance; and if she correctly identifies the train that traveled at the faster speed, she is said to have mastered the concept of velocity.

In each of these tasks, the child does not have to attend to more than one dimension in order to arrive at correct answers. For example, to say which of the two trains went for the longer time does not at all require the consideration of their speeds and distances traveled. Correct time (duration) comparisons can be made on the basis of time information only, starting and stopping times being of particular importance when "logical" comparisons, as emphasized by the logical–operational approach, are of interest (Gréco, 1967). Consideration of distance and velocity information would be necessary only if time information were not given, or if just that dimension about which the question was asked were ignored. This does not seem very likely. Mastery of the time concept could thus be assessed for a child who does not have any idea of how time is related to distance and/or velocity.

One might wish to qualify this argument for some of the classical Genevan studies since Piaget gave great importance to the relations introduced by the children when they justified their answers. However, when justifications are taken as the data base for concept assessment, several other problems arise (Fraisse & Vautrey, 1952a, 1952b). If, for example, a child justifies her response on the velocity comparison by saying, *"The blue train went at the same speed as the red one, because it went the greater distance and took more time,"* this justification may legitimately be taken, as Piaget did, as an indicator of some knowledge about dimensional relations—although this justification cannot explain sameness of velocities in general. On the other hand, consider a child who justifies her velocity response by saying, *"The trains went at the same speed, because I saw that they went at the same speed."* For Piaget, this "tautological" justification would probably be as bad as no justification at all; although, on logical grounds, it is even better than the former one that referred to the relations between the dimensions. It can be concluded from the foregoing analysis that the previous studies addressed to the development of the concepts of time, distance, and velocity cannot tell much, if anything, about children's knowledge of the relations that exist between the dimensions.

Research on Nonmetric Relations

OVERVIEW OF PREVIOUS STUDIES

Two researchers have recently begun to study explicitly children's knowledge of the relations that exist between time, distance, and velocity: Crépault (1978,

1979, 1980) and Montangero (1977, 1979). Using tasks apparently derived from
the Piagetian paradigm previously outlined, both researchers have restricted
themselves to nonmetric relations. Whereas Montangero's research has concentrated on the age range from 5 to 8 years, Crépault has investigated children 10
years and older, as well as adults. The study by Montangero (1979) may serve to
illustrate this approach.

The child is shown, for example, two toy houses, one representing Geneva and
the other Paris and, in addition, a blue and a red toy car. The experimenter tells
that the blue car takes a whole day, from sunrise to sunset, to go from Geneva to
Paris, and that the red car takes a half day, from sunrise to noon. After this
information has been given, three types of questions are asked: (*a*) Which car, if
either, took more time to go from Geneva to Paris? (*b*) Did the blue car, which
took more time than the red car, travel at the same speed as the red car? (*c*) Was
the distance the two cars traveled the same?

The logic behind each task is that information for two dimensions of the
time–distance–velocity set is given. For one of these dimensions, the two events
to be compared share a common, constant value (distance in the example above);
for the other dimension (time), the two events have different values. On the basis
of this information, the relative value of the third dimension (velocity) has to be
inferred. Different types of tasks are used, such that each of the three variables
serves in turn as a dimension for which constant values are given, as a dimension
for which different values are given, or as a dimension for which the relative
value has to be inferred.

Children 5 and 6 years of age gave correct answers as to the nonmetric
relations existing between two dimensions at a time, provided that the values on
the third dimension were held constant. However, children of this age were
unable to coordinate all three dimensions. In the preceding example, these children would make the correct inference that the car that takes less time goes at the
faster speed. But when asked about the third dimension (i.e., distance), the
children no longer realized the constancy of this variable, but answered as if now
one of the other variables were held constant. For example, a child may have said
that the red car went further because it took the longer time. Possible reasons for
this behavior will be given in the next section.

The 7- and 8-year-olds, by comparison, coordinated all three dimensions. In
general, this coordination was accomplished by putting together two two-by-two
relations, for example, the velocity–time and the time–distance relation. A main
result of Montangero's research is that some of these two-by-two relations appeared to be more easily understood than others, and that this asymmetry may
give rise to certain types of errors. For example, many children proved to prefer
relations starting with the velocity term. Therefore, if asked about a relation
starting with another term, such as distance → velocity, these children tended to
make a detour that allowed them to start with the velocity term and to put the

two-by-two relations together as follows: velocity → time, time → distance, distance → velocity. Such a detour, however, most often leads to typical errors that can be observed in studies investigating nonmetric relations. In the preceding example, such an erroneous inference would be: more velocity → less time, less time → less distance; hence, less distance → more velocity.

Crépault (1979, 1981) has investigated, in more detail, the different psychological status of the nonmetric relations existing between time, distance, and velocity. Based on this research, he has proposed a structural model that serves to explain the pattern of errors at different ages. Crépault also maintains that the child's comprehension of the time–distance–velocity system is gradually constructed by the coordination of two-by-two relations. In a recent article (Crépault, 1980), he proposed the following developmental order of three possible two-by-two relations: (a) inverse relation between velocity and distance, (b) direct relation between velocity and distance, and (c) inverse relation between distance and time.[1]

PROBLEMS WITH STUDIES ON NONMETRIC RELATIONS

By separating time, distance, and velocity information and asking the child to infer the value on a dimension that was not perceptually present, Crépault and Montangero adopted the necessary procedure to investigate knowledge about relations between the dimensions. Unfortunately, both researchers remained within a Piagetian framework as to critical features of method. In particular, they adopted the Piagetian choice–task method, which always requires two objects or events to be compared. Inherent in the choice task are some serious problems. The most important problems for the issue at hand will be briefly discussed in this section. In the sections that follow, it will be shown how these problems can be overcome.

Processing Capacity

To succeed in the choice tasks that investigate knowledge of nonmetric relations, the child has to consider many different pieces of information. Each of the

---

[1]It should be noted that, besides the research outlined in this section, the development of interdependencies between time, distance, and velocity information has been investigated in a quite different psychological framework (e.g., Bonnet, 1965; Matsuda, 1977; Ono, 1975). This research has been concerned with perceptual interdependencies presumably operating on an unconscious level. In particular, the question of how children's time estimations are influenced by the distance of stimuli that mark the beginning and end of the temporal interval (kappa effect), or of how children's distance estimations are influenced by the temporal interval between the information marking the two end points of the distance (tau effect) has been of interest to these investigators. Such phenomena, which are usually classified as perceptual illusions, will be excluded from the present chapter because its emphasis is on knowledge, that is, on cognitive aspects of time, distance, and velocity interrelations.

two events to be compared contains information on two relevant dimensions. When the dimensions are time or distance, each of these four pieces of information may be derived from two more basic facts, namely, starting and stopping times or starting and stopping points on the distance dimension, respectively. Thus, there are eight pieces of information on which the child must operate when asked to make a "logical" inference on relative velocity. This amount of informational input may overburden the young child's processing capacity and thus prevent her from showing knowledge of dimensional relations.

Language

An implicit assumption of the comparison task used in previous studies has been that the child has an adequate understanding of relational terms and comparative adjectives, such as *more* and *less* or *same* and *different*. However, research on developmental psycholinguistics in the past decade has shown that these terms are often ambiguous for young children and have a different meaning for them than for adults (e.g., Donaldson & Wales, 1970; Palermo, 1974). It seems probable that similar difficulties as found for the terms in English language also apply to the analogous French terms used in these studies on nonmetric relations (e.g., Montangero, 1979). These language difficulties may mask a young child's understanding of relations existing between time, distance, and velocity.

Form of the Relationship

The studies on nonmetric relations are silent about the form of the relationships. Consider, for example, the following questions: If a child correctly answers that a car that takes half a day to go from Geneva to Paris travels at a faster speed than that that takes a whole day for the same distance, will she know that the velocity of the first car is twice as much as that of the second? Does an increase in time have the same effect on a decrease in velocity at all levels of time? Is there any possibility at all of predicting an exact value of velocity from time and distance information, or are relative values the only predictions that can be made? These and other questions bearing on the form of the relation between the variables cannot be answered by the results of studies on nonmetric relations.

The choice-task paradigm used in the previous studies is, in principle, not capable of investigating quantitative, functional relations as they are involved in the physical laws. Knowledge of these laws, however, is the issue of interest— even in a Piagetian framework. One problem of the logical-operational approach is that findings on nonmetric relations cannot be generalized to knowledge of continuous, quantitative relations (see Wilkening & Anderson, in press, for further discussion).

Holding One Variable Constant

Crépault and Montangero were right in realizing that, within a nonmetric framework, one of the three variables out of the time–distance–velocity set always has to be held constant. Otherwise, knowledge of nonmetric relations cannot be studied. This can be easily seen by considering the following example based on Montangero's paradigm. When the values on two dimensions were varied at a time, one possible task could be to compare the velocities of two cars: Car A travels from Geneva to Paris from sunrise to noon and Car B travels a greater distance in a longer time, say, from Geneva to Brussels from sunrise to sunset. A "logical" answer as to which car went faster is impossible unless quantitative information is given, e.g., as to distance in kilometers and as to times of sunrise and sunset in hours and minutes. If such quantitative information is not given, as is generally the case in the nonmetric approach, it is a logical necessity to hold one of the three variables constant in order to be able to investigate knowledge of relations between the other two.

Unfortunately, there is a problem with holding one variable constant in these tasks. The problem is that the child's responses leave open the question of whether the dimension with constant values has been considered or ignored. A child who totally disregards this dimension would arrive at the same answers as a child who correctly uses the information. However, only in the latter case would the assessment of knowledge about nonmetric relations be justified.

Holding one of the three variables constant delimits the investigation of inter-dependencies between all three dimensions to separate two-by-two relations. One might be interested, however, in learning about children's knowledge of the system of interrelations within the time–distance–velocity set all at once, that is, by not putting together two-by-two relations obtained in different tasks. How this can be accomplished and how, at the same time, the other problems with the nonmetric approach can be overcome will be shown in the following section.

A GENERAL METHODOLOGY FOR STUDYING KNOWLEDGE OF FUNCTIONAL RELATIONS

The problems inherent in the previous studies (outlined in the preceding section) can be avoided by using functional measurement methodology, which was developed as part of information integration theory (Anderson, 1974, 1981). Functional measurement neither requires two-object choice tasks nor does it rely on comparative judgments. Thus, demands on processing capacity are relatively low, and an adequate understanding of relational terms is not a prerequisite for succeeding in the task. Furthermore, functional measurement is capable of studying the form of functional relations on a metric, quantitative level, and of investigating interrelations of more than two variables simultaneously in one and the same experiment. As will be elaborated, these ends are served by the use of numerical, continuous rating scales and of factorial design.

Most studies conducted within an integration–theoretical framework have not directly asked for knowledge of dimensional relations. Rather, the central question of these studies may be put in a more general way: How do people integrate different pieces of information in their overall judgment of multidimensional input? For example, it has been investigated (Anderson & Cuneo, 1978; Wilkening, 1979) how children integrate width and height of rectangles in their overall judgment of area; and it has been found in these studies that young children integrate width and height according to an adding rule (area = width + height), while older children and adults integrate this information according to a multiplying rule (area = width × height). Evidence for the operation of simple algebraic rules such as addition, multiplication, averaging, or division has been found in many other areas, ranging from psychophysics to moral judgment (see Anderson, 1980, 1981, for overviews).

For the three variables, which are the minimum number involved in each integration–theoretical experiment, two functional relations can be read off directly from the algebraic model. For example, it follows from the adding, as well as from the multiplying, rule for judgment of rectangle area that each of the two dimensions to be integrated (i.e., perceived width and perceived height) are directly and linearly related to the third dimension (i.e., judged area). The following shows how the integration–theoretical approach can be applied to the time–distance–velocity set of dimensions and to the study of their psychological interrelations.

In Newtonian mechanics, velocity is defined by the distance–time ratio:

$$\text{velocity} = \text{distance} \div \text{time} \tag{1}$$

It follows that

$$\text{distance} = \text{time} \times \text{velocity} \tag{2}$$

and

$$\text{time} = \text{distance} \div \text{velocity.} \tag{3}$$

That is, when the physical values on two dimensions are known, the value of the third dimension can be obtained by the algebraic operation of multiplication or division.

The physical rules are thus quite clear. However, when people make inferences about time, distance, or velocity in everyday life, they almost never know the exact physical values of the information that is given. Rather, they base their inferences on subjective estimates in most instances. Also, people might have no explicit knowledge of the physical rule, that is, multiplication or division, according to which the information has to be integrated. How do people handle the two pieces of information in these situations? How this question would be tackled within the framework of information integration theory may be illustrated best by an example.

Imagine that Equation 3 was to be tested; that is, the question of interest would be, How do people integrate distance and velocity information in their inferences about time? A more specific question might be whether the psychological integration rule mirrors the physical division rule. According to functional measurement methodology, some distance and some velocity levels would be selected, and the child would be asked to judge each factorial distance–velocity combination on a linear scale of time.

A reasonable task might be to show the person, in the open country or on a map, three different distances and ask how long it would take to cover each of these distances by foot, by bicycle, or by car. For physical distances of 1, 2, and 3 km, and velocities of 6 km/hr, 15 km/hr, and 50 km/hr, for example, the correct physical time values are shown in Figure 4.1. Of course, the physical distance and velocity values chosen here are arbitrary; and, as noted previously, the subjective values might be quite different and are usually unknown. But whatever they may be, the general pattern of time judgments will exhibit a linear fan shape (as shown for the physical values in Figure 4.1) if the distance and velocity information is integrated by a dividing rule, and as long as the subjective values are linearly related to the physical values. (Nonlinear relations between objective

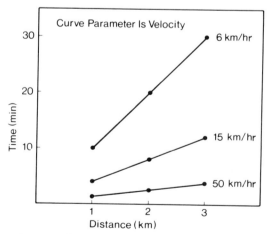

Figure 4.1. Bilinear fan pattern for values of physical time as a function of physical distance and velocity in a hypothetical example.

and subjective values can also be handled by functional measurement, but these techniques are excluded here for the sake of simplicity; see Anderson, in press, for details.)

In the present context, the point of major importance is that three conclusions can be made when time judgments follow a linear fan pattern as in Figure 4.1. First, as already noted, distance and velocity information have been integrated according to a dividing rule. Second, subjective time and subjective distance are directly related; this can be seen from the increasing slope of the curves. Third, subjective time and subjective velocity are inversely related; this can be seen from the inverse order of the curves for the velocity levels (increasing from top to bottom). The second and third conclusion given here follow directly from a dividing rule and thus are usually not explicitly mentioned in the integration-theoretical studies. In the present chapter, however, with its emphasis on knowledge of relations, this implication of an algebraic integration rule should be referred to and be kept in mind.

Figure 4.2 shows some other general patterns of possible results that might be obtained in the above time judgment task. Each pattern refers to a different rule. The leftmost pattern indicates a multiplying or a dividing rule, as already discussed. The distinctive feature between these two rules is the order of the levels of the curve parameter, an increasing order from bottom to top indicating a multiplying rule and a decreasing order indicating a dividing rule.

A parallel pattern as shown in the second panel indicates an adding or subtracting rule, the distinctive feature again being the vertical order of the curves—analogous to the order for a multiplying or dividing rule, respectively. The patterns in the third and fourth panels indicate nonintegration, "centration" rules, the missing slope or the missing vertical separation of the curves indicating that distance or velocity information has not been considered, respectively. For these

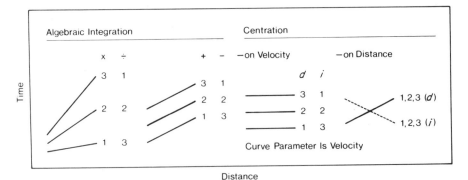

Figure 4.2. Judgment patterns for some hypothetical rules for integrating distance and velocity information in the judgment of time (d = direct relation; i = inverse relation).

centration rules, direct or indirect relation between the independent and dependent variable can again be seen from the vertical order of the curves (third panel) or from their slope, which can be positive or negative, respectively (fourth panel).

Of course, empirical data usually do not exhibit the degree of regularity shown in the schematic patterns of Figure 4.2. Various sources of error can hardly be avoided. Analysis of variance provides a useful tool to determine the significance of the deviation of any given judgment pattern from the theoretical pattern predicted by a multiplying, dividing, adding, subtracting, or centration rule. This is not only true of analyzing integration rules on the group level. If a person judges each factorial combination more than once, analysis of variance can be applied on the individual level and a rule can be assessed for each child, as has been shown, for example, in recent applications of functional measurement in the developmental field (e.g., Wilkening, 1980).

The experiments to be reported in the following section are based on the integration–theoretical approach and employ functional measurement as a rule-assessment methodology to represent children's knowledge of time, distance, and velocity interrelations.

INTEGRATING AND RELATING TIME, DISTANCE, AND VELOCITY

Two experiments were designed to study how the integration of time, distance, and velocity information develops, and what children know about the interrelations between these dimensions. The emphasis of the first experiment is on the detection and assessment of integration rules, and the second experiment is aimed at processes that underlie these rules.

Experiment 1: Detecting Algebraic Integration Rules

In each of three tasks, Experiment 1 tested one of the normative integration rules designated by Equations 1, 2, and 3 in the preceding section. Task 1 studied integration of time and velocity information in judgment of distance; Task 2, the integration of distance and velocity information in judgment of time; and Task 3, the integration of distance and time information in judgment of velocity. In each experiment, 15 5-year-olds, 15 10-year-olds, and 15 adults participated, with no subject serving in more than one task. Since details of methods and results have been reported elsewhere (Wilkening, 1981), only a brief outline will be given here.

TASK 1: JUDGED DISTANCE = TIME × VELOCITY?

Method

Three levels of velocity and three levels of time were combined in a factorial design. The velocity levels were presented by a turtle, a guinea pig, and a cat. These animals were portrayed as fleeing from a barking dog, who would bark for 2, 5, or 8 sec, which were the three levels of time. The child's task was to judge how far an animal could run during that time.

The judgment scale was depicted on a screen that was 3 m long and 1 m high. On the left side of the screen, there was a frightening-looking dog. A straight footbridge led away from the dog to the right. This footbridge served as the scale for judgments of distance. Small cardboard pieces, each of them showing one of the three velocity levels (turtle, guinea pig, or cat) could be attached by a magnet anywhere onto the judgment scale.

For each trial, one of the three animals was placed at the left end of the footbridge, close to the dog. Then one of the three barking times was presented by a tape recorder. After the barking had stopped, the child was asked to put the animal at that position on the footbridge she thought that animal would have reached. This judgment was read by the experimenter on a centimeter scale, which was not visible to the child. Each child judged all nine factorial combinations in three replications, with different random orders in each replication.

Results

Figure 4.3 shows mean distance judgments for the three age groups. As to the pattern of judgments, no substantial difference between the age groups is visible. The data of each group follow the diverging fan pattern indicating a multiplying integration rule. That is, children as well as adults took account of both dimensions and integrated the information by a rule that mirrors the physical rule; distance = time × velocity. This rule implies direct, linear relations between time and distance and also between velocity and distance. Analyses of variance yielded the pattern of results to be required for an assessment of a multiplying rule in each age group.

TASK 2: JUDGED TIME = DISTANCE ÷ VELOCITY?

Method

Apparatus and general procedure paralleled those of Task 1, except for some modifications that were necessary to allow investigation of distance and velocity integration in judgment of time.

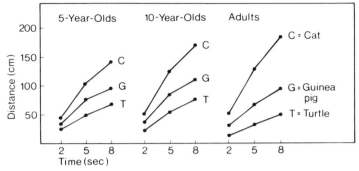

Figure 4.3.   Mean judgments of distance as a function of time and velocity for the three age groups in Experiment 1.

The same velocity levels as in Task 1 were used, that is, turtle, guinea pig, and cat. Distance levels were 70, 140, and 210 cm. For each trial, one of the three animals was placed at one of the three distance levels on the footbridge and the child was asked to judge how long the dog would have barked to cause that animal to run that distance. The children made their judgments by pressing a key to let the dog bark on the tape recorder. On releasing the key, the dog stopped barking, and the barking time could be read by the experimenter on a stopwatch, which was' connected to the key.

Results

Figure 4.4 shows mean time judgments for the three age groups. The dividing model; judged time = distance ÷ velocity, implies that the data should form a diverging fan pattern, with the difference from the multiplying model of Task 1

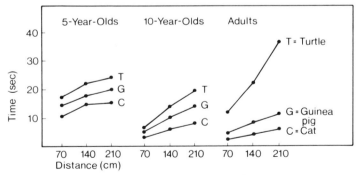

Figure 4.4.   Mean judgments of time as a function of distance and velocity for the three age groups in Experiment 1.

(Figure 4.3) being that the order of the curves for the velocity levels should be reversed.

This diverging fan pattern was obtained for the 10-year-olds and adults. The judgments of the 5-year-olds, on the other hand, do not follow the diverging fan pattern but are approximately parallel. Parallelism, with the same vertical order of the curves as required by the dividing rule, is indicative of a subtracting rule; judged time = distance − velocity.

This difference in judgment patterns of the 5-year-olds, on the one hand, and the 10-year-olds and adults, on the other hand, was reflected in the results of analyses of variance, which yielded a significant interaction for the two older age groups but not for the youngest.

TASK 3: JUDGED VELOCITY = DISTANCE ÷ TIME?

Method

Distance and time levels were the same as used before, that is, 70, 140, and 210 cm, and 2, 5, and 8 sec. Distance levels were presented by a marking on the footbridge; time levels were again presented by the dog's barking. The response scale for velocity judgments consisted of seven animals, each painted on a piece of cardboard: a snail, turtle, guinea pig, mouse, cat, deer, and horse. These animals laid in this order on a table in front of the child.

For each trial, first the dog barked, and then the experimenter put the marker on one of the three distance levels. The child was asked which out of the seven animals would have run that distance over that time. In other respects, details of procedure paralleled those of Tasks 1 and 2.

Results

Figure 4.5 shows that the data in no age group follow the diverging fan pattern required by the dividing rule, judged velocity = distance ÷ time. The judgment patterns of each of the two older age groups, 10-year-olds and adults, appear to be parallel. This parallel pattern, with inverse order of the curves for the three levels of time, indicates a subtracting rule: judged velocity = distance − time. For the 5-year-olds, in contrast, the curves for the three time levels are not clearly separated, while the upward slope of all three curves shows a clear effect for the distance dimension. This pattern implies a distance-only "centration" rule: judged velocity = distance.

Results of analyses of variance were in line with the above graphical analyses. For the youngest age group, only the main effect of the distance dimension was

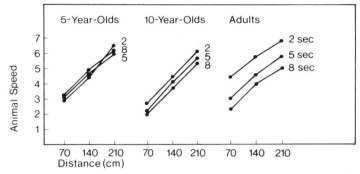

Figure 4.5. Mean judgments of velocity as a function of distance and time for the three age groups in Experiment 1.

significant, whereas for each of the two older age groups, main effects of both dimensions were significant and the interaction was insignificant.

DISCUSSION

The purpose of the three tasks of Experiment 1 was to study if and how people of different ages integrate time, distance, and velocity information. Integration of information was found in all tasks and at all ages, except for the 5-year-olds in one task. In all other instances, children and adults considered information from two different dimensions and integrated this information to infer a value on the third dimension. The integration followed algebraic rules: multiplication, division, or subtraction. For time and velocity integration in judgment of distance (Task 1), the psychological rule obeyed the normative multiplying rule in all age groups. For distance and velocity integration in judgment of time (Task 2), the data for the 10-year-olds and adults followed the normative dividing rule, whereas the 5-year-olds employed a subtracting rule. An analogous subtracting rule was found for the 10-year-olds and adults for integration of distance and time in judgment of velocity (Task 3).

These findings about integration rules have straightforward implications for our understanding of children's knowledge of dimensional relations. Each of the various rules obtained here reveals knowledge that children and adults have about the physical two-by-two relations existing between the dimensions.

Children as young as 5 years related time directly to distance and inversely to velocity, and they related distance directly to velocity. That is, all three two-by-two relations that exist within the time–distance–velocity set were conceived in accordance with the correct physical rule. The centration rule obtained for the 5-year-olds in the task investigating distance and time integration in inferring velocity (Task 3) can hardly be seen as an exception, for the inverse time–velocity relation that was missing in this task did appear in Task 2, when time had to be inferred on the basis of distance and velocity information.

The three tasks of Experiment 1 differed as to their demands on short-term memory and on information processing capacity. In Task 1, the information to be integrated, that is, time and velocity, could be processed simultaneously by employing a relatively simple eye movement strategy. Since in each trial the velocity information was given before the presentation of time information began, it was possible for the child to imagine an animal with a particular speed fleeing over the footbridge during the time the dog barked. It could easily be observed in the experimental trials that almost all children and adults employed such a strategy. They followed an imaginary movement on the footbridge with their eyes and, after the dog had stopped barking, pointed to that position the imaginary movement had reached. Since, for each child, the speed of the eye movements was different for each animal, and because the order of these eye movement speeds agreed with the objective order of the velocity levels, the distance judgments produced the diverging fan pattern of a multiplying model.

A similar eye movement strategy was possible in Task 2 also, which investigated distance and velocity integration in inferences on time. The strategy required imagining the animal on the footbridge back at the starting point, letting the dog bark while imagining the animal fleeing over the footbridge, and stopping the barking when the imaginary movement had reached the distance end point presented. The 10-year-olds and adults apparently employed this strategy. The 5-year-olds, however, seemed to have difficulties in the initial imaginary replacement of the animal and in temporarily ignoring the animal presented on the scale at the end point selected for that trial.

Theoretically, an eye movement strategy was possible in Task 3 also. This required imagining the simultaneous movement of all seven animals of the velocity judgment scale for the time that the dog barked. Thereafter, the seven imaginary positions of the animals on the footbridge would have to be stored until the distance level was presented, and then the animal nearest to that distance point would have to be selected as velocity judgment. Even for the adults, the information processing demands imposed by this strategy were apparently too high to use it as an aid for information integration in this task.

As a consequence, time information had to be retrieved from memory at the moment the judgment was asked. However, this retrieval may have been much more difficult for the young children than for the older children and adults. Evidence for this argument comes from the well-known studies by Trabasso and his colleagues (e.g., Trabasso, 1977), who showed that young children's failure to integrate the information necessary for logical inferences is often due to the difficulties they have in retrieving all that information from memory. If the 5-year-olds of the present study were in fact unable to remember the time information in Task 3, this would easily explain their centration on distance in judging velocity—the only nonintegration rule obtained in any age group.

Experiment 2:
Varying the Information Processing Demands

The results of Experiment 1 provide clear evidence of algebraic rules in children's and adults' integration of time, distance, and velocity information. However, as already discussed, the tasks used differed as to their information processing demands, and therefore the results do not allow unambiguous conclusions about developmental differences in knowledge, independent of information processing demands. For example, it does not necessarily follow from the distance-only centration rule found for the 5-year-olds in the task investigating inferences on velocity that these children have no understanding of the relation existing between time and velocity, or that the concept of velocity develops later than the concepts of distance and time. Rather, the centration rule may be an effect of the unique memory demands of this particular task.

Experiment 2 was an attempt to make the information processing demands of the tasks used in Experiment 1 more similar to each other. To this end, two of the three tasks were modified. The task studying time and velocity integration (Task 1), which was apparently the easiest one, was made more difficult by ruling out the possibility of employing a simple eye movement strategy. On the other hand, the task studying distance and time integration (Task 3), which was apparently the most difficult, was facilitated by visualizing time information and thus not requiring its retrieval from memory. These two tasks were presented to children and adults (comparable to those of the youngest and oldest age group of Experiment 1) and it was studied how the variations in information processing demands affect the integration rules at different ages.

METHOD

Task 1: Distance = Time × Velocity?

Apparatus and general design were the same as in Experiment 1. The only difference in procedure was that the order of presenting time and velocity information was reversed: in each trial, first the dog barked, and only then one of the three animals was placed at the left end of the scale. Thus, during the time the dog barked, the child did not know the velocity level about which, in combination with that particular time level, the question was going to be asked. If an eye movement strategy was to be employed in this modified task also, it would require imagining the movement of not just one but of three animals simultaneously, all moving at a different speed.

Task 3: Velocity = Distance ÷ Time?

This task was also the same as in Experiment 1, except for one modification: Time information was visually represented. This was done as follows: when the dog began to bark, a bubble with the words "bow wow," such as in a cartoon, came out of the dog's mouth and moved with constant speed upward to the right until the barking stopped. For the time levels of 2, 5, and 8 sec, lengths of the bubble were 20, 50, and 80 cm, respectively; its width was 10 cm throughout. This visualized time information was present, together with the distance information, at the moment the velocity judgment was asked so that time information did not need to be retrieved from memory.

At the beginning of the experiment, the child's attention was drawn to the correspondence between barking time and its visual representation by showing that length of barking time could be read off from the length of the bubble with the words.

Subjects

From each of the two age groups, 5-year-olds and adults, 10 subjects participated in each task. Each subject served in only one task. The children attended a kindergarten in Braunschweig; the adults were mostly psychology students at the University of Braunschweig, Germany.

RESULTS

Figure 4.6 shows the mean distance (upper panel) and velocity judgments (lower panel) obtained in the two tasks for each age group. Comparison with Figures 4.3 and 4.5 shows that the only change in the integration rule from Experiment 1 to Experiment 2 appears to have happened for the 5-year-olds in Task 1.

Their judgments followed a parallel pattern, thus indicating an adding integration rule: distance = time + velocity. Analysis of variance yielded significant main effects of time, $F_{(2, 18)} = 7.31$, $p < .01$, and of velocity, $F_{(2, 18)} = 9.59$, $p < .01$, whereas interaction was not significant, $F_{(4, 36)} = .18$. This pattern of an adding rule contrasts with the multiplying rule found for this age group in Experiment 1.

The three other judgment patterns in Figure 4.6 are very similar to the respective patterns obtained in Experiment 1. For the 5-year-olds, velocity judgments in Task 3 (lower left panel) again follow a distance-only centration rule. Distance information, $F_{(2, 18)} = 49.19$, $p < .01$, but not time information, $F_{(2, 18)} = 3.53$, $p > .05$, had a significant effect on judgments of velocity.

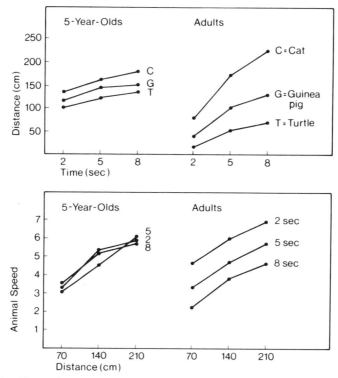

Figure 4.6. Mean judgments of distance as a function of time and velocity (upper panel) and of velocity as a function of distance and time (lower panel) for the two age groups in Experiment 2.

For the adults, judgments again followed a multiplying rule in Task 1 and a subtracting rule in Task 3. Interaction was significant in Task 1, $F_{(4, 36)} = 19.94$, $p < .01$, but not in Task 3, $F_{(4, 36)} = .34$. Main effects were always significant in this age group, $F_{(2, 18)} = 102.44$ and 69.69, $p < .01$, for time and velocity in Task 1, and $F_{(2, 18)} = 193.05$ and 137.09, $p < .01$, for distance and time in Task 3, respectively.

DISCUSSION

Effects of Eliminating the Eye Movement Strategy in Task 1

The purpose of changing the distance = time × velocity task in the present experiment was to study how the integration rule would change when the possibility of using a simple eye movement strategy was repressed. There are two kinds of evidence that the eye movement strategy, which underlay children's and adults' distance judgments in Experiment 1, was in fact not employed in Experiment 2. First, it could easily be observed during the experiment that neither the children nor the adults followed an imaginary movement on the judgment scale with their eyes. Second, the results shown in Figure 4.6 demonstrate that the eye movement strategy had not been employed, for this strategy would yield data that follow a diverging fan of straight lines.

For the children, a parallel pattern was obtained, which agrees with an adding rule for time and velocity integration. This adding rule is analogous to the subtracting rule found for distance and velocity integration in the respective age group of Experiment 1. In both the adding and the subtracting rule, the child considers both dimensions that have been manipulated by the experimenter, and the subjective values on each dimension contribute independently, without interaction, to the overall judgment.

Thus, the results of Task 2 of Experiment 1 and of Task 1 of Experiment 2 appear to tell the same story: If young children are prevented from using the eye movement strategy as an aid for integrating the information according to a multiplying or dividing rule, they fall back on a simpler adding or subtracting rule. This finding is important because the judgments based on the eye movement strategy may be considered as reflecting an as-if integration only (Wilkening, 1981). However, the adding and subtracting rules found here show that young children can integrate time and velocity as well as distance and velocity information even without the facilitating tool of an eye movement strategy. Both rules can be seen as further instances of the general purpose adding rule suggested by Anderson and Cuneo (1978) to operate in young children across a variety of situations. The implications of this rule for the issue of children's knowledge about time, distance, and velocity interrelations will be discussed later under "General Discussion."

For the adults, the downward bowing of all three curves in Figure 4.6 is further evidence that the eye movement strategy was not employed in this age group either. Following an imaginary movement on the judgment scale with constant speed until the barking stopped would require a straight line for each level of velocity. The downward bowing of the curves indicates that subjective time is not linearly related to objective time in this age group. Approximately straight lines could be obtained by moving the points representing 5-sec distance estimates to the right on the abscissa, which then—according to functional measurement methodology—would represent the subjective time scale. Thus, the diverging fan pattern obtained for the adults shows that they, in contrast to the young children, can integrate time and velocity according to the normative multiplying rule even without employing the eye movement strategy.

Effects of Visualizing Time Information in Task 3

The purpose of changing the velocity = distance ÷ time task was to study how the integration rule would change when time information was visualized so that it did not have to be retrieved from memory. This task variation apparently had no effect on the integration rule in either age group. The judgments of the adults again followed a subtracting rule: velocity = distance − time, and the 5-year-olds again employed a centration rule, in which velocity was judged on the basis of distance information only.

Concerning the adults, it has to be asked why the visualization of the time information did not help them to shift to the correct dividing rule; however, speculations about this question should not be carried too far. It might be that, because of a scaling artifact, the subtracting rule obtained in both Experiments 1 and 2 in fact mirrors an underlying dividing process. The scale used for velocity judgment in this task differed from the distance and time scales in that it was not objectively linear. As noted by Wilkening (1981), there is some evidence that the scale might be logarithmic. If this is true, a covert dividing of distance and time information will yield a parallel pattern of velocity judgments, as with a subtracting rule obtained with a linear scale. Thus, the present experiment leaves the possibility open that adults integrate distance and time information according to the normative dividing rule.

For the 5-year-olds, visualizing time information was apparently inefficient. Therefore, the difficulty of retrieving time information from memory appears not to be the only reason for young children's reliance on distance only in judgments of velocity. The failure of these children to integrate time information when judging velocity (Task 3 of Experiments 1 and 2) contrasts with their abilities to integrate velocity information when judging time (Task 2 of Experiment 1).

Two kinds of problems may account for this asymmetry. First, although young children seem to understand visual representations of time in simple situations, this information may be too superficial to be considered along with more salient information—particularly in tasks that impose further demands on the child, such as relating the time information inversely to another dimension. That is, processing visual representations of time may be as difficult for young children as retrieving time information from memory. Visual representations of distance and velocity, by comparison, are usually much more concrete and direct than is possible of time information and, therefore, appear to be easier to process, particularly for the young child.

The second reason for the psychological asymmetry of the time–velocity relation may be that, irrespective of information processing demands, time and velocity in everyday life differ as to the likelihood of each dimension acting as a dependent or independent variable. For young children, in particular, velocity seems much more often to have the status of an independent variable than is true of time. At this age, speed is typically conceived as a given, fixed property of an object or a living being, or as a variable that can be manipulated at will to produce changes in length of time. Conversely, the idea that time acts as an independent variable that can have an influence on speed seems to be strange to young children because they are not as used to time limits as determinants of speed as older children and adults are. The difficulty young children may have in conceiving of time as a variable that can determine speed would explain their reliance on distance only, which has the additional advantage of being directly related to velocity.

GENERAL DISCUSSION

Integration Rules and Knowledge of Metric Relations

Both experiments reported here provide evidence of children's knowledge of the relations that exist between time, distance, and velocity. Whereas previous studies in this field have dealt with nonmetric relations (e.g., Crépault, 1979; Montangero, 1979), the knowledge found here is on the level of metric relations. The evidence comes from the integration rules. At all ages, the integration of time, distance, and velocity information followed algebraic rules: multiplication, division, addition, or subtraction. Each of these algebraic rules requires a metric of the two dimensions to be combined, and also a metric of the third, resulting dimension.

Whether the psychological integration rule mirrored the normative, physical rule depended on age and task. The judgments of the adults followed the normative rules in all but one task. On the other hand, the judgments of the 5-year-olds followed a physically incorrect rule in all but one task. These children considered the relevant information from both dimensions in all but one instance, but to integrate the information, they employed an adding instead of a multiplying, and a subtracting instead of a dividing rule. However, although addition and subtraction are incorrect rules for combining time, distance, and velocity, these rules do not differ from the correct multiplication and division rules as to the metric relations involved. That is, even the adding and subtracting rules employed by the 5-year-olds reveal that these children relate time directly and linearly to distance and inversely and linearly to velocity, and relate velocity directly and linearly to distance—in agreement with the physical interrelations governing the time–distance–velocity system.

A word of caution against overrating the knowledge of the young children seems necessary. The judgments obtained here do not allow the conclusion that the children have an explicit understanding of the dimensional interrelations in the sense that they know all their implications and can conceive of time, distance, and velocity in the formal language of physics. Rather, the children (as well as the adults) know procedures that can be used to relate the dimensions such that the physical rules are not violated. Such a level of understanding may be classified as an implicit one; and it may be of interest to note that it seems to be just this level of conceptual understanding that most of the Piagetian tasks also investigated (Greeno, 1980).

Relations as Constituents of Concepts of Time

In classical physics, time is "absolute"; it passes independently of the objects and events in the world. That is, to define time as a "concept" does not require relating it to any other dimension. Since the laws of classical physics have proven to be acceptable approximations of reality in practically all situations of everyday life, one might ask, therefore, why knowledge of dimensional relations is of any interest in the issue of assessing a concept of time in children.

Within the absolute, unidimensional concept of time, only some operations are possible. Points of time can be compared as to their simultaneity or succession, and lengths of time can be (logically) compared on the basis of their beginning and end points—provided the interval that began earlier did not also end earlier. When successive time intervals are to be compared, either perceptual estimates have to be taken as a basis or, if a more "logical" level is desired, time has to be measured by objective instruments. Time measurement, however, almost always relates time to another dimension. Usually, the other dimension is velocity (which is held constant), be it the movement of the hand of a clock or the rotation of earth. Another important case in which time has to be related to another dimension is relativity theory, in which time is not absolute but has to be defined in terms of velocity and space.

The Piagetian studies on developmental aspects of time appear to have been addressed almost exclusively to the nonmetric concept of time, which allows some duration comparisons by referring to points in time only, but is of no use when time has to be measured on a metric level. Accordingly, the Piagetian paradigm has investigated children's abilities to ignore velocity and distance in comparisons of time. However, time concepts in physics are more complex, as indicated previously. Faced with this complexity, it is of minor interest in modern physics how the concept of time is defined; much more important is the question of how time should be measured. Given this state of affairs in physics, it seems meaningless to speak of "mastery" or "full understanding" of the concept of time, as has been done in the Piagetian studies (e.g., Siegler & Richards, 1979). The preceding discussion has shown that relations of time to velocity and distance are involved in at least two other important concepts of time than the previous studies have dealt with.

Research Prospects

The empirical findings and theoretical analyses presented in this chapter suggest two lines of future research. The first should be concerned with representing children's basic knowledge of the dimensional relations involved in concepts of time, space, and velocity. The present experiments have shown that perceptual and memory demands play an important role and have to be considered more seriously than they have in the past when children's knowledge of time, distance, and velocity interrelations is to be assessed (see also Levin, Gilat & Zelniker, 1980). Research in this field becomes even more difficult when the development of children's knowledge about time, distance, and velocity is to be investigated as it relates to the acquisition order of the concepts. Tasks addressed to each of these concepts typically differ in aspects that are not logically related to the concept in question. Memory, for example, almost always plays a role in tasks on time but seldom in tasks on distance or velocity. Experiment 2 (reported in this chapter) was but one attempt to equalize the assessment tasks as to their information processing demands. Other attempts in this direction will be necessary if one wished to obtain deeper insights into the development of children's cognition of the time–distance–velocity system and into the role of perception and memory in the acquisition of each of these concepts.

The second line of research should emphasize applied issues, and focus on complex time, distance, and velocity interrelations as they relate to everyday life situations. From the viewpoint of an applied developmental psychology, for example, it is of interest to know under what conditions children can integrate time, distance, and velocity in everyday life decisions, and what rules they employ at a given age in situations that impose certain demands on perception and short-term memory. This research need not be restricted to simple combinations of the dimensional information like those investigated in the present study. More complex tasks of information integration should also be used. For example, it would be of interest to know how children combine two or more velocities of objects moving in different directions at different distances, when estimating time of collision or safe passing—as is often required in everyday decisions. Such situations cannot be mastered by cognitive capacities only; perceptual estimates, for example, play an important role. Research on the interplay of these perceptual processes and children's cognitive capacities for relating time, distance, and velocity is practically nonexistent. The methodological approach employed in the present study can be extended to complex situations and therefore seems to be useful for the proposed line of investigation.

SUMMARY

Previous research on children's knowledge of time, distance, and velocity interrelations has been conducted within a nonmetric framework. This contrasts with the fact that, in the physical world, time, distance, and velocity are metric concepts that cannot be defined by nonmetric relations. In addition to this conceptual problem, the previous studies share some methodological shortcomings that even call into question the conclusions that have been drawn on knowledge structures at the nonmetric level.

The present study shows how these problems can be overcome by using functional measurement as a rule-assessment methodology. In three tasks, two of which were varied in a second experiment, children and adults had to infer values of time, distance, or velocity from information that was given on the other two dimensions. These inferences were made by children as young as 5 years. In all but one task, the integration of information followed algebraic rules: multiplication, division, addition, or subtraction. While the multiplying and dividing rules mirrored the physical laws for the respective dimensional combinations, these physically correct rules shifted to the incorrect adding or subtracting rules in some instances. Nevertheless, each of these algebraic integration rules gave clear evidence of children's knowledge about the metric relations that exist between time, distance, and velocity. The relevance of these findings to the issue of development of time concepts in children was discussed, and two lines of future research were proposed.

ACKNOWLEDGMENTS

This research was supported by a grant from the Stiftung Volkswagenwerk, Hannover, Federal Republic of Germany. I wish to thank Norman Anderson, Jacques Crépault, Iris Levin, and Jacques Montangero for comments on an earlier version of this chapter.

REFERENCES

Anderson, N. H. Algebraic models in perception. In E. C. Carterette & M. P. Friedman (Eds.), *Handbook of perception* (Vol. 2). New York: Academic Press, 1974, pp. 215–298.

Anderson, N. H. Information integration theory in developmental psychology. In F. Wilkening, J. Becker, & T. Trabasso (Eds.), *Information integration by children*. Hillsdale, N.J.: Erlbaum, 1980, pp. 1–45

Anderson, N. H. *Foundations of information integration theory*. New York: Academic Press, 1981.

Anderson, N. H. *Methods of information integration theory*. New York: Academic Press, in press.

Anderson, N. H., & Cuneo, D. O. The height + width rule in children's judgments of quantity. *Journal of Experimental Psychology: General*, 1978, *107*, 335–378.

Bonnet, C. Influence de la vitesse du mouvement et de l'espace parcouru sur l'estimation du temps. *L'Année Psychologique*, 1965, *65*, 357–363.

Bourne, L. E., Jr., Dominowski, R. L., & Loftus, E. F. *Cognitive processes*. Englewood Cliffs, N.J.: Prentice-Hall, 1979.

Crépault, J. Le raisonnement cinématique chez le préadolescent et l'adolescent: I. Esquisse d'un modèle théorique: concepts de base. *Archives de Psychologie*, 1978, *178*, 133–183.

Crépault, J. Influence du repérage sur la durée: Etude génétique des inférences cinématiques. *L'Année Psychologique*, 1979, *79*, 43–64.

Crépault, J. Compatibilité et symétrie: Etude génétique des inférences cinématiques chez des sujets de 11 et 13 ans. *L'Année Psychologique*, 1980, *80*, 81–97.

Crépault, J. Etude longitudinale des inférences cinématiques chez le préadolescent et l'adolescent: Evolution ou régression. *Canadian Journal of Psychology*, 1981, *35*, 83–92.

Donaldson, M., & Wales, R. J. On the acquisition of some relational terms. In J. R. Hayes (Ed.), *Cognition and the development of language*. New York: Wiley, 1970, pp. 235–268.

Fraisse, P., & Vautrey, P. La perception de l'espace, de la vitesse et du temps chez l'enfant de cinq ans: I. L'espace et la vitesse. *Enfance*, 1952, *5*, 1–20. (a)

Fraisse, P., & Vautrey, P. La perception de l'espace, de la vitesse et du temps chez l'enfant de cinq ans: II. Le temps. *Enfance*, 1952, *5*, 102–119. (b)

Gréco, P. Comparison "logique" de deux durées et jugements corrélatifs de distances et de vitesses chez l'enfant de 6 à 10 ans. In J. Piaget (Ed.), *Etudes d'épistémologie génétique* (Vol. 21). *Perception et notion du temps*. Paris: Presses Universitaires de France, 1967, pp. 3–103.

Greeno, J. G. Analysis of understanding in problem solving. In R. H. Kluwe & H. Spada (Eds.), *Developmental models of thinking*. New York: Academic Press, 1980, pp. 199–212.

Levin, I., Gilat, I., & Zelniker, T. The role of cue salience in the development of time concepts: Duration comparisons in young children. *Developmental Psychology*, 1980, *16*, 661–671.

Matsuda, F. Effects of time and velocity on path-length estimation in children and adults. *Studia Psychologica*, 1977, *19*, 19–31.

Montangero, J. *La notion de durée chez l'enfant de 5 à 9 ans*. Paris: Presses Universitaires de France, 1977.

Montangero, J. Les relations du temps, de la vitesse et de l'espace parcouru chez le jeune enfant. *L'Année Psychologique*, 1979, *79*, 23–42.

Ono, A. Etude expérimentale des interrelations entre temps distance et vitesse subjectifs: Etude de l'effet kappa-tau. *Journal de Psychologie*, 1975, *72*, 261–290.

Palermo, D. S. Still more about the comprehension of "less." *Developmental Psychology*, 1974, *10*, 827–829.

Piaget, J. *The child's conception of time* (A. J. Pomerans, trans.). London: Routledge & Kegan Paul, 1969. (Originally published, 1946.)

Piaget, J. *The child's conception of movement and speed* (G. E. T. Holloway & M. J. Mackenzie, trans.). New York: Basic Books, 1970. (Originally published, 1946.)

Siegler, R. S., & Richards, D. D. Development of time, speed, and distance concepts. *Developmental Psychology*, 1979, *15*, 288–298.

Trabasso, T. The role of memory as a system in making transitive inferences. In R. V. Kail & J. W. Hagen (Eds.), *Perspectives on the development of memory and cognition*. Hillsdale, N.J.: Erlbaum, 1977, pp. 333–366.

Wilkening, F. Combining of stimulus dimensions in children's and adults' judgments of area: An information integration analysis. *Developmental Psychology*, 1979, *15*, 25–33.

Wilkening, F. Development of dimensional integration in children's perceptual judgment: Experiments with area, volume, and velocity. In F. Wilkening, J. Becker, & T. Trabasso (Eds.), *Information integration by children*. Hillsdale, N.J.: Erlbaum, 1980, pp. 47–69.

Wilkening, F. Integrating velocity, time, and distance information: A developmental study. *Cognitive Psychology*, 1981, *13*, 231–247.

Wilkening, F., & Anderson, N. H. Comparison of two rule assessment methodologies for studying cognitive development and knowledge structure. *Psychological Bulletin*, in press.

Paul Fraisse

The Adaptation of the Child to Time

INTRODUCTION

The central question at issue in the developmental psychology of time is the development of mankind's adaptation to time. The most advanced form of this adaptation is the capacity to think about time, that is to acquire a notion of time that permits man to hold a coherent and objective discourse about the past, the present, and the future and to behave according to it. Many of the chapters in this volume investigate the development of the notion of time during childhood. This notion is based on the child's experiences which constitute the raw materials from which the child will begin to develop the notion of time.

In this chapter our objective is to take into account all of the child's experiences that precede a mastery of the notion of time. We will present a synthesis of our laboratory work that remains, for the most part, unknown to English-speaking psychologists.

We begin our discussion by making two observations. First, we must overcome the traditional opposition between subjective time (or *temps vécu*) and objective time, or between the internal experiences of the subject (whether active or passive) and those tied to events in the environment. The psychology of time—which is not the same as the physics of time—is necessarily that of our

113

experiences. Specifically, it is a psychology of the experiences of changes that
are produced in us, by us, and around us. At time $t + 1$ our experience is not at
all the same as that which we had at time t, whether it concerns our thoughts, our
affects, or our perceptions of the environment. We have underlined the successive character of the changes; to this one must add the quality of duration. Except
in limited cases, none of these changes is instantaneous; each has a certain
duration, and between each change there may be intervals of greater or less
duration. Perceptually each experience of change has the character of a figure on
a background.

Certainly, the raw materials that enable us to experience changes in the environment and those that constitute our mental life do not have the same accuracy
and do not permit the same controls. But all these experiences are treated by the
same types of processes, processes that play a role in a person's life well after
early childhood. It is futile, therefore, to contrast the period in which the child
acquires the capacity to make a logical appraisal of time and to measure time with
the period when he would have only preoperational experience of changes in
terms of succession and duration. In the same way that we have a notion of space
that does not modify our perception of space, our notion of time is not a substitute for our experience of time. Time, like space, gives rise to perceptual illusions or, in other words, to systematic distortions that may be found in the child
as well as the adult. Our task will be to show in what way they are the same and
in what way they differ.

The second preliminary observation, which we have presented in an earlier
work (Fraisse, 1957, 1963), is that there are three modes of adaptation to time.

1. *Conditioning to time*. Like all other animals, we are prone to rhythms of
both endogenous and exogeneous origin. We are also conditioned to the intervals
between signals. They provide us with useful information for orienting ourselves
in time, at both a practical and a cognitive level.

2. *Perception of time*. This refers to the perception of brief durations. On this
basis we are able to perceive and adapt to rapid changes.

3. *Mastery of time*, or, in other terms, knowledge of time. This has two
levels. One remains at the preoperational level and involves the representation of
past or actual changes. The other, which corresponds to what W. J. Friedman
(1978) calls "logical time," makes possible "the deduction of temporal relations
between events," and permits one to construct an exact representation of these
changes and anticipate and master future changes.

Both conditioning to and perception of time are common to humans and
animals, though we must note that humans can use the information furnished by
these processes at other levels.

With respect to the mastery of time, the distinction between preoperational
experience and logical reasoning corresponds to two different processes. From

the point of view of developmental psychology, it is important to understand how the transformation is made from one to the other, even if the two coexist thereafter.

In this chapter we reconsider these three modes of adaptation, which obliges us to take into account the information they provide about the adaptation of the child to time. It is not our purpose to present a complete review of previously published work, syntheses which we have already made (Fraisse, 1957, 1963) and which is brought up to date by many of the chapters in this volume. What we do intend is to present the contribution of our own laboratory to these problems.

CONDITIONING TO TIME

The phenomenon of "time conditioning" must be mentioned first. It reminds us, first of all, that the animal is also capable of adaptation to time. What is more, we will show that this process has a role to play in adults and therefore in the child. But much remains to be done in this area.

Circadian Rhythms

Before discussing conditioning, which implies the idea of an acquisition at the level of the individual, it must be recalled that not only plants but also animals possess temporal biological activity. These phenomena come currently under the heading of chronobiology (Aschoff, 1965; Bünning, 1967; Halberg, 1969) and, more particularly, the field of circadian rhythms.

Without entering into detail, it is obvious that the child, like the adult, is subject to biological rhythms that evolve from early childhood (Hellbrügge, 1968). They are apparent, above all else, in the rhythms that are linked to the successive periods of waking and sleeping. These rhythms are so strong that they are capable of making us commit gross errors, even as adults, when we are deprived of the means of measuring time. Thus Siffre (1964) lived *hors du temps* in a darkened cave for 58 days. In trying to estimate the duration of his sleep and other activities, he thought that he had only lived in a cave for 33 days. During this period he had 57 alternations between sleep and waking. Had he placed his confidence in this natural sleeping/waking rhythm, his error would have been only 1 day instead of 25. It appears that in some cases our body gives us quite precise information, but that our perceptual estimations of time seem more credible to us than the organic responses produced by our circadian cycle. Nonetheless, this information plays a considerable and practical role, for example in determining mealtimes or bedtimes.

Conditioning Proper

Besides these endogenous rhythms, our adaptation to time is also constructed on the basis of conditioning of exogenous origin. Behavior is programmed on the basis of previous experiences or on a regular time interval intervening between a signal and an adapted reaction without any reference to a biological cycle.

Two types of conditioning in particular have been studied: classical and operant.

CLASSICAL CONDITIONING

Classical conditioning, demonstrated by Pavlov (1927), has two temporal forms, conditioning to time and delayed conditioning.

1. Conditioning to time is characterized by the fact that the organism adapts to periodic stimuli; for example, the dog that Pavlov fed every 30 min and who did not salivate until the end of each period.

2. Delayed conditioning corresponds to conditioning in which an interval of time elapses between the conditioned and unconditioned stimuli. To take the same example, if we feed a dog 3 min after the blow of a whistle, it will salivate more and more abundantly towards the end of the 3-min interval. In both cases, the animal takes account of information about the duration of the pauses to which it is subject, and applies this in its neurovegetative or motor reactions.

Animals can be conditioned to respond discriminately to stimuli differentiated only by their durations (Gibbon, 1977). All these behaviors show that the animal, lacking an advanced conceptual apparatus, is capable of taking durations into account.

It is important to emphasize that the child, like the adult, adapts to this type of conditioning even at a very early age. Marquis (1941) studied two groups of infants in a nursery, one of which was fed every 3 hours, corresponding almost exactly to the natural feeding rhythm of these children, and the other of which was fed every 4 hours. Adaptation was measured by growth of agitation before meal times, as recorded using actographic beds. Each group adapted to its respective rhythm although the 4-hour rhythm group took somewhat longer. On the ninth day, children fed on the 3-hour schedule were placed on the 4-hour schedule. Their agitation between 3 and 4 hours was conspicuous and completely different from that of the children fed on the 4-hour schedule. There was, therefore, conditioning to time. From a practical perspective, parents and teachers know that infants are calmer when they live according to regular rhythm, that is, when conditioning to time facilitates successive adaptations.

The adult does not escape this conditioning although cognitive psychologists may have underestimated its importance. Following Jasper and Shagass (1941) we studied alpha-rhythm blockage using a luminous signal with a periodicity of 8 sec. We measured the electroencephalogram (EEG) of subjects who were asked to predict the return of the light and respond in synchrony. With eight subjects, it was found that alpha-rhythm blockage was regularly produced after an average interval of 7.4 sec ($\sigma = 1$ sec). Synchronized motor responses were produced on average after 8.1 sec ($\sigma = 1.2$ sec). The process of alpha blocking, which corresponds to a delayed conditioning, is therefore at least as regular as that of a motor response, based on a voluntary estimation (Fraisse & Voillaume, 1969).

But delayed conditioning, in which the subject takes into account an interval between the signal and his response, must be even more important in the life of the child. In the absence of experimental findings, we recall the familiar observation that a child of only a few months of age stops crying as soon as it sees that the preparation of a bottle has begun. Between the animal and the adult there is an important field of study to be developed.

OPERANT CONDITIONING

Ferster and Skinner (1957) studied the temporal variable in behavior under two principal headings: fixed interval (FI) and delayed response learning (DRL).

Animal Studies

Schedules of reinforcement of the FI type are similar to Pavlovian conditioning to time. It has been established that the rat adapts to the distribution of food at fixed intervals: after taking the food, it takes a pause and then begins to press the lever with a constant acceleration until its action is reinforced.

The adaptation to duration is particularly specific in DRL programs where the animal, after pressing the lever, must wait a certain amount of time (10, 20, 30 sec) for its action to be reinforced. Here, explicit account is taken of the duration between two responses, but the animal is obviously not *measuring* time.

In order to explain these adaptations, the existence of a biological clock has been suggested. But as yet no one has been able to localize it or to explain exactly how it functions. The existence of such a clock would imply that there is also some kind of counter that uses this time base. Viviane Pouthas (1979), who carried out research in our laboratory, showed the existence of two processes, each depending upon the duration of the interval studied. One process consists of the animal repeatedly coming and going from the food box to the farthest corners of its cage—though one cannot suppose that a count is being made of these journeys. On the other hand, if the waiting times are rather long, one may find inhibition phenomena such as sleeping. The animal then wakes violently from this subdued state to press the lever immediately, a behavior reminiscent of people who can wake at a fixed time (Fraisse, 1963; Block, 1980).

Operant Conditioning in Children

Techniques of operant conditioning are being applied currently by Pouthas (1981) to children aged 2 to 4 years. Substituting for the role of the lever in a Skinner box was a large red button, very attractive to the child. In order to get around the problems linked with giving sweets as a reinforcement (dental problems, frequency of distribution, the duration of chewing or sucking, etc.), Pouthas had the ingenious idea of using a cognitive reinforcement, corresponding to the child's interest. For the 2.6-year group, the presentation of a slide on a screen, similar to a television, was used and a sound was associated with the image, for example, the image of a chick with peeps, an orchestra of dolls with music. The stimuli were grouped in series: birds, means of locomotion, etc. In order to maintain the reinforcing effect of the stimuli, there was a change in the series for each experimental session. The principle was the same for the children in the 4.6-year group. The reinforcing stimuli consisted of the projection of a color slide for two, three, or four sec on a screen placed in the window of a puppet theater at a distance of 1 m from the child. Slides were grouped in series defined by content: zoo animals, toys, stores, Snow White, and so forth. During an experimental session, slides from one series were presented successively. The series was changed for each experimental session.

Observation showed that the reinforcing effect of the stimuli chosen was very strong. The principal problem was that corresponding to "shaping" in the animal. It was decided to use two successive instructions. The first minimal instruction was given to all subjects: "*You are going to play a game in which you will try to make pictures appear on the screen* (or in the window of the puppet theater)."

The pauses to be taken between each press of the button were successively 1, 2, 3, 4, 5, 7, and 10 sec for the 2.6-year-olds, and 2, 3, 5, 7, 10, and 15 sec for the 4.6-year-olds. Augmentation of the delay was made by the experimenter when the number of reinforced responses was 30% or more after 60 trials. Most often children pressed the button with a frequency apparently equivalent to a spontaneous tempo. However, among the children from the 2.6-year group, 3 out of 9 developed behavior adapted to the DRL. Among the 4.6-year group, 6 out of 12 adapted to a delay, 4 to the 15-sec pause, 1 to 10 sec, and 1 to 7 sec.

Those subjects who failed to find the rule of the game spontaneously in the course of three experimental sessions were given a second instruction that we called informative: "*You should not press the button all the time, but you should wait a little to see the pictures.*" Following the informative instruction two out of six children in the 2.6-year group then met the criterion for the 4-sec pause. Three children in the 4.6-year group achieved a DRL of 10 sec and one of 5 sec, but two children still failed on all delay intervals.

One conclusion is clear: At least some children between 2 and 5 years old are capable of adapting to intervals of 10 to 15 sec. It is possible to obtain better results with rats, but only after a tremendous number of trials. With infants it is impossible to perform many trials a day during many weeks with a single task. On the other hand, it is evident that this task does pose a problem for the child, perhaps because many irrelevent solutions are attempted. These include pressing the button at an increasingly fast rate, pressing harder on the button, etc. This is why the second, or informative, instruction was helpful to many of them.

Given the observations made from animals, we should ask ourselves how the child occupies the interval between reinforcement and the following response. It is clear that children of this age do not count during the interval. Certain children who received the second instruction waited passively. As for the others, their behavior can be interpreted as an effort to occupy their time talking to themselves or the experimenter, singing or other motor activities, tapping the table, or tracing around the button with their fingers.

The 2½-year-old who did adapt to a 10-sec DRL moved around the room after each press of the button, and when the delay was extended, complicated his route. The length of the wait, therefore, became a relevant variable for the child's behavior. The values found by Pouthas are, however, only indicative. Perhaps it was confusing for the children to see the delay getting longer, especially when they had adapted to a previous delay. In one sense it is doubtful that these experiments concern only the use of delays to bring about an effect, and not also the capacity to resist frustration—a capacity that, as we know, increases with age.

We will conclude this section by noting that both animals and children are capable of adapting to intervals of duration, whether repetitive or not. These adaptations also suggest, as we have already said, the possible existence of a biological clock, but the vagueness of this hypothesis only masks our ignorance. We can only assert that neural processes must exist that have nothing to do with the cognitive processes with which we are familiar.

In the case of exogenous adaptations to enduring or periodic stimuli, we might make a guess that inhibition processes are important. Examples are the so-called collateral activities that can be observed in both animals and young children. Pouthas believes that these activities are related to time counts. However, the author sees them as failures of inhibition—partial discharges that have no value as measurements but that manifest difficulties of adaptation in what we would otherwise call a waiting period.

There remains a great deal of work to be done in this area if we are to understand better the role of conditioning in children, the precision of its operation, and also the information, both cognitive and biological, that contributes to such processes.

PERCEPTION OF TIME

The experience of change, which is at the base of our concept of time, always implies the perception and memory of changes. However, among such changes, only the briefest give rise to perception without reference to memory.

In order to understand, let us use the analogy between time and space. I live in a space that I can consider in terms of an abstract plan, like a geometric form. I also have a memory of the space that I move around in: my house, my garden, my street, my town. But in one given moment, t, if I open my eyes I can perceive a space that is simply in my line of gaze. With respect to time, changes succeed changes, but in an instant I can perceive, in a quasi-simultaneity, successive events. I have just been asked, "Do you want some tea?" and this succession of phonemes has been grasped as a perceptual and semantic unity, without there being any mnemonic relation between the first and last phoneme.

This problem has been recognized in general terms since William James's idea of "a sensitive present" (1891), which we prefer to call "the psychological present" and which others today call a very "short-term memory." This area of looking at the successive can be defined as that which can be perceived as a group or unit, whether it concerns sounds in rhythms, tones in melodies, or phonemes in a sentence.

Because many authors ignored that there is a specific mode of perception of durations (varying from some hundredths of a second to 2 or 3 sec), many problems in the psychology of time have been obscured by confusing experiments dealing with heterogeneous modes of knowledge. Let us take one example. We will see later that the 6-year-old child, asked to reproduce 20 sec durations, makes systematic errors that are greater in number and more variable than those made by adults (Fraisse, 1948). On the other hand, the same children can reproduce a 1-sec duration with as much accuracy as an adult, even if their variability is a little greater. The processes in the two tasks are not the same.

In this area of the present, we can distinguish a limiting case, often called "the psychological moment," which corresponds to a "point" in space, determined by the threshold of acuity. In this case, succession is not discerned and successive events appear to be simultaneous. Bloch (1978) reported various experiments from which he concluded that the point of time could vary from 50 to 200 msec. Thus if we project successively onto a screen, but within a limit of 125 msec, four points which form a square, the subject perceives the square without realizing that the presentation was successive (Lichtenstein, 1961). We have shown (Fraisse, 1966) that this integration does not depend on whether the material is meaningful (letters forming a word) or not (points forming a geometric figure).

It has since been shown that very young children can perceive rhythmic structures and distinguish one from another. In our laboratory, Demany, McKenzie,

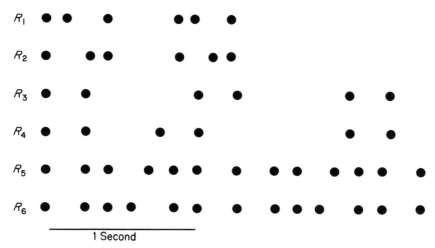

Figure 5.1. Sequence of sounds in six situations (adapted from Demany *et al.*, 1977).

and Vurpillot (1972) found, using a habituation technique, that children of 70 ± 15 days could discriminate between two different sound sequences. (The rhythmic sequences are shown in Figure 5.1.)

The children were seated 40 cm from a uniform visual field containing, on the left, a bright target to attract their attention. A small hole was pierced in the target that permitted the experimenter to follow the movements of the subject's eyes. As soon as the subject looked at the target, the experimenter set off a sequence of sounds that lasted for the period during which the subject continued to look at the target. The loudspeaker that produced the sounds was placed just behind the target. The dependent variable was the duration of visual fixation. The sound sequences were always identical (for example, R_1) so as to create habituation and a loss of interest—in other words, briefer fixations of the target.

When habituation stabilized, the experimenter substituted a new sequence for the first, for example R_2 instead of R_1. If the baby detected a change, the period of fixation would increase briefly. The distinctions between R_1 and R_2 and between R_3 and R_4 were easily perceived. Following Fraisse (1956, 1974), it may be assumed that the rhythms constituted units of duration, or that the law of proximity played a major role. The intervals between the units make it easier to structure them. The structures in R_1 and R_2 were different but the interval was the same. In R_3 and R_4 the structures were the same (two sounds 291 msec apart), but R_3 had equal intervals (873 msec) and R_4 had intervals of two values successively (582 and 1164 msec).

The results show that children of 2½ months are sensitive to differences of structure as well as differences of interval, or to put it another way, to all the aspects of the temporal structure. However, infants of 75 days did not discriminate R_5 from R_6 but children 157 days old (± 14) did. These structures are more difficult because there is no interval between them. We have called these chained structures (Fraisse, 1956). The order of the subgroups alone—1-2-3 versus 1-3-2, or 3-2-1—provides the basis for distinguishing these rhythms from one another. The task is difficult even for an adult, but chilren aged 5 months can cope with it.

In spite of the inability of most infants to discriminate the difficult chain structures, it is clear that there is perception of temporal structures at a very early age and this perception is apparent in the first months of life. Chang and Trehub (1977) provide additional support by showing that children aged 5 months could discriminate a temporal base of multitone patterns composed of identical component tones. In their study, a 2-4 stimulus pattern was distinguished from a 4-2 stimulus pattern. Each sound lasted for 200 msec and within each subgroup the interval was also 200 msec. The interval between the two subgroups 2 and 4 was 600 msec. Again, the technique used was that of habituation, but identified in terms of cardiac deceleration.

Another demonstration of this phenomenon is provided in the work of Humphrey, Tees, and Wheeler (1979) in which children aged 4 months perceived synchronized sound and visual signals during the habituation phase. Following this, the periodicity of the sound signal remained the same (950 msec), but the luminous signal accelerated to 890 msec. The subjects were extremely sensitive to this change, but the result is only clearly shown when the stimulus sources are spatially concomitant. When there is no concomitance one wonders whether or not the child focuses attention on only one or both of the two sources (Spelke, 1979).

The precocity in the perception of brief durations and rhythmic structures shown in these studies is concordant with current observations of children who react to musical rhythms by more or less synchronized shifts of balance (Fraisse, 1974).

There is indeed room for a number of studies concentrating on the limits of discrimination from newborns to 5-year-olds. We have tried—although the results have not yet been reported—a game of imitation with a 3-year-old child, varying the duration of a sound and telling the child to give a response of the same duration. The perception of duration here is very precocious. It is no doubt facilitated by its integration into repetitive structures of a rhythmic type. Indeed, it has been shown (Fraisse, Pichot & Clairouin, 1949) that mentally retarded children aged 6-17 with an IQ between 29 and 48 can produce much the same results with rhythmic structures as normal children (3-6 years) with the same mental age.

Even if there is no problem of memory in perceiving duration, it nonetheless remains that perceived durations are always durations of something. Has the content of this something any repercussions on the duration perceived? Recent research with adults has shown that the content of the stimulation slightly modifies the perceived duration. There is in fact an interaction between the duration and the information it carries. Brefford (1971) and Thomas and Brown (1974) found that when intermittent auditory stimuli are more frequent, durations of 800 to 1600 msec are perceived to be longer. Mo (1971, 1975) found that of two visually presented slides, the one containing more points is perceived as having a longer duration. Warm and McGray (1969) asked subjects to judge the duration of a 1-sec presentation of short or long words. The duration of short, frequently used words was estimated to be greater than that of longer or less frequently used words. The easier the task, the greater the duration was perceived to be.

Fraisse (1979) has verified this. Previous research had shown that reading a word, for example, *carré* (in English, "square"), was faster than naming the corresponding object (a drawing of a square) (Fraisse, 1969). We suggested the hypothesis that a reading task was easier than a naming task. We asked subjects, after familiarizing them with a 1-sec beat, to read at this rhythm a strip with 48 names of simple geometric figures (circle, square, triangle, diamond) and to do the same for a strip carrying 48 drawings of figures corresponding to these names. The experiment was also carried out with 12-year-olds (in the sixth-grade) with 80 names of four colors to be read and 80 colored pencils to name. The results are shown in Table 5.1. The differences are significant by t-tests in both groups; children $p < .001$, adults $p < .01$.

In order to understand this result it must be remembered that we are talking about a production task. The more rapid replies during reading correspond to an overestimation of the 1-sec norm. Thus, overestimation occurs in the easier task. This overestimation, like the previous result, could be explained in terms of the model proposed by Thomas and Weaver (1975). According to this model, during activity, attention "is placed between two parallel processors, a temporal information processor f (timer) and a cognitive processor g. As information increases,

TABLE 5.1
Mean Duration of Reading and Naming in the Imitation of a 1-Second Rhythm

	Task	
Age group	Reading	Naming
12-year-olds	814	932
Adults	1021	1077

NOTE: Times are in msec.

more attention is allocated to the cognitive processor; as cognitive information decreases, more attention is given to the timer.'' In our case it brings about overestimation of time during reading.

We find here a law that is just as valid for the estimation of longer durations. The more we attend to the passage of time itself, particularly in the case of waiting, the longer it seems. One can formulate the same relation (particularly in the case of perception) by using models of information processing. Our capacity is limited and when we are more interested in the nature of a change, our attention cannot be given equally to duration, and vice versa.

It should be possible to study these relations between duration and content in the child. It is important to learn much more about the evolution of these perceptual processes that play such a large part in our lives, whether in crossing the road, in driving a car, or in games of skill.

KNOWLEDGE OF TIME

With respect to conditioning, as with perception, humans as well as animals depend on time. But during a long process, the child gradually becomes capable of objectifying the changes to which he or she is subject and is also able to represent time in terms of successions and durations. The child learns to use these experiences to construct increasingly abstract representations, finally leading to a knowledge of time that will permit him or her, to a certain degree, to master time; each will be capable of speaking about the past and making plans for the future. The passage is a gradual one—from the ability to perceive brief durations and to make estimates of waiting intervals, to the capacity to categorize durations and successions, using all the temporal indices to reason logically about time.

The period from 5 to 7 years of age is a particularly interesting one for us, given also the dissatisfaction we experience reading Piaget's (1946) book. I will not return to the controversy surrounding the accuracy of Piaget's description already mentioned in other chapters in this book. I wish only to remind the reader of our study and its results.

Estimation of Duration

Let us discuss a point that has already been demonstrated in a number of experiments using operant conditioning. The young child, quite apart from anything else, is capable of estimating duration.

In order to characterize these situations, let us return to the old distinction made by Strauss (1928) between time of self and time of the world. This distinction implies that we should separate those cases of estimating time when something is happening in the environment from those cases when there appears to be nothing happening or when we succumb to an internal experience. However, this opposition is relative since we have seen in Pouthas's experiments that some children try to fill in time with overt activities. It is not inconceivable that others react in a similar way but in a manner unobservable to others, by lapsing into mental activity. In these cases adults have a tendency to count, something that 5-year-olds are not yet capable of doing. With older subjects we have always forbidden counting and have always verified afterwards that this restriction was respected.

If the child of 2–5 years is capable of estimating a duration, we must nevertheless underline the fact that these estimations are very imprecise. Pouthas's criterion for success for a given DRL duration was 30%. For three subjects aged 5½ who succeeded with a DRL of 10 sec, the interval produced varied from 2 sec to more than 20 sec. We recorded the reproductions made of unfilled intervals of 20 sec (two sounds marking the interval) by 6-year-olds (Fraisse, 1948). The reproductions fell within a range from 1 to 60 sec, with a relative variability $\left(\dfrac{\sigma}{\bar{x}} \times 100 \right)$ of 90%. The corresponding figure for adults was only 30%.

In another experiment (Fraisse, 1963), children aged 6 years had to reproduce an interval of 30 sec. After each reproduction, the subjects were informed of their results in qualitative terms: "correct" (the criterion was ±5 sec), "too long," or "too short." Out of 10 responses for each of 20 children, the percentages obtained were as follows:

Correct	Too long	Too short
36%	43%	20%

We extended the experiment and found that, in the absence of any objective criterion, the children were still capable of improving their performances. Crowder and Hohle (1970) found that with durations of 2.7 and 5.41 sec, 5-year-olds were capable of doing just as well as 7- or 9-year-olds if they were given feedback about their performances. E. Friedman (1977) trained groups of children aged 2½ and 5½ to reproduce a 15-sec interval using a stopwatch. After this the children produced, on the average, a 15.5-sec interval ($\sigma = 4.5$ sec).

As soon as the child estimated in one way or another something with duration—whether it was an external event or his or her own action—we found that the systematic errors were of the same type as those of the adult despite a greater variability.

Thus, in our 1948 experiment, if we asked a 6-year-old to reproduce a filled duration of 20 sec (in the context of this experiment, a sound that continues during the stimulus and during the response) these filled durations were, as with adults, overestimated by comparison with unfilled intervals.

Comparison of Two Durations

In order to compare two durations with precision, the adult does not generally rely on the capacity to estimate time directly. He measures the duration of some event with an instrument. In the absence of such means of computing time, the adult uses elements inherent in the events themselves. One takes into account, for example, the succession of beginnings and endings of the two concomitant events. Children before 8 or 9 years are not capable of using an instrument to measure time. Neither are they capable of the logical reasoning that could integrate durations and successions. We are interested therefore in the criteria used by children to compare two contemporaneous or successive durations, and in their progression towards the operational stage.

THE COMPARISON BETWEEN TWO JOURNEYS

When two objects move along parallel trajectories, what are the indices used by 5-year-olds (4 years 6 months to 5 years 6 months) to judge the relative duration of the journeys? In a study designed to address this question (Fraisse & Vautrey, 1952), we used figures representing racing cyclists that moved a distance of 25 to 50 cm, for a duration of 2 to 3 sec. In these experiments we reached the following conclusions:

A. When the duration of the routes is proportional to the amount of distance covered at a constant speed, the durations are estimated fairly correctly. Therefore, with the following routes:

(1) $m_1 \longrightarrow$
         $m_2 \longrightarrow$

when the departure time is simultaneous and the speeds are equal, and where consequently m_1 follows the journey after m_2, the number of correct replies (that $t_1 > t_2$) is 79%.[1]

This percentage diminishes slightly, however, if the finishing points are not spatially displaced. Thus if we have:

(2) $m_1 \longrightarrow$
         $m_2 \longrightarrow$

when m_1 leaves first and m_2 begins to move when m_1 reaches its level, we still find that $t_1 > t_2$, but in only 69% of the cases. The simultaneous finish elicits

[1]These figures should be compared with those that would be obtained by chance, which would give 33%. There are three possible choices: equal, or that one or the other object moves for a longer period.

a judgment of equality of duration in 29% of the responses, an error that we find repeatedly and on which we will comment.

B. When departures and arrivals both coincide, no matter what route is followed, logical reasoning allows the adult to conclude that the durations were equal.

Let us take the two preceding spatial interactions again, but this time varying the speed of the two moving objects in such a way that the moments of departure and arrival are simultaneous.

(3) $m_1 \longrightarrow$
         $m_2 \longrightarrow$

(4) $m_1 \longrightarrow$
         $m_2 \ \longrightarrow$

In the first example (3), only 17% of the responses were correct, that is, specifying equality. The responses of the remaining subjects were equally divided between the other two possibilities. The percentage of correct responses increased to 39% in the second situation (4) because the coincidence of the finishing points raised the number of responses of equality.

If the distances are equal and the speeds are also equal but with a displacement of the respective starting and finishing points, we have the following situation:

(5) $m_1 \longrightarrow$
         $m_2 \ \longrightarrow$

The percentage of correct responses was only 14%. It increased, however, to 55% if we removed the effect of displacing the finishing points by making the objects disappear into tunnels located at these points. (This technique was used by Berndt and Wood [1974] with the same effect.) The equality of distances and of speed then becomes a relevant criterion that is otherwise masked by displacing the finishing points.

The importance of the finishing points, mentioned earlier by Piaget (1946), has been taken up again by Montangero (1977). In fact, in order to judge duration, the child often uses as a criterion the succession (or simultaneity) of finishes. These are a very simple form of perceptual data. We also use them to make judgments about the durations of athletic and horse races. Montangero has shown that the perception of the successive switching on and off of lights, for example, makes the subject's task even easier because the problem is no longer complicated by the amount of distance covered. Berndt and Wood (1974) have already found the same thing. Levin (1977) compared the duration of "sleep" of two dolls and reached the same conclusion.

The comparison of situations (3), (4), and (5) shows, therefore, that the child of 5 is not yet capable of logical reasoning, and is incapable of judging the equality of two durations in this way. The rather better results of experiments (4) and (5) show that the child can only make a correct judgment by using an inadequate criterion. In (4) it is the simultaneity of finishes; in (5) it may be by attributing equality to the durations by contagion with the equality of the parameters of distance and speed, but only in the condition where the effect of the spatial displacement of the finishing points is attenuated by masking them.

In the five situations we have looked at so far, the judgments of duration, whether they were right or wrong, leaned heavily on perceptual data, that is, on indices that were not temporal, such as distance covered and the simultaneity or nonsimultaneity of starting and/or of finishing points. However, in the same research, it was found that in some situations subjects were capable of using indices that did not adhere to environmental data or to "time in the world." Instead, they projected the "time of the self," a phenomenon Piaget would call articulated intuition.

The situations studied within this perspective are:

(6) $m_1 \longrightarrow$
        $m_2 \longrightarrow$

The departure of the two objects is simultaneous, but the speed of m_1 is more than double that of m_2 which, therefore, comes to a halt after m_1.

Situation (7) is the same but with a displacement in the starts rather than the finishes:

(7) $m_2 \longrightarrow$
        $m_2 \longrightarrow$

The two objects start simultaneously, but m_2 (which is slower) finishes after m_1.

In situations (6) and (7), m_2 continues for a longer time than m_1 although its speed is much less. According to Piaget, subjects should judge the durations on the basis of speed (the faster it is = the more time it takes) and attribute the journey of greater duration to m_1. But this is not so; 54% of the subjects in (6) and 67% in (7) judged that m_2 continued to move for a longer time. If they were asked why, they said incorrectly that m_2 had to make more effort. There occurs a projection of the intuitive reactions of the self, reminding us of the child who finds the time too long when the outing does not please him, or when he is obliged to eat something he dislikes.

These experiments indicate that the child can employ different cues to support judgments that do not rest on logical inference. He is thus able to use either environmental indices or introspective reactions of a projective form. The latter were favored in our experiment because of the fact that the moving objects were miniature cyclists.

These experiments, all conducted with the same children do not, therefore, allow us to conclude with Piaget (1946) that children go through two successive stages before arriving at the operational stage: one in which they judge duration by external criteria—space covered or, even better, speed—and one in which they separate the work accomplished by the activity itself and judge duration by its introspective characteristics. There should be, according to Piaget, a passage from an intuitive and irreversible egocentrism to the operational grouping. In fact, it appears from other experiments that the development of the judgment of duration is more complex. When the situation does not permit logical (or operational) reasoning, with increasing age the child gradually ceases to trust the extrinsic data when comparing durations. Nor is the young child's problem one of perception of the data. Longobardi and Wolff (1973), who conducted experiments of the same type on children between 5 and 8 years, found that children who could reproduce exactly the situations presented were nevertheless incapable of comparing the durations correctly. This is true not only for children aged 5 years but for some older children, as well.

THE COMPARISON OF TWO SUCCESSIVE DURATIONS

In the experiments that follow children of different ages and adults had to compare two successive durations. It must be said initially that the results indicated that irrespective of the situation, there was an overestimation of the second duration in relation to the first—an error frequently made by adults (Fraisse, 1978), but which is more marked and more systematic in children. We will only present here, for the clarity of the discussion, one particular order of presentation.

The Comparison of Two Activities

The principle of this experiment (Zuili & Fraisse, 1966) is taken from Piaget. It involves children's comparisons of the lengths of time taken to carry two kinds of objects that differ in carrying difficulty. In one case the child must carry rings from one box to another (Task A). In the other, the child must carry disks with tweezers (Task J). The time taken to carry these objects varied with age but within each of the age groups studied (5-, 9-, and 13-year-olds), carrying a disk always took two and one-half times longer than carrying a ring. In the main part of the experiment the child carries rings (or disks) for 20 sec. At the end of this period he is told to stop and is then asked to carry disks (or rings). After 20 sec he is told to stop this second activity. The experimenter then asks the child which task lasted longer. After replying, the child is then asked to justify his response. Relative duration judgments are shown in Table 5.2.

To the 5-year-old, carrying the rings seemed to take longer than carrying the disks. This was also true for the 9-year-olds, but at 13 the percentage of such

TABLE 5.2
Percentage of Subjects Judging the Transportation of Rings Longer
Than That of the Disks

	Age group	
5 years	9 years	13 years
70	60	45

replies corresponded to chance. It is more interesting to consider the reasons given by the children. Table 5.3 gives a global view of the results. We should note first of all the difficulty that young children had in justifying their own replies. In addition, at 13 only 32.5% of the children used the two criteria that were inherent in the task, namely the number of pieces carried and the difficulty or slowness of carrying disks as compared to rings.

In the case where carrying the rings was judged to take longer, subjects mention the relatively greater number of pieces carried, as follows: age 5 years: 62%; age 9 years: 92%; age 13 years: 63%.

On the other hand, in the cases where subjects judged that carrying the disks took longer, they mentioned the difficulty of carrying each piece nearly every time: age 5 years: 75%; age 9 years: 94%; age 13 years: 100%.

These two criteria are thus present at every age level, but they are not given the same weight. Furthermore, it is only toward age 13 that number and difficulty (or slowness) of the task seemed to be balanced against one another.

Comparison of Two Series of Slides

In another experiment (Fraisse, 1966) we asked five groups of subjects (aged 6:5, 8:5, 10:5, and 12:5 years and adults) to compare two periods of time,

TABLE 5.3
Percentage of Subjects in Each Age Group Citing Different Numbers
of Criteria

Number of criteria cited[a]	Age group		
	5 years	9 years	13 years
None	81	44	17.5
One	17	37	50
Two or three	2	19	32.5

[a] Acceptable criteria for these tasks are relative number, speed, and difficulty.

TABLE 5.4
Percentage of Different Judgments in Each Age Group

Judgment	Age group				
	6:5	8:5	10:5	12:5	Adults
A = B	18.8	9.5	11.1	27.2	44.4
A < B	81.2	85.7	77.8	72.8	33.4
A > B	0	4.8	11.1	0	22.2

both in reality equal 32 sec but differing in the number of slides presented. In Series A 8 slides were presented for 4 sec each and in Series B 16 slides for 2 sec each. (These slides depicted various kinds of animals.) After viewing the second series, the subject had to compare its duration with that of the first without using words, but only rods of different lengths (from 5 to 20 cm) according to the convention that the duration of the first series be represented by a rod of 10 cm. The results for the A–B order are shown in Table 5.4. The results were in the same direction for the B–A order but less marked because the time order error, already mentioned, attenuated the illusion.

It is thus necessary to reach adult age before the effect of number ceases to be decisive. When asked to justify their responses, subjects replied by mentioning either the number, the frequency (or the speed of presentation), or the duration of each presentation. Reasoning of a logical kind should involve balancing number (or frequency) against the duration of each slide or the inverse of their frequency. In fact, replies combining two criteria, no matter what their nature, were rarely given by the young children. The proportion of such cases varied from 8.5% for the 6 : 6-year-olds to 70.6% among the adults (see Table 5.5). The percentage of cases in which subjects took into account two contrasting types of indices remained small and even among the adults only reached 22.8%.

This experiment points to several conclusions. Adults are capable of reasoning logically about such situations but they do not always do so. In our estimations of duration, we seem to express two attitudes:

TABLE 5.5
Percentage of Subjects Having Used One or Several Criteria

Number of criteria cited	Age group				
	6:5	8:5	10:5	12:7	Adults
One	57	60	65	48	29
Two or three	9	19	35	48	71

1. An intuitive attitude in which we judge the duration from our immediate reactions. The number of changes is the most salient variable determining our responses, distance with respect to moving objects, or the number of events with respect to successive events.

2. A metrical attitude in which we analyse all the information in the situation.

This double attitude is ubiquitous in the adult. We can say at the end of a pleasant evening, "How quickly the time has passed, but it must be so late." The young child does not possess this double attitude. In this situation he gives priority to one cue and judges the duration on the basis of this one index. This can often be information from the environment. For example, in our experiments, it is distance covered, the number of objects carried, the number of slides presented; that is, more of _____ = more time. But the cue can also be the subjective difficulty of the task. The double attitude develops slowly in the child. Even children who possess operational reasoning (7 or 8 and older according to Piaget) do not use exclusively metrical approaches in judging duration, nor are such attitudes necessarily predominant. As a result, adults and children have the same illusions about duration. But is this not also true with respect to space?

Use of Temporal Indices in Succession

In all of the preceding experiments on duration we have seen that perception of succession plays a major role. In the experiments that we are now going to present, conducted by Estaun-Ferrer (1981), we tried to determine the temporal indices that enable children to judge the succession (or nonsuccession) of two events. The principle of the task was simple. The child saw two slides that represented two scenes from everyday life and from these he must tell a story that takes into account the two pictures (there was a preliminary session to explain the task to them).

There are four types of relations between slides:

1. Pragmatic (P): A temporal order inherent in the action; that is, a pragmatic type. For example: Write a letter. / Put it in a mailbox.

2. Contextual (CON): A temporal order indicated by the context of the action. For example: Five children playing in a swimming pool. / The same children making a snowman.

3. Cognitive (COG): A succession or order marked by cognitive indices (a clock, a calendar). For example: A child who plays a flute under a conspicuously placed calendar showing May 10th. / The same child in the same situation with the calendar showing June 10th.

4. Nonsuccessive (SS): An absence of succession that is a negative form of temporal relation. For example: Two views presented as if a photograph had been

cut in half. For example: In one we see a man eating and in the other a woman sitting opposite him doing the same. All the details of the table and furniture are the same and are completed by the two slides.

There were three items on each type of relation. The question we examined was whether there are certain cues that are better understood by children in situations analogous to those found in cartoon strips or cartoon films. In this vein we also asked whether successive presentation favors comprehension of succession and if, correspondingly, simultaneous presentation of the two scenes favors comprehension of nonsuccession.

For the successive presentation condition, each slide was presented for 7 sec (14 sec for both slides). In the simultaneous presentation condition, exposure was prolonged until the child gave a response. Subjects were 6 years $\pm$ 2 months, 8 years $\pm$ 2 months, and 10 years $\pm$ 2 months and came from middle-class backgrounds with normal education. Order of relation types was randomized for the children in each age group and condition. The children's responses were classified as follows:

0 point: Description of a single image.
1 point: Description of two images but without setting them in temporal relation to one another.
2 points: Setting the two images in an incorrect temporal relation with one another.
3 points: Correct temporal relationship of two images, but erroneous interpretation of cues.
4 points: Correct temporal relationship and adequate justification of the relationship.

Children in each presentation condition could obtain between 0 and 12 points (3 items × 4 points per item) for each relation type. Table 5.6 shows the average number of points obtained by subjects in each group.

Three results must be stressed. First, a successive presentation of scenes is often more difficult to interpret than a simultaneous presentation. This phenomenon can be explained by the fact that successive presentation requires the intervention of short-term memory. It must also be remembered that the duration of presentation of each successive image was limited to 7 sec, while the duration of the simultaneous presentation was unlimited. This makes the exploration and verification of the relevant cues easier. Second, successions of the pragmatic type are easier to understand. Even at age 6 they present no difficulty. Finally, the change from 6 to 8 years is the greatest in the case where the relevant cues are cognitive or, if one prefers, conventional. This finding is consistent with W. J. Friedman's (1978) summary of age trends in children's knowledge of conventional time.

TABLE 5.6
Mean Number of Points Received For Each Relation Type as a Function of Age and Presentation Condition

| Relation type | Age | Presentation Condition | |
		Successive	Simultaneous
Pragmatic	6	11.1	10.7
	8	11.7	11.8
	10	12.0	12.0
Contextual	6	4.8	5.6
	8	7.3	8.8
	10	7.8	9.9
Cognitive	6	5.5	5.2
	8	6.3	11.3
	10	9.7	11.8
Nonsuccessive	6	7.0	7.8
	8	9.1	8.8
	10	10.3	10.4

To summarize, then, the difficulty for children is not in the perception of succession but in the interpretation of certain types of temporal cues. If these are inherent in the action, there is no difficulty at 6 years. If they are of a conventional type, we must wait until 8 years before children begin to use them. When the indices are linked to a context, we can state that they are still difficult to use at 10 years of age. Could it not be, then, that the child who is so sensitive to the figure–ground distinction only takes into account the actions of people and neglects the temporal cues?

Waiting and Hurrying

Estimation of duration is not the only case in which we are confronted with time. As Janet (1928) said, our first encounter in our lives with time occurs in situations of waiting. There is a wait every time a delay is imposed between a desire and its realization. This delay provokes a conflict.

The next experiment shows that children find it difficult to wait and that waiting affects other behaviors. We have tried, experimentally, to determine the relationship between this difficulty and a child's age. As children develop they learn to control their reactions better, and emotional stability increases as well. We wanted to measure the effects of age and of the differences in emotional stability at each age on waiting behavior (Fraisse & Orsini, 1955; Orsini & Fraisse, 1957). In these studies, we tried to measure emotional stability by using a task of manual dexterity. The difference between the score in the normal situation and the stress situation (in which a bell sounds for every error) gives a measure of the perturbation brought on by stress. Scores on this index decrease with age.

The effects of waiting are measured by two tests:

1. A relative increase in reaction time as the delay between the preparatory signal and the executive signal is increased from 1 to 10 sec.

2. Projective tests. For example, a picture is presented of a child receiving a gift. The experimenter explains the situation in the form of a story recounting how the child could not open the present until his father returned. The subject must continue the story, describing the reactions of the child waiting to open his present. The replies are scored on a 5-point scale going from refusing to wait to smiling acceptance.

The results show that waiting is easier to tolerate when children are older (between 6 and 10 years) and that the smaller the increase in reaction time, the better the acceptance of the delay. Emotional stability also increases with age and is, at every age, a significant correlate of the waiting scale.

While waiting, the child must put up with a time interval that is longer than he desires. The inverse situation is that of hurrying. The time granted for a reaction is insufficient and he must react more rapidly than usual. We asked three groups of children, aged 6, 8, and 10, to do our stress test in a situation where the child must carry out a precision task (e.g., placing the pieces of a game without touching the sides). The child must then complete the same task but in less time (time is made overt by a verbal count—1, 2, 3, . . . —played on a tape recorder). It was clear first of all that the 6-year-olds did not understand the situation of hurrying. At 8 years there was a deterioration in performance (fewer pieces placed in the same amount of time and with more errors). This deterioration was less at 10 years. In each age group, there was also a correlation between emotional stability and adaptation to the situation of hurrying (Orsini & Fraisse, 1959).

Whether in conflicts provoked by waiting or by hurrying, with increasing age the child learns better to take into account the temporal constraints of action. There is, no doubt, a better evaluation of durations, but there is also doubt that there is an increasing capacity to control the emotional reactions that give rise to conflicts.

SUMMARY AND CONCLUSIONS

We are tempted to think that humans are not adapted to time until they are capable of reasoning about time in what Piaget (1946) described as formally operational terms or by, according to W. J. Friedman's (1978) formulation, mastering logical time. But as the latter explicitly states, logical time "is an abstraction beyond perceptible order or duration."

In order to understand how the child adapts to time before adolescence, we must distinguish between the different modes of adaptation. Conditioning to duration, particularly periodic, already exists in the animal and it is clearly evident in the child during the first few days following birth. This conditioning to time does not imply a cognitive process, but it facilitates adaptation to regular changes and furnishes information that the child will integrate little by little into his or her experiences of temporal change. This development has not yet been properly explored.

In the first few months of life children also perceive rapid changes, on the order of 1 sec. They can discriminate durations and by 3 years of age are capable of reproducing them with some precision. In considering changes of rather longer duration, we should stress that children, before the age at which they are capable of reasoning about time, have experiences—or perhaps we should say intuitive notions—with succession and duration.

Certainly, the younger the child the more he is interested in the actual nature of the changes. As we have already stated, the first experience of duration occurs, no doubt, when the interval frustrates us; in particular, when we must wait before satisfying our desires. It is remarkable that in Pouthas's experiments children of 2½ years who did not adapt spontaneously to a DRL schedule were able to succeed in observing the delay as soon as one suggested to them that they should *wait* (using this word). There is a cognitive regulation even at this early age. Estimations of durations of 20 to 30 sec are much more imprecise in the child than in the adult. However the child is able to achieve an estimation almost as precise as the adult if he receives feedback about his performance. This is true in the absence of all external cues and before he has learned to count.

This simple result forbids us to contrast the duration of changes in the environment with that of internal experiences. In both cases the child is in possession of information that he uses just as the adult does, with the same systematic errors and the same illusions linked to context or to the nature of the changes. However, above all, it is external change that the child takes into account, whether in reactions to unexpected successions or to events that he either produces or is subject to.

Our experiments have concentrated on children's successes and failures in comparing two durations. When the durations are contemporaneous, appropriate and correct responses are only possible if the child can deduce the durations from the order of the beginnings and endings of the two events. But the errors of young children (5 and 6 years old) inform us about the preoperational criteria that they use. The child certainly does have a notion of duration, but it is insufficient for comparison. Most often the child refers to his immediate perceptions. In the race between the two cyclists, stopping the competitors on the same line facilitated judgments of equality for the duration of the journeys, while displacing the finishing points led to judgments of inequality. Distance covered was also a very salient cue.

If we draw together these results and those obtained in the comparison of successive durations, we can state that 5-year-olds are characterized by the fact that they only take into consideration one cue of the situation. This can be a perceptual element: finishing points, distance covered when this is not obviously dissociated from speed, the number of objects carried, the number of slides viewed, etc. It can also be a subjective consideration: effort, the difficulty of the task. In every case the child makes a judgment of the kind, more of _____ = more time. This type of judgment struck Piaget who, in 1946, foresaw that it did not only apply to speed. Several authors have made the same observation. Recently Levin (1979) underlined that this type of reasoning applies to many dimensions of experience other than speed.

The subsequent development that leads to the possibility of logical reasoning involves taking into consideration the several types of perceptual information in the situation. This information is often redundant; more distance covered and greater speed; or, more slides presented and greater frequency of presentation. But gradually the child discovers the considerations that I call complementary— the greater the number of objects carried in an interval, the shorter the duration of carrying each; or, the less the distance covered, the more effort required.

Berndt and Wood (1974) have shown that this decentration from a misleading cue (which is more common in experiments involving the passing of one train by another) can be produced at age 5 by creating conflicts in which the train running for the longer time finishes behind the other, or by using tunnels as we also did. In such conflict situations the child often changes criteria and more frequently arrives at a correct response.

It is the perception of several aspects of the situation that opens up the possibility of logical reasoning. We are not pretending, however, that logical reasoning is simply the result of perceptual progress. The latter is only a condition. Our experiments also show that adolescents and adults can make errors of estimation by only retaining one aspect of the changes. The difference between adults and children evidently depends on their capacity for reasoning but also on their attitudes and motivations.

In the face of one or several changes, we may be interested first of all in the event, or, in other words, "that which changes." We may also be interested in the duration of the change. In the latter case research shows a tendency to overestimate duration. The child, in contrast, takes the first attitude except in circumstances where there is no external change, as in simply waiting. The adult moves more easily between one attitude and the other, and when he turns his attention to duration he can also take into account information of a type that constitutes a measure of time, that is, homogeneous changes with a fixed periodicity.

The attitude that accords a privileged position to one aspect of the situation does not mean that the child of 3 to 5 years is unable to consider several dimensions. He does not know how to integrate the data successively in order to reach—when the situation permits—a correct conclusion about duration. But he is capable (under certain circumstances) of taking into consideration a number of aspects of these changes, and his estimations of duration are then more precise. Wilkening (1981) shows, in a new and fruitful paradigm, that the 5-year-old is capable of estimating that more time is needed for a turtle than a guinea pig or a cat to go a given distance. But the child remains incapable of working out the proportionality between the distance to be covered and the time taken, which the 10-year-old can do. The 5-year-old is able to estimate that more time is needed for the slowest animal to cross a given distance. Does he think, the slower the object = more time, or does he make the opposite inference, "less fast = more time"? I think that he takes into account past experiences in which slowness was associated with duration. But the results show that he does not truly reason because if we triple the distance to be covered, he will not triple the necessary duration. He just makes it slightly longer.

We conclude that the child estimates durations by the contents of changes, or else takes into consideration the order of successions while giving priority to more recent events. The child will be able to make logical comparisons or estimations when he is capable of analyzing the multiple data of experience and of establishing relations between changes; then memory of previous events will facilitate the processing of perceptual information.

REFERENCES

Aschoff, F. *Circadian clocks*. Amsterdam: North-Holland, 1965.

Berndt, T., & Wood, D. The development of time concepts through conflicts based on a primitive duration capacity. *Child Development*, 1974, *45*, 825–828.

Block, R. Time and consciousness. In G. Underwood, & R. C. Stevens (Eds.), *Aspects of consciousness* (Vol. 1). London: Academic Press, 1980.

Buffardi, L. Factors affecting the filled-duration illusion in the auditory, tactual and visual modalities. *Perception and Psychophysics*, 1971, *10*, 292–294.

Bünning, E. *The physiological clock* (2nd ed.). New York: Springer-Verlag, 1967.

Chang, H. W., & Trehub, S. E. Infant's perception of temporal grouping in auditory patterns. *Child Development*, 1977, *48*, 1666–1670.

Demany, L., McKenzie, B., & Vurpillot, E. Rhythm perception in early infancy. *Nature*, 1977, *266*, 718–719.

Estaun-Ferrer, S. La compéhension des indices temporels chez l'enfant. Unpublished thesis, University René Descartes, Paris, 1982.

Ferster, C. B., & Skinner, B. F. *Schedules of reinforcement*. New York: Appleton-Century-Crofts, 1957.

Fraisse, P. Etude comparée de la perception et de l'estimation de la durée chez les enfants et les adultes. *Enfance*, 1948, *1*, 199–211.

Fraisse, P. L'estimation de la durée. In *Psychologie et épistémologie génétique*. Paris: Dunod, 1966. Pp. 253–269.

Fraisse, P., Pichot, P., & Clairouin-Oléron, G. Les aptitudes rythmiques. Etude comparée des oligophrènes et des enfants normaux. *Journal de Psychologie Normale et Pathologique*, 1949, *42*, 309–330.

Fraisse, P., & Vautrey, P. La perception de l'espace, de la vitesse et du temps chez l'enfant de cinq ans. II. Le temps. *Enfance*, 1952, *5*, 102–119.

Fraisse, P., & Orsini, F. Etude expérimentale des conduites temporelles. I. L'attente. *L'Année Psychologique*, 1955, *55*, 27–39.

Fraisse, P. *Les structures rythmiques*. Louvain: Editions Universitaires, 1956.

Fraisse, P. *Psychologie du temps*. Paris: Presses Universitaires de France, 1957. (English translation: *The psychology of time*. New York: Harper & Row, 1963.)

Fraisse, P. Visual perceptive simultaneity and masking of letters successively presented. *Perception and Psychophysics*, 1966, *1*, 285–287.

Fraisse, P. L'estimation de la durée. In *Psychologie et Epistémologie Génétique*. Paris: Dunod, 1966, 253–269.

Fraisse, P. Why is naming longer than reading? *Acta Psychologica*, 1969, *30*, 103.

Fraisse, P., & Voillaume, Cl., Conditionement temporel du rythme alpha et estimation du temps. *L'Année Psychologique*, 1969, *69*, 7–15.

Fraisse, P. *Psychologie du rythme*. Paris: Presses Universitaires de France, 1974.

Fraisse, P. Time and rhythm perception. In E. C. Carterette & M. P. Friedman (Eds.), *Handbook of perception* (Vol. 8). New York: Academic Press, 1978, pp. 203–254.

Fraisse, P. (Ed.) *Du temps biologique au temps psychologique*. Paris: Presses Universitaires de France, 1979. (a)

Fraisse, P. Influence de la durée du traitement de l'information sur l'estimation d'une durée d'une seconde. *L'Année Psychologique*, 1979, *79*, 495–504. (b)

Friedman, E. R. Judgments of time intervals by young children. *Perceptual and Motor Skills*, 1977, *45*, 715–720.

Friedman, W. J. Development of time concept in children. In H. W. Reese & L. P. Lipsitt (Eds.), *Advances in child development and behavior*. London: Academic Press, 1978, pp. 267–298.

Gibbon, J. Scalar expectancy theory and Weber's law in animal timing. *Psychological Review*, 1977, *84*, 279–322.

Helbrügge, T. Ontogenèse des rythmes circadiares chez l'enfant. In J. de Ajuriaguerra (Ed.), *Cycles biologiques et psychiatrie*. Symposium Bel-Air III, September, 1967, Geneva, Librairie de l'Université, George et Cie, 1968, pp. 159–183.

Halberg, F. Chronobiology. *Annual Review of Physiology*, 1969, *31*, 675–725.

Humphrey, K., Tees, R. C., & Werker, J. Auditory-visual integration of temporal relation in infants. *Canadian Journal of Psychology*, 1979, *33*, 347–352.

James, W. *The Principles of psychology*. (2 vols.). London: McMillan, 1891.

Janet, P. *L'évolution de la mémoire et de la notion de temps*. Paris: A. Chahine, 1928.

Jasper, H., & Shagass, C. Conscious time judgments related to conditioned time intervals and voluntary control of the alpha rhythm. *Journal of Experimental Psychology*, 1941, *28*, 503–508.

Killeen, P. On the temporal control of behavior. *Psychological Review*, 1975, *82*, 89–115.

Levin, I. The development of time concepts in young children: Reasoning about duration. *Child Development*, 1977, *48*, 435–444.

Levin, I. Interference of time related and unrelated cues with duration comparisons of young children: Analysis of Piaget's formulation of the relation of time and speed. *Child Development*, 1979, *50*, 469–477.

Lichenstein, M. Phenomenal simultaneity with irregular timing of components of the visual stimulus. *Perceptual and Motor Skills,* 1961, *12,* 47-60.

Longobardi, E. T., & Wolff, P. A. A comparison of motoric and verbal responses on a Piagetian rate-time task. *Child Development,* 1973, *44,* 433-437.

Marquis, D. P. Learning in the neonate. *Journal of Experimental Psychology,* 1941, *29,* 263-282.

Matsuda, F., & Matsuda, M. Effects of spatial separation as a cue of time estimation in children and adults. *Japanese Psychological Research,* 1979, *21,* 132-138.

Mo, S. S. Judgment of temporal duration as a function of numerosity. *Psychonomic Science,* 1971, *24,* 71-72.

Mo, S. S. Temporal reproduction of duration as a function of numerosity. *Bulletin of the Psychonomic Society,* 1975, *5,* 165-167.

Montangero, J. *La notion de durée chez l'enfant de 5 à 9 ans.* Paris: Presses Universitaires de France, 1977.

Orsini, F., & Fraisse, P. Etude des conduites temporelles. II. Etude génétique de l'attente. *L'Année Psychologique,* 1957, *57,* 359-365.

Orsini, F., & Fraisse, P. Etude expérimentale des conduites temporelles. La précipitation. *Psychologie Française,* 1959, *4,* 117-126.

Pavlov, I. P. *Conditioned reflexes.* New York: Dover Edition, 1960. (Originally published, 1927.)

Piaget, J. *Le développement de la notion de temps chez l'enfant.* Paris: Presses Universitaires de France, 1946. (English translation: *The child's conception of time.* London: Routledge & Kegan, 1969.)

Pouthas, V. Analyse des conduites observées au cours de conditionnements au temps chez l'animal. In Fraisse, P., et al. (Eds.), *Du temps biologique au temps psychologique.* Paris: Presses Universitaires de France, 1979, pp. 149-160.

Pouthas, V. Adaptation à la durée chez l'enfant de 2 à 5 ans. *L'Année Psychologique,* 1981, *81,* 33-50.

Siffre, M. *Beyond time.* New York: McGraw-Hill, 1964.

Spelke, E. S. Infant's intermodal perception of events. *Cognitive Psychology,* 1976, *8,* 553-560.

Strauss, E. Das Zeiterlebnis inder endogenen Depression und inder psychopathischen Verstimmung. *Monatsschrift für Psychiatrie und Neurologie,* 1928, *68,* 640-657.

Thomas, E. A. C., & Brown, I., Jr. Time perception and the filled-duration illusion. *Perception and Psychophysics,* 1944, *16,* 449-458.

Thomas, E. A. C., & Weaver, W. B. Cognitive processing and time perception. *Perception and Psychophysics,* 1975, *17,* 363-367.

Warm, J. S., & McCray, R. E. Influence of word frequency and length on the apparent duration of tachistoscopic presentation. *Journal of Experimental Psychology,* 1969, *79,* 56-58.

Wilkening, F. Integrating velocity, time, and distance information: A developmental study. *Cognitive Psychology,* 1981, *13,* 231-247.

Zuili, N., & Fraisse, P. L'estimation du temps en fonction de la quantité de mouvements effectives dans une tâche. Etude genetique. *L'Annee Psychologique,* 1966, *66,* 383-396.

Lorraine Harner

Talking about the Past and the Future

The notions of past, present, and future are central to the ways we organize our lives and to how we think and talk about events, experiences, and ourselves. Some of us are more influenced by past events in terms of what we think and talk about. Others live largely for the future, always planning, waiting, or dreaming. Still others have a ''now'' orientation and are mainly concerned with the present moment's experiences. We all vary in our temporal orientations and in our subjective interpretations of time and the ideas of past, present, and future. Yet there is certainly a widely accepted, more objective view of these temporal relations.

This chapter will explore how the more objective aspects of the notions of past, present, and future time are gradually acquired and differentiated by young children. Both the conceptual and the linguistic frameworks that guide our thinking about such temporal notions will be considered. After the cognitive and linguistic frameworks have been explored, experimental and observational research in developmental psycholinguistics will be drawn on to discuss key issues. In addition, I will present some of the findings concerning factors that may influence our personal and subjective temporal perspectives after we have mastered the basic linguistic and cognitive systems. Consideration will also be given to the effect of subjective factors on the acquisition of the objective system.

141

The Developmental Psychology of Time

ISSUES IN OBJECTIVELY DEFINING CONCEPTS OF
PAST, PRESENT, AND FUTURE TIME

Temporal Models of the World: Are They Valid?

For centuries philosophers have argued about whether or not temporal ideas are a valid way of describing the world (Gale, 1967; Whitrow, 1961). Despite the lack of unanimity on this point, it is nonetheless the case that throughout different cultures and periods, the division of experience into present and nonpresent has been a common description or categorization of human life (for examples, see J. T. Fraser, 1965, 1975; Thompson, 1965). The division of the nonpresent into past and future, and the relation between these two and the present may have taken different forms or models in different cultures (e.g., spiral, circular, straight line). But the existence of our memories and our abilities to plan and anticipate make it seem probable that regardless of how they were conceptualized, notions of the past and the future must have existed in some form throughout human history. For the purposes of this chapter, I will consider only our Western linear model of time in which past and future are categories ordered in relation to a continually shifting ''present'' reference time.

Key Features of Western Society's Linear Model of Time

In order to relate the meaning of past, present, and future categories to their experience in the observable world, children must grasp the basic concept of temporal seriation. *Seriation* refers to the order of successive events or changes; young children can generally perceptually discriminate a succession of changes more easily than they can correctly recall them (Fraisse, 1963). We can distinguish two basic aspects of temporal seriation. The first is that any two events on the time continuum occur relative to each other; if they do not occur simultaneously, then they either precede or follow one another. The second is that any set of events must also be considered in terms of its position in the overall time continuum. Thus, although judgments of the relative order of two events will be consistent over time, the same two events do not always belong to the same past, present, or future category of experience, but are at some time a member of each in turn.

Learning the relative order of events seems essential to the development of past and future categories in two ways. First, if the idea of the past originates from a collection of discrete memories, then at some point these memories must begin to be sequenced so that in recollection certain events precede others. The same might hold for the future. The idea of the future may originate as intentionality or potentiality, but children must learn the probable sequence of occurrence of future events if they intend to have any effect on their shaping. Second, an ordered relation must be established among the three categories of past, present, and future as well as within each. That is, past, present, and future must be ordered among themselves. Such an ordering of the categories is clearly essential to the notion of a continuing sequence of events maintaining constant relation to one another (either before or after one another), but moving in a regular way from one temporal category to another.

Another important feature is that the boundaries of both the past and the future are determined by a present reference time. Thus it is clear that according to our Western linear model, the past and the future are mutually exclusive. Although they are both nonpresent times, they neither overlap nor are they interchangeable. However, even though the temporal dimensions of past and future are conceptually distinct, the events we experience are not completely independent of each other. Future predictions are made based on past events. While the future is never an exact duplicate of the past, it often seems influenced, if not determined by events that have already occurred. The linear conceptual model, which clearly specifies the mutual exclusiveness of past and future, does not account for the interconnectedness of events or for our desire to predict and control the future. It may be that young children first understand the future as a recurrence of the past. If that is their initial experience of the future, learning that past and future are mutually exclusive may not be as easy for young children as the conceptual model would lead us to expect.

A further potential problem in learning the ordered relations of past, present, future categories may result because the boundaries of each category are not fixed, but are expandable, contractable, and shifting. There are two reasons for these variable boundaries. The first is that the present is not only a reference point separating what has happened from what is about to happen; it is also a category of experience in itself. The duration of the present can range from a split second to a longer time such as this minute, this mealtime, this morning, or this day. We subjectively perceive the extent of the present, and we can expand it to include the immediate past or the immediate future. Thus when we note the present consequences of an event that just occurred, such results are both part of a past event and our present experience. Similarly, our anticipations of future actions seem to be a part of both an extended present and the immediate future. Although children must realize that the past and future are separate from the present as well as from each other, they also must realize that there is no set time span for the present, and that the past and future domains of experience merge into the present.

The limits of the present are impossible to fix for yet a second reason. In addition to the subjectively perceived present having expandable limits, the present moment is continually changing. The remote future becomes the immediate future which, in turn, becomes the present. The present moment quickly becomes the past. Thus the actual contents of past, present, and future categories are always changing. In order to fully understand the continually changing and relational nature of past, present, and future times, children must have a sense of the present as a shifting reference point on a linear temporal continuum. Children must be able to separate their subjective experiences of the present from the notion of the present as a reference point. Once children implicitly comprehend the notion of the present as a continually changing reference point that does not always correspond to their own, they may understand past and future relations from points of view other than their own. The ability to adopt a temporal point of view that differs from one's own immediate temporal viewpoint has been referred to as temporal decentering (Cromer, 1971; Harner, 1980). Temporal decentering is characteristic of the adult's mastery of our temporal system and is yet another skill that must be mastered by children.

Smith (1980) discussed the notion of temporal decentering until further and drew implications for specifying our time system in relation to our linguistic system. She noted that it is not enough to simply reference an event in relation to the present to determine its pastness or futurity. Often we compare an event's temporal relation to some other event or time that is not concurrent with the present. Thus, there are three important "times" in our cognitive–linguistic system. First is the *event time,* the time at which the event actually occurs; next is the *speech time,* the time at which reference is made to the event; the third is a *reference time,* a time that may or may not be parallel to the speech time. According to Smith, young children's temporal reference systems reflect the existence of the first two times—event time and speech time. Only when they have developed the ability to temporally decenter do children demonstrate the existence of a flexible reference time in their temporal system. Smith's theory is based upon her review of current research on children's acquisition of time language and upon her earlier theoretical work on adult use of temporal reference (Smith, 1978).

To summarize, the key features of a cognitive map of the Western model of time include: (*a*) temporal sequencing of two events in relation to one another; (*b*) past and future as mutually exclusive categories; (*c*) the duality of the present as both a reference point and an expandable category of experience in itself; (*d*) the shifting boundaries between the past and the present as well as between the present and the future; (*e*) the continually changing nature of the present and the shifting contents of each of the temporal categories, past, present, and future; (*f*) the existence of three "times" as the conceptual system intersects the linguistic system—event time, speech time, and reference time; and (*g*) the need to decenter and consider a reference time other than one's own immediate present. Later in this chapter I will review the available research data in relation to how children master these conceptual distinctions.

Are Past and Future Categories Really Equivalent?
Subjective Considerations

If we conceive of the past and future as segments of a time line, segments that exist in relation to a changing present reference point, then past and future categories appear to be logically equivalent. However, the quality of our experience is not the same for all nonpresent events. Our past experiences are familiar and known, whereas our sense of the future is characterized by a measure of uncertainty. Clearly there are important subjective factors influencing both our perceptions of past events and our projections of future events.

It seems likely that some past events achieve more salience than others because of the social and affective contexts in which they occur. In his chapter on "Pastness," Miller (1978) notes the personal origins of our early notions of the past. He argues that young children's linguistic expressions of pastness usually refer to concrete experiences that have some present-moment personal relevance. Thus young children's understanding of the past is not as complex as that of adults. Only later do children understand the idea of the past as separate from the present. For Miller, the earliest notions of pastness are embedded in a kind of extended present. Werner (unpublished paper, n.d.) also refers to a present that extends into and includes the immediate past and future.

The emergence of such abstract notions as past and future is most likely rooted in the child's daily experiences. The achievement of satisfying past events may lead to a desire for recurrence. Such a wish for recurrence is one possible origin of the idea of the future. But the future is essentially unknown and untried. Nothing is ever an exact repetition of the past, and events never occur exactly as predicted. We may wonder how the unknown aspect of the future is conceptualized. We can project new images based on past knowledge, but how do we maintain an openness towards future possibilities that are not variations on a past theme? We may know the range of possibilities, but it is less clear how we think about the unexpected and unknown. Thus, despite the objectively defined equivalence of past and future as ordered temporal relations, there is an important sense in which our personal understanding of past and future categories is quite asymmetrical.

LANGUAGE: THE MEDIUM THROUGH WHICH
NOTIONS ABOUT PAST AND FUTURE EVENTS
ARE TRANSMITTED

Knowledge about the present can be acquired and shared by those who witness the same events in the objective world. Language is not required for perceptions to be shared—it is enough that two or more people watch the same events from the same social, physical, or temporal perspective. However, knowledge of the past and ideas about the future are unlike perceptual knowledge of the present; we cannot see or touch the past or the future. Such knowledge exists in our minds or in recorded history and has no immediate, external, physical reality. We depend on language as the primary medium through which we can communicate ideas about nonpresent events. Consequently, it is important to consider how language encodes ideas of past and future time. Language provides structures for thinking and communicating. These linguistic structures may well influence the psychological processes involved in conceptualizing past and future events.

Language forms that encode notions of nonpresent time have varied greatly among different societies as well as within any particular language community. Most languages do code notions of past, present, and future time (Bull, 1971). However, these languages vary from one another in the forms that they provide and the distinctions that they make. The most common way of indicating the time of an action in relation to the time at which the action is spoken of is through the system of verb tenses. Jesperson (1938), Lyons (1968), and Palmer (1974) note that verb tense is distinguished by morphological inflections (e.g., in English, -ed for past, -s for present); if the verb system in a language does not have inflections, then the language does not have verb tenses, according to these linguists. The tense inflections order the time at which an event occurs in relation to the time at which the event is spoken of. Thus, the event occurs either before it is referred to (past), at the same time it is being spoken of (present), or after the time it is mentioned (future).

The inflections indicating past, present, and future times are most commonly—though not exclusively—attached to the verb. Bull (1971) notes instances in which these temporal order morphemes are attached to the subject of a sentence: in languages such as Zulu and Haitian French, and other instances in which they occur as free forms, not attached to any word (subject or verb) as, for example, in Mandarin Chinese or Hawaiian.

Linguistic variety is so great that the language of the Hopi Indians has no system to indicate whether an event is past, present, or future (Whorf, 1962). Their verbs are inflected, but for other reasons. The inflections indicate the sort of validity that the speaker assigns to a statement. The types of validity include: (a) a report of an event that can be either present or past; (b) a report of an event from memory, which is always past; (c) the expectation of an event, which is similar to our future; and (d) a law or generalization about events, which is like our "timeless" present (Whorf, 1962). The lack of time references in a language is quite uncommon. Whorf has argued that the lack of temporal order morphemes in the Hopi language reflects and perhaps even influences their conceptual model of the universe. The Hopi language mirrors the Hopi world view in that both ignore notions of past and future time. In addition, insofar as language guides thought and thought is dependent on language, the Hopi language influences its speakers to think of a world in which past and future are not relevant distinctions.

The form of a linguistic system may be determined by the existence of key concepts in the culture. However, the linguistic system itself then becomes a transmitter of the culture's essential notions. For the Hopi, ordered time relations do not seem essential to their cosmology and consequently to their language. For a young English-speaking child, however, the situation is quite different. There are important temporal distinctions to be mastered, and the structure of the English language is an important data source.

At this point, having given a brief sense of the ways languages encode time, it seems useful to consider how English, in particular, encodes the scheme of past, present, and future relations. Clearly, there is no one-to-one correspondence between the temporal relations existing in the world of objects and actions and the linguistic forms available to refer to those relations. Rather, there are several alternative ways to refer to such relations. For instance, the pastness of an event can be communicated by simple past tense, present perfect tense, past perfect tense, past progressive tense, or by the adverbials *yesterday, before, already, last week,* and so on. There is, then, an elaborate linguistic system related to notions of time that children must gradually master. Researchers have studied, through naturalistic observations and experimental methods, how children come to understand "time language." These studies will be reviewed in the next section.

A central subsystem in our linguistic expression of past, present, and future relations is the use of verb forms to indicate the time of the action. However, there is a linguistic asymmetry in the way the English verb system expresses temporal reference. As Jesperson (1938), Lyons (1968), Bull (1971), and Palmer (1974) noted, verb tense is characterized by inflections. Thus in English, *s* is the present tense inflection and *ed* signifies past tense. English, however, unlike Russian, French, Hungarian, Spanish, and many other languages, has no inflection for future verb forms. Consequently, linguists describe English as having no "proper" future tense. Instead we have a system of modal auxiliary verbs (*can, may, will, must,* etc.) that convey varying degrees of certainty that the event the speaker mentions will actually occur. This asymmetry in the verb system corresponds to the asymmetry of our personal experiences of past and future as discussed in the preceding section. How the linguistic and experiential asymmetries may influence the development of children's understandings of past, present, future relations will be considered in the following section.

RESEARCH FINDINGS ON THE DEVELOPMENT OF PAST AND FUTURE CONCEPTS IN CHILDREN

Prelinguistic Origins: Early Seriation

The ability to order events in a temporal sequence is basic to an understanding of past, present, and future relations, and one can first locate the emergence of this ability to seriate in the prelinguistic period. In Piaget's work on the sensorimotor period, he observed the development of temporal relations in infants up to 18 months (1954). He described children's earliest understandings of temporal relations largely in terms of temporal seriation. In mastering seriation, children perceptually discriminate, imitate, and later recall a succession of changes. Through describing the development of temporal seriation, he attempted to explain how children accomplish the transition from a personalized, often action-embedded time to a sense of time that has broader scope and is more objective.

In discussing the transition from sensorimotor to representational modes of thought, Piaget has referred to the notion of an extended present. At the sixth stage in the sensorimotor period children are able to retrieve objects hidden in a sequence of places. Piaget has explained this new ability by pointing out that children no longer depend upon their immediate perceptions and acts for the existence of objects. Children are now able to maintain ordered images that correspond in some way to the order of preceding events and states. On the basis of the analysis, Piaget has pointed out that the present has been "extended" to include the immediate past (1954).

Although Piaget did not comment on the possibility of an extended present that includes the immediate future at this point in development, there might be an earlier point when such an awareness exists. For instance, during the fourth stage when children move one object to have an effect on another object, one could say that the child's present actions, perceptions, and anticipations are indications of a primitive notion of the immediate future. It may be that Piaget did not suggest this possibility because of his concern with distinguishing between an action knowledge of temporal series and knowledge based on a more representational framework, such as a series of images. Based on Piaget's ideas, one can suggest that the past, as a concept, has its origins in sensorimotor memory and the future in the early practical intentionality of the child.

Psycholinguistic Studies: How Children Use and Understand Language that Refers to Past and Future Events

PAST AND FUTURE: ORDER OF ACQUISITION

Much of the early work examining the emergence of temporal reference in child language has focused on whether references to past and future events emerge simultaneously or sequentially. Diary studies of children's spontaneous speech production (Stern & Stern, 1907) have suggested that the emergence of grammatical tense forms has not corresponded to the growth or frequency of references to past or future times. Future reference preceded past reference in the speech of the children studied by the Sterns. Although the children used verbs to refer to future events before they used verbs to refer to past events, the inflected or temporally marked verb occurred first in reference to the past. The appropriate form for the future emerged later. In reviewing three diary studies (English, German, and French), Clark (1969) also found that tense markings for the past preceded those for the future. The Sterns noted that the infinitive form of the verb was a part of the future verb form in German (as it is in English) and, as such, seemed to suffice for the children as an indicator of future time. Stern and Stern also reported that among the first temporal adverbs they collected from several diary studies, those that denoted the immediate future preceded those that denoted the immediate past.

A detailed longitudinal study of temporal reference was done by Cromer (1968). Cromer analyzed the spontaneous speech production of Adam and Sarah, two of the children studied by Brown (1964). Cromer's appendices of utterances show, as Clark found in reviewing three other studies, that irregular past verb forms preceded future verb forms. But his data also show that inflections in past forms of verbs occurred at about the same time as the use of the modal *will* in the future forms. At the close of the study, when the children were approximately 5 years 6 months of age, neither past nor future verb forms were consistently being used correctly. At the youngest ages (2 years 3 months and 2 years 7 months), future references were more frequent than past references—16% future as compared with 5–6% past. When the children were between 5 and 6 years old, the gap closed considerably with the percentage of future and past references at approximately 18% and 13%, respectively. Such results suggest that reference to future events, if not learned earlier, at least is more common for the young child. In sum, then, the evidence does not indicate clearly whether children learn to refer to either past or future events first or to both at the same time.

ORDER OF EMERGENCE AND EARLY MEANING OF TEMPORALLY MARKED VERBS AND ADVERBS

With respect to the sequence in which temporal forms emerged, Bloom's data (1970) on the spontaneous speech of three children from 1 year 7 months to 2 years 6 months confirmed Werner's observations (unpublished paper, n.d.). Both researchers agreed that in the acquisition of time language, verb tense was the first form to appear; temporal adverbs followed. Werner suggested that the adverbs *yesterday* and *tomorrow* at first referred to nonpresent time because they were often used interchangeably without regard to whether they actually referred to past or future times. He also noted that when adverbs were first combined with verbs, the verbs signaled whether the reference was past or future, thus implying that the verb and the adverb were not consistent with respect to either future or past time reference. The utterances collected by Bloom in which there are both nonpresent verbs, either past or future, and temporal adverbs demonstrated temporal concord.

However, although these early sentences with temporally marked verbs and adverbs were grammatically correct, they did not accurately describe the real events referred to. Thus when Kathryn said, *"You came here last night—when my mother was ironing,"* the verb tenses and the temporal adverb agreed; the past time reference was correct, but the statement was not true. Her mother did not iron *"last night,"* nor was the observer to whom she was speaking present *"last night."* However, it was true that the observer had been present at a previous time when Kathryn's mother was ironing.

Whether the early understanding of temporal adverbs is that of nonpresent time, as Werner suggested, or clearly either past or future is an interesting question. One could argue on the basis of Bloom's data that the child has a sense of the past as separate from the present and future since the two events (mother ironing and observer visiting) did occur in the past and at the same time, and the child correctly encoded them as being past. One might say that the child was in error because she did not have the metric system (that is, the objective quantitative system) for measuring and ordering past events.

The following interchange also suggests that Kathryn had a clear sense of the past and a small set of terms for past reference. The observer asked Kathryn, *"Did you play with me tomorrow?"* to which Kathryn replied, *"Yes."* The observer then asked, *"Will you play with me yesterday?"* Again Kathryn responded without appearing troubled by or even cognizant of the temporal inconsistency of the questions. She said, *"Yes, last yesterday, last night."* Kathryn responded to the temporal adverb in the second question with two other temporal adverbs also past in reference. Although her affirmation about the previous night was incorrect, it was true that the observer had played with her in the past.

One could interpret her first response, *"Yes,"* to mean that she was referring to the nonpresent, that is, to another time of playing, either earlier or later. However, her second response, *"Yes, last yesterday, last night"* suggested that she realized that some experiences had already happened and were past. Why she responded to the adverb rather than the verb in the adult's utterance is not clear. Perhaps it was a term she was just acquiring and therefore particularly motivated to use it. Or perhaps her language was more developed in the domain of past reference than in the domain of future reference.

Examples such as the previous one give us a sense of children's efforts to master the complex linguistic system that enables us to refer to nonpresent events. Their acquisition of the system seems to begin with temporally marked verbs, after which nonpresent adverbs appear. It may be that the acquisition pattern for temporally marked nonpresent adverbs does not parallel the acquisition pattern for nonpresent verbs. Children may initially learn different distinctions for verbs than they learn for adverbs. According to Werner, nonpresent verbs are more clearly understood as having either past or future implications than are temporally marked adverbs. There may be a stage in which adverbs signify a generalized "not now" for young children. This stage of understanding could coexist with an understanding of verbs as either past, present, or future. Gradually the understanding of time relations coded by verbs and adverbs becomes synchronized by children, but the combination of verb and adverb, each signifying a temporal distinction, requires complex coordinations and is a later achievement than the use of either form alone.

PAST TIME: WHAT IS THE NATURE OF THE EARLY USE OF PAST VERBS?

Children's early references to past events have been the topic of several studies and theoretical papers (Antinucci & Miller, 1976; Bloom, Lifter & Hafitz, 1980; Bronckart & Sinclair, 1973; Kuczaj, 1977; Miller, 1978; Sachs, 1979; Smith, 1980). In a theoretical paper, Miller asked how children's early use of past verbs differs from adult use. Smith also focused on the conceptual distinctions children encode and how these differ from the adult notion of past time. Both Miller and Smith concluded that children's early meanings are less complex than the adult notion of pastness. Miller described the earliest use of past verbs as referring to a kind of past-in-the-present. He argued that children's personal motivation results in their speaking about immediate events that have current meaning. Support for Miller's ideas can be found in a study of a Hebrew–English bilingual child, in which Berman (1978) found that from 22 to 25 months the function of most verbs was to communicate the child's needs and desires. As a later development (from 25 to 27 months), verbs were also used to report on events that were not of immediate personal significance.

Whether very early past verbs can be said to have general past reference or whether they refer instead to the present consequences of past events is a question that has engendered a series of studies. The issue has been whether early past verbs are used to code the time of an event or the aspect of an event.

Tense and aspect both code time-related characteristics of actions, but there are significant differences between the two systems. Verb tense is inherently relational in nature while verb aspect is not (Friedrich, 1974). The verb tense codes the time at which an action occurs in relation to a reference time, usually the time at which the speaker refers to the event. On the other hand, the verb aspect codes temporal features that pertain to the action without reference to any other time or event. For instance, if an action is spread out over time (i.e., is continuous), then progressive aspect would be appropriate (-*ing* in English). Or, if an event is completed with an extrinsic goal achieved, then the completive aspect would be used (-*ed* or irregular past in English).

The first study to raise the issue of tense versus aspect was done with French-speaking children (Bronckart & Sinclair, 1973). Bronckart and Sinclair elicited descriptions of past actions from children ranging in age from 2:11 to 8:4. The children were more likely to use past verbs to describe actions with obvious goals or ending points than they were to use past forms to describe continuous past actions with no clear goals or ending points. Children under 6 years tended to use the present tense to describe a continuous past action. Children who were 7 or 8 years old used past verbs for both kinds of actions. Bronckart and Sinclair claimed that the early use of past verbs by the children in their study did not signal ordered time relations, that is, that the action being mentioned occurred at a time prior to the moment at which they were speaking about the action. Instead, the argument went, the children were encoding a more salient aspectual feature of the action—its completedness. Bronckart and Sinclair further argued that the abstract relational system underlying verb tenses is too complex for young children who are in Piaget's preoperational stage to have mastered.

Support for Bronckart and Sinclair's position that young children are coding aspect and not ordered time relations can be found in studies by Bloom, Lifter, and Hafitz (1980) and Antinucci and Miller (1976). These researchers studied the spontaneous language of children from 1:6 to 2:6 years and found that the children used past verbs only with certain types of past events. Events that were goal-oriented and had completive aspect were most likely to be coded with past verbs.

However, Kuczaj (1977) and Di Paolo and Smith (1978) presented an alternative view. They found English-speaking children were able to use past verbs to refer to a variety of past events, not just to goal-oriented ones with completive aspect. Kuczaj's children ranged in age from 2:6 to 5:6 while Di Paolo & Smith's ranged from 4:7 to 6:6.

It may be that the age differences can account for the different findings of Bloom et al. and Antinucci and Miller on the one hand and Kuczaj and Di Paolo and Smith on the other. Sachs (1979) found that although the very earliest instances of past reference were to events with clear end results (age range: 1:8 to 2:1), from 2:2 to 2:7 years references to continuous, non-goal-oriented past events occurred. Sachs' findings suggest that English-speaking children are able to use past verbs to code ordered time relations well before 3 years of age.

Children's ability to encode both ordered time relations and aspectual features of actions from 3 years of age on emerged as a clear finding in a recent study of elicited language production (Harner, 1981). The children were more likely to use the simple past tense with goal-oriented actions (completive aspect) and more likely to use progressive verbs with non-goal-oriented actions (continuous aspect). However, even the progressive verbs were more likely to have a past auxiliary (*was*) than a present auxiliary (*is*).

The issue of aspect versus tense can be thought of as a reformulation of a question raised earlier in the chapter. That is, do children learn first of an extended present that includes the immediate past and future, or do they learn of past and future as separate from the present? Data from the youngest children studied suggest that nonpresent verb forms are first used to refer to *aspects* of an extended present. Data gathered from children over 2 : 6 years suggest that children are able to refer to both the present consequences of past events (completive aspect) and the past as an event preceding and separate from the present (tense).

However, despite children's earliest tendencies to use past forms in their own speech to signal a "present completedness of a past action," they may understand references to past events in the speech of others. Language production and language comprehension do not always develop in a lock-step manner. Children sometimes seem to understand words and linguistic structures that they do not produce. At other times they use words inappropriately, signaling a lack in their knowledge of the meanings of the words. Miller (1978) noted that it may not be cognitive complexity that determines early topics of time talk. Children may be capable of understanding and remembering more remote past events. In a comprehension study, Harner (1976) found that children from 24 to 36 months understood past reference equally well when the events occurred either the preceding day or the preceding moment. Such studies have not been done with children from 1 : 6 to 2 years, whose earliest use of past verbs seemed to signify aspectual distinctions rather than past time.

Parental input may be the determiner of what children talk about as being past, according to Sachs (1979). If parents talked about past events for which there were no observable present consequences, their children might be more likely to use past verbs for similar purposes at an earlier age than would be the case if parents talked only about the observable present. Parents, however, tend to simplify their utterances to be sure that they communicate with their children.

In sum, the available data indicate that the very earliest uses of past verb forms (under 2 years of age) refer to the completed aspect of events, a kind of past-in-the-present. We do not know whether these youngest children, before they refer to such events, understand references to past events with no present consequences. However, there is evidence that by 2 years of age children both understand and produce past verbs in reference to more remote past events. Miller (1978) has argued that children talk first about events that are of immediate personal significance to them. It may also be the case that children realize that parents are more likely to respond to a comment about something present and observable (Sachs, 1979).

PAST AND FUTURE: ARE THEY MUTUALLY EXCLUSIVE CATEGORIES FROM THE START?

Is it possible that children confuse the notions of past and future? For instance, if children learn first about a notion of the nonpresent, they might confuse what has happened with what they want to happen again. Or, alternatively, the two temporal domains of past and future may be clearly separated from each other in the understanding of young children.

There is reason to think that children's first understandings of past and future are of distinct categories separate from each other, although they each may be perceived as emanating from the experience of an extended present. Research on early language (Bloom, 1970) has shown that in their earliest two-word utterances, children are using different words to comment on the absence of a recalled object or event than they use to request the recurrence of the same absent object or event. ''Milk allgone'' is a statement of the current nonexistence of a quantity that was formerly present. Underlying the comment is a comparison of a memory of a filled glass and the observable empty one. ''More milk'' is a request to have the glass filled up. Thus it seems that from a very early age children use language that both differentiates between past and future and communicates their personal desires and reactions. Expression of their desires for the recurrence of some past event results in the use of a linguistic form that differs from the expression of a present nonexistence. It may be that subjectively experienced needs, feelings, and memories are at the root of early linguistic and conceptual differentiations of nonpresent time as past and future.

Another source of information about whether past and future develop as mutually exclusive categories is an analysis of the types of errors children make in using words that have past or future reference. There has been little discussion of children's confusion of past and future reference in the literature on spontaneous language production—perhaps because such confusion is infrequent. Ames (1946) reports a number of misuses of past tense, but no supporting, contextual, nonlinguistic evidence is presented to indicate that past and future verbs are confused with each other. She reports that children make mistakes with the adverbs *yesterday* and *tomorrow*. Furthermore, children combine past and future verbs with adverbs that have inappropriate and often contradictory temporal reference, according to Ames (e.g., ''*I had a bath tomorrow*''). But that type of error indicates a difficulty in (*a*) understanding the meaning of the temporal adverbs and (*b*) coordinating two temporally marked linguistic forms (verbs and adverbs) rather than either a conceptual confusion of past and future or a confusion of past and future verbs with each other. (See the preceding section, ''Order of Emergence and Early Meaning of Temporally Marked Verbs and Adverbs.'')

Comprehension studies have been designed that consider whether past and future reference are confused by young children. In a study of the terms *yesterday* and *tomorrow,* with 2-, 3-, and 4-year-old children, it was found that *yesterday* was not misunderstood as meaning *tomorrow* any more often than it was misunderstood as meaning *today* (Harner, 1975). However, the findings of the same study indicated that when the 3-year-olds made a mistake in understanding *tomorrow,* they were more likely to think that *tomorrow* meant *yesterday* than *today*. This pattern of misunderstanding was limited to the 3-year-olds;

errors for the 2- and 4-year-olds were randomly distributed for the terms. The data suggest that there may be a stage for some children when the term *tomorrow* is understood as having primarily a nonpresent time reference, either the day preceding or the day following the present day.

In two other comprehension studies (Harner, 1980; Herriot, 1969), children understand the distinction between the past and the future early, but they did not understand the present-past distinction and the present-future distinction until later. Herriot used three movable toys: One that had completed an action (past referent); another that had not yet begun the action (future referent); and a third that was actually performing the action (present referent). In his descriptions of the toys, he used either past, future, or present progressive verbs. When the past and future referents were paired together, the children (from 3 to 6 years) were better able to select the correct referent than when either past or future referent was paired with the present referent (the moving toy).

In Harner (1980) three sequential pictures were used as referential choices. Children from 3 to 7 years were asked questions about the pictures using the linguistic forms *before, after,* past verbs, and future verbs. The children indicated no systematic confusion of past with future; however, they were much less clear about the present-past and the present-future distinctions. In sum, then, it appears that distinguishing past and future as mutually exclusive domains is accomplished relatively easily by most children, particularly when the linguistic reference is made with past or future verbs, or when the adverbials *before* or *after* are used to order an event in relation to a present reference point.

THE ASYMMETRY OF PAST AND FUTURE CATEGORIES

As previously mentioned, the linguistic forms for past and future verbs are very dissimilar in English. The future time of an action is conveyed through a set of modal auxiliaries such as *may, shall, will, must,* and *can* instead of verb inflections. Lyons (1968) explains that the auxiliary verbs signaling future reference convey more than just the notion of temporal order (i.e., a time after the present moment). In addition to order, the auxiliaries express the linguistic mood of the speaker. Mood refers to the degree of certainty the speaker has that what is being stated will actually occur in the future.

Research has indicated that children are able to understand reference to immediate past and immediate future events equally well (Fraser, Bellugi & Brown, 1963; Harner, 1976; Herriot, 1969; Lovell & Dixon, 1967). However, when the reference is to an event one day removed from the present, utterances with past verbs are significantly better understood than utterances with future verbs (Harner, 1976, 1981b). These findings do not imply that children have trouble thinking about a more remote future event because the same children in both studies understood references to the following day quite well when it was referred to as "the day after this day." It seems then that the traditional future verb form, "*will* + a main verb" has a meaning component that implies immediacy for young children.

The interconnectedness of immediacy and certainty in future reference seems reasonable since the sooner a future event is to occur, the fewer the possible interventions that will prevent it from occurring, and, consequently, the greater the certainty that it will occur (all other factors being equal). Thus it seems that our linguistic form for future verbs and our personal uncertainty about distant events combine to make children less able to handle future verbs when they refer to events that are not a part of the immediate future. To date, comprehension studies dealing with future reference have looked only at future verbs with the auxiliary *will*. It may be that children will do better on comprehension tasks in which the modal auxiliary referring to a remote future event is one that implies less certainty than does *will*. More work needs to be done exploring the circumstances under which other modal auxiliaries are best understood.

Although the research on children's comprehension of future reference has almost exclusively used the modal auxiliary *will*, that is not the linguistic form most commonly used by children to refer to the future. When children from 3 to 7 years are describing an action that is just about to occur, they use the auxiliary—*'s gonna/is going to* from 80% to 90% of the time (Harner, 1981). Unfortunately there is no comparable data available on the preferred auxiliary in reference to more remote events. Often the earliest inflected verb form to appear in children's speech is the progressive *-ing* (Cazden, 1968). As it is first used, it implies that a present action is spread out over time and not yet completed. Perhaps it is just this meaning of temporal extension that makes it the preferred auxiliary of children when they refer to an immediate future event. The progressive may imply a continuation of the speaker's intention or anticipation into the future and up to the onset of the action.

Kuczaj and Daly (1979) have examined children's reference to hypothetical future and past events and also found an asymmetrical pattern. Children were more likely to use hypothetical constructions in relation to future events than in relation to past events. Examples of auxiliaries used in hypothetical reference are *might, would, could*. Kuczaj and Daly discuss their findings in terms of the likelihood or probability of the hypothetical events occurring. Children are more likely to use hypothetical forms in reference to events that are likely to occur than in reference to an event whose occurrence is highly unlikely or even impossible. Since past events have already occurred, the likelihood of a hypothesized past event occurring is zero. Hypothesized past reference is counterfactual, and children can have no certainty about its occurrence. Consequently, they may refer to hypothetical past events much less frequently.

A useful line of further inquiry would be to consider what conditions elicit regular and hypothetical modal auxiliaries in the domain of future reference. For instance, would children understand reference to remote future events better if hypotheticals were used as auxiliaries?

Still another difference in the early use of past and future verbs is in the emphasis placed on aspectual features of an event. Recent research has indicated that as early as 2 years of age children begin to code past actions in terms of their completive aspect (goal-oriented actions with new present consequences) or their progressive aspect (non-goal-oriented actions that are continuous and have no new consequences) (Antinucci & Miller, 1976; Bloom, Lifter & Hafitz, 1980; Sachs, 1980). Event aspect remains a significant feature to be coded by older children as well (Bronckart and Sinclair, 1973; Di Paolo & Smith, 1976; Harner, 1981). But despite the importance of aspect in children's references to past events, aspect has been almost completely absent in their descriptions of immediately impending future actions (Harner, 1981a).

Perhaps the reason that event aspect is so significant in past verbs (but not in future verbs) is due to the asymmetry of our experience of past and future time. What helps us to know that an event is past is the ending point of the event (completive aspect). But in understanding and conceptualizing the future, we are less concerned with endings than with beginnings. Will this event actually occur? Will it *begin* to happen? Thus, in the future condition, temporal order is interwoven with a degree of certainty that the event will occur. It is mood and not aspect that is of primary concern in the future conditions.

The issue of degree of certainty or uncertainty about the future can partially explain the finding that 3-year-olds understood the term *yesterday* significantly better than the term *tomorrow* (Harner, 1975). (The pattern for the 2-year-olds in the same study showed similar differences, although they were not significant. The 4-year-olds did not appear to differ in their comprehension of the two terms.) The line of reasoning about the influence of degree of certainty on the findings is as follows: Because the children had experienced the past event on the preceding day (*yesterday*), they had no uncertainty about its having occurred, except in those instances when they may have forgotten the events of the preceding day. However, in the situations where an event was referred to as one that would occur *tomorrow,* the children may have been uncertain just how likely it was for the event to actually occur. *Yesterday* refers to past events that can be recalled and therefore one can be more certain of them than of future events that are named as occurring *tomorrow.* It seems, then, that the asymmetry of past and future domains may influence the acquisition of linguistic terms even when those terms do not reflect the asymmetry in their surface form as the verbs do (inflections for past verbs versus modal auxiliaries for future verbs).

TEMPORAL DECENTERING

Past and future are most simply conceptualized as existing in relation to a present reference time—either having preceded the present or following the present. Thus, when we encode an event as past or future, we are temporally ordering the event in relation to the present time at which we are speaking. However, Miller (1978) and Smith (1980) have talked about adult time language as coordinating three times: event time, speech time, and reference time. Usually we order the time of the event in relation to the time at which we mention it, as for example, "I played tennis with Lynda." But sometimes we order the past event in relation to another past event, as in, "Lynda and I had finished our tennis match before the rain began." Both Miller and Smith agree that young children are not likely to be able to coordinate event time, speech time, and a reference time that differs from speech time.

The ability to shift one's reference time from the moment one is speaking to another point in time has been called temporal decentering. Cromer (1971) described children's reactions to a set of questions about picture–story sequences in terms of their ability to decenter temporally. The children in his study ranged from 4 to 7 years. As the sequence of five pictures was placed in front of the children, a corresponding narrative was told to them. At the time of questioning, the actions were all past from the children's point of view. The children were then asked to show the correct picture for each in a series of sentences. The verbs in the sentences were all marked for either past or future time. The children did much better with the past verb forms than with the future verbs. Cromer explained his finding in terms of temporal decentering. He reasoned that to choose the correct referent for the sentences with future verbs the children had to coordinate their own points of view and present reference points with another reference point and a different point of view.

In another study in which children were shown a sequence of three pictures and presented with sentences with past and future verbs, as well as sentences with the adverbs *before* and *after,* the future verbs were poorly understood (Harner, 1980). Linguistic factors were thought to have a strong influence on the results since references to the same pictures were well understood when *before* was used, but poorly understood when future verbs were used. However, in addition to linguistic influences, temporal decentering requirements were offered as an explanation for the poorer comprehension of future reference. It was argued that to decode the linguistic description that used a future verb, the children may have had to mentally return to the origin of a sequence of actions that had already occurred. The decentering requirement would have meant that they had to reverse the action sequence in their minds; otherwise, they would have had difficulty in coordinating their own points of view—that the actions had occurred in the past—with the linguistic description of the actions as about to occur in the future. The children ranged in age from 3 : 0 to 7 : 11 years, and though the older children did much better on the task, they were still having difficulty. At age 7, the children were selecting the correct referent for future verbs 69% of the time and the correct referent for past verbs 84% of the time.

Temporal decentering has been proposed as a cognitive prerequisite to certain linguistic descriptions of action sequences—descriptions in which the order of mention of the events is the reverse of their actual order of occurrence (Ferreiro & Sinclair, 1971). In a study done with 4- and 5-year-olds, it was found that children who could describe a sequence of two actions by beginning with the second action (e.g., *"The dog jumped up after the cat climbed the ladder"*) also demonstrated reversibility in a conservation test. It was argued that children who lack reversibility see two successive actions as existing completely independently of each other rather than as constituting potential reference points for each other. Children who have reversibility were said to be able to see events from more than their own subjective view, and therefore when asked to describe two events by beginning with the second event, they were able to deduce the ordered relationship and code it linguistically. The linguistic complexities of subordination were not considered in the study.

Temporal decentering, of course, is not required in most of our commonplace daily discussions about future plans and events. Thus the findings of the studies should not be interpreted to mean that children have difficulty understanding reference to the future in their daily lives. However, the studies do confirm the notion that there are some situations in which the cognitive demands placed on the listener result in the temporal reference being more difficult to grasp.

INTEGRATING THE LEXICON AND SYNTAX OF PAST VERBS

English "time language" is far from simple; it presents a major challenge for young children. Not only are there significant asymmetries in the way we code past and future time, but in addition, the system of past verbs is further complicated by subdivision into two categories, regular and irregular. The rules for forming the past are different for each category, so the young child is confronted with two apparently contradictory sets of rules. The first rule is that to form the past, add *-ed*. The second rule is more difficult: it is that to form the past, don't add *-ed,* but instead either change the actual form of the lexical item radically (*go/went*), or less radically (*teach/taught*), or still less radically (*make/made*), or not at all (*hurt/hurt*). How children coordinate and gradually master the past forms of irregular and regular verbs has been studied by Kuczaj (1977).

Kuczaj found a developmental trend in children's overgeneralization errors with past verbs. Overgeneralization errors result when children apply the rule for forming the past of regular verbs (add *-ed*) to irregular verbs (e.g., *goed, wented*). Kuczaj used two approaches : one was to analyze the errors in spontaneous speech samples; the other was to elicit children's judgments about the "correctness" or "incorrectness" of different overgeneralization errors. The 15 children whose speech was analyzed ranged in age from 2.6 to 5.6. The younger children were much more likely to err by adding *-ed* to the verb base (e.g., *eat +*

ed = *eated*) than to the past tense form (e.g., *ate* + *ed* = *ated*). Interestingly, the older children seemed to make more, or at least as many, of the second type of error (*ated*) than the first type (*eated*). The experimental studies in which children judged past verb forms as grammatical or ungrammatical were consistent with the production findings.

Kuczaj explains how the different types of overgeneralization errors could be a function of an age-related, increasing linguistic competence. He focuses on children's early understandings of the meaning of pastness and on their difficulty in coordinating the semantics of past action with the available syntactic forms in English. He argues that children who use irregular past verb forms understand the pastness that the verbs imply. However, they may not understand the syntactic relation of the irregular past form (*ate*) to the base form of the verb (*eat*). Thus the children may see these as two different and unrelated words that have the same action meaning but different temporal meaning. Kuczaj proposes that children gradually, verb by verb, learn that the irregular past verbs are related to the base form (*ate* to *eat*) and that therefore the *-ed* ending is redundant and should not be used.

It has long been recognized by researchers that children's errors often occur because of overgeneralization by the children. Certainly errors that are just occasional random mistakes and not a part of any larger pattern do occur. However, it is through the examination of consistent error patterns that we hope to learn more about the underlying thought patterns. When these error patterns change with age, there is the further hope that they will reveal a development in the underlying conceptual organization. In this instance they revealed a change in the linguistic organization of the syntax and lexicon of time language. Kuczaj's research indicates that mastery of the linguistic system that encodes temporal realtions may in some ways be a more difficult task than mastery of the basic underlying conceptual distinctions. Further support for the notion that some of the language we use to talk about time may be more complex than the basic temporal concepts is found in Harner (1980), a study in which the ability to understand past or future references depended in large part on the particular linguistic form used to express the temporal reference.

UNDERSTANDING THE DUALITY OF THE PRESENT

Children need to learn about the dual nature of the present. The present is both a reference point that sets the boundaries of past and future time, and a category of experience in itself with expandable and contractable boundaries. Although researchers have talked about early notions of the past and future as emanating from a kind of extended present, little attention has been paid to the extent of the present as a domain of experience. What, for instance, are the outer limits of the present, and where do the past and future begin? Psycholinguistic research has largely assumed the present is limited to the actual moment of speaking. This is a reasonable assumption since the linguistic system either orders events in relation to the speech event through past, present, or future verb forms, or it provides adverbials to signal an extended present (*today, this morning,* etc.). However, from a more subjective perspective, the extent of the present is highly variable. Furthermore, for young children the boundaries of the past and the present and the boundaries of the present and the future are not always so clear.

Error data have been used to argue that children are less clear about the past–present boundaries and about the future–present boundaries than they are about the mutual exclusivity of past and future events (Harner, 1980; see the preceding section, "Past and Future"). In this comprehension study children chose the correct referent from one of a sequence of three pictures arranged so as to tell a story. The children were presented with a series of statements with past or future verbs. When the sentence called for a future referent, the children rarely made the mistake of choosing a picture with a past meaning. It was just as unusual for the children to mistakenly choose a picture with future reference when the sentence expressed a past time. By age 7 no children were making this type of error, and it was concluded that children rarely confused past and future with each other.

However, in the same study there was a pattern of errors for both past and future verbs that was significant. When the children made errors, they chose the picture that was the "present" referent. This was interpreted to mean that they had difficulty in establishing the boundaries of the present. The extent of the present was not clear, and the picture that the researcher thought of as serving as a present reference point became instead an expanded present capable of including immediate future and immediate past. This interpretation of the finding is in agreement with Werner's (unpublished paper, n.d.) observation of an extended present and with Miller's (1978) notion of the past-in-the-present.

The finding can also be understood as a developmental progression in the gradual mastery of the dual nature of the present. Errors in which children choose the present referent for a statement with past or future reference reflect their struggle with a paradox in our Western conceptualization of time. The present is both a reference point in our objective understanding of ordered temporal relations, and it is a category of experience in our personal knowledge of the world and the sequence of events in it. From our subjective points of view, we can expand or contract our experience of the present so that it includes as much of our immediate past or future as feels right. Children gradually learn about the duality of the present—as both a reference point and a category of experience. This learning is a part of their gradual objectification of time.

AFTER THE OBJECTIVE SYSTEM HAS BEEN MASTERED

Integration of Subjective Time and Objective Past, Present, Future Relations

Our personal experiences with time are very much rooted in the here and now. Whether we experience time as moving slowly or quickly depends on how interested we are in what is occurring. Our deep involvement in an ongoing activity can result in an objectively very long, extended present that seems very short to us. Similarly, our boredom with a present activity can make the time, however brief, seem unendurably long. And, as the child development literature has indicated, even our first notions of the past and the future seem to be rooted in an extended present.

Once we have developed an internal model of the past, present, future relations as we understand them to exist in the outside world, we still do not give up our more subjective experience. Instead, we have to reconcile the duality of an objective system that can be consensually validated and a subjective experience that is unique for each of us.

The objective system that we share with others gives us a feeling of order, reason, and well-being in the world. But it can also predominate over our personal sense of time. Many parts of our modern world are regulated by time. Our productive work lives often seem to be governed more by time than by a commitment to high quality output. Time determines salary as well as beginnings and endings. Rather than being just an objective system used to organize and improve interpersonal communication and social functioning, time is often treated as a commodity in our technological and commercially oriented world.

The ways in which people preserve their subjective experience of time in the world while maintaining a grasp of the objective system are varied. Some people are more oriented toward one domain of experience than another. However, even those whose temporal focus is primarily the future may bring very different attitudes to it. For instance, some may look to the future with gloom, seeing it as a loss of youth and trying to deny the aging process. Others may see it as a time to prepare for by saving and planning. Others may have a feeling of weakness, or of a lack of power and control over what will occur. As wide a range of attitudes can apply to past or present orientations also. Thus, clearly, many factors influence the quality of our subjective temporal experience, attitudes, and orientations. Some of these factors are cultural, social, economic, age-oriented, sexual, and personality-centered.

Temporal Perspectives from Adolescence to Adulthood

By the end of the middle years of childhood (6–7 to 10–11) children have mastered the basic objective system of time relations and the varied linguistic structures we use in referring to temporal distinctions. The question of interest is no longer "how are they mastering the language and the underlying ideas," but rather, "what is their conscious perception of their own past and future, and what factors influence such perceptions." Adolescents are capable of self-reflection, of comparing self and other, and of self-evaluation. These developing abilities bring with them a change in significant issues and concerns as well as a change in the methods used to study past and future time orientation.

The methods used in gathering data from young children have been of two main types: first, children's spontaneous and elicited language has been analyzed to assess the mastery of temporally marked linguistic forms in varying contexts; second, children have been asked questions about actions, and their answers have been recorded and taken as indicators of their linguistic and cognitive understanding of temporal reference. Children's time language and their time concepts have been compared with adult norms, and the children's errors have been analyzed to gain insight into the nature of the acquisition process.

Adolescent and adult use of time language has not been examined in normal populations since it has been assumed that the adults can use the full range of the linguistic system to express temporal distinctions. The methods used with adults and adolescents commonly involve an interview in which the person is asked questions about his or her personal temporal orientation or about the most probable outcome of a contrived situation. Measures that have been used include rating scales and analyses of projective techniques including circular and linear representations of time. It is not easy to find established norms for the subjective perceptions of adolescent and adult populations, although some research efforts have been devoted to just that issue (Bortner & Hultsch, 1972; Bühler, 1968). Others have focused on the effects of variables such as sex and ethnicity on future perspectives (Moerk, 1974).

During adolescence the consciousness of time increases and, consequently, there is much more planning for the future than there was during the earlier years of childhood. Furthermore, as adolescents become older, their future plans become more realistic. Moerk and Becker (1971) interviewed adolescents from 14 to 17 years. As their ages increased, the subjects increased the optimal age of marriage for males; they increased the optimal time span for having children; and the male adolescents decreased the optimal number of children in a family. Furthermore, the acceptability of birth control procedures increased dramatically as the age of the adolescents increased.

In another study. Moerk (1974) explored the effects of sex and of membership in ethnic minority groups on the goals of boys and girls from 12 to 15 years. The subjects were asked questions about their educational, occupational, and economic aspirations. The results indicated that memberships in different ethnic groups affected aspirations as did the sex of the subject. In a longitudinal follow-up, it was found that the changes over time varied for the different groups depending on ethnicity and sex.

The effects of age, sex, and social class on adolescents' perceptions of time has been explored by Cottle, Howard and Pleck (1969). Using a variety of procedures, they interviewed upper- and middle-class adolescents from 12 to 18 years. They found that as the ages of the children increased, there was a corresponding shift in temporal orientation from recall to expectation. Furthermore, the older adolescents had more of a sense of the relatedness of past, present, and future. Middle-class children were more interested in distant future whereas upper-class children were more interested in zones closer to the present as well as in historical zones. This finding was corroborated in a related study (Cottle & Pleck, 1969) in which it was found that the linear marking off of a personal life line varied as a function of age, sex, and social class. Cottle and Pleck hypothesized that achievement strivings or instrumental activism resulted in middle-class boys having a much greater future orientation than middle-class girls or upper-class children of either sex.

Recent years have seen an increased concern with development throughout the human lifespan, a concern reflected even in the popular literature (Sheehy, 1974). One approach to examining the understanding of past, present, and future relations over the lifespan is to determine the orientations of people to their own lives at different ages. Bühler (1933, 1969) has examined people's attitudes towards their own life goals such as careers, interpersonal relationships, activities, and self-concept. She defined five broad phases that revolve around the issues of intentionality, self-determined goals, and self-assessment of achievement and satisfaction. Her data base consisted of 202 biographies that were analyzed.

The first period is characterized by a lack of self-determination of life goals and is clearly the childhood years up to early or mid-adolescence. In the second period there develops a preliminary set of life goals that are not yet firm commitments; the age range is mid-adolescence (about 15 years of age) to the mid-twenties. The third period sees a more definite decision about life goals and also more significant efforts to implement these goals; the age range is from 25 to 45 or 50. In the fourth period there is a reassessment of the time that has passed and of the relative satisfaction and achievement of goals (from 45 or 50 to 60 or 67 years). The fifth period is described as consisting of rest and retirement.

In another effort to examine personal time perspectives in the adult years, Bortner and Hultsch (1972) compared present life satisfaction with recalled life satisfaction (5 years prior) and anticipated future satisfaction (5 years hence). They found that present life satisfaction was relatively constant among people from 20 to over 70 years when a rating scale from 1 to 10 was used. However, the evaluations of the past and the future changed with increasing age. Up until 60 years of age the present was evaluated more positively than the past, and the future was evaluated more positively than the present. However, after age 60 the pattern began to reverse itself. For the oldest people in the study, the past was evaluated most favorably; next was the present, and last, the future. Thus the source of positive self-evaluation for the oldest group seemed to rest in their assessment of the past rather than in their hopes for the future. The youngest people in the study felt that they had made considerable progress in achieving life goals and satisfactions, and that they would continue to do so. They evaluated the future higher than the present and the present higher than the past.

We may unconsciously alter our views of the past and the future to maintain a sense of internal consistency and continuity, according to Fischhoff (1975, 1980). For instance, when we acquire a new piece of information about the outcome of some past event, we unconsciously reorganize our earlier perceptions of the event to correspond to the later data. Fischhoff presented people with a past situation with which they were not familiar and told them one of several different outcomes. Regardless of which outcome they were told, the subjects insisted that it was obvious from the previous information that this particular outcome was inevitable.

Fischhoff (1976) also considered whether the greater uncertainty generally associated with the future would result in adults being more certain about the outcome of past actions than future actions. The issue of certainty of occurrence can be seen as a parallel to some of the research in developmental psycholinguistics. Studies with young children have indicated that immediacy of occurrence and degree of certainty that an event will actually take place have an important influence on children's understandings of future reference, especially when future verbs are used (Harner, 1976, 1981). Fischhoff's findings were that adult judges had no greater certainty about the outcome of past than future events.

However, Fischhoff raised a question about the language forms he used in his verbal presentation to the subjects. For both past and future conditions, a short story was told in the past tense. Then a stimulus question was phrased using either past or future verb form, for example, *"What are the chances that X happened?"* or *"What are the chances that X will happen?"* When he tried to tell the story using future verb forms and then asked about the likelihood of a particular outcome, the subjects were reluctant to participate, "expressing discomfort" with the linguistic description. Thus the issue of the degree of certainty expressed by the modal auxiliary in the future verb form may still be causing some problems, even for adult speakers.

The development of our temporal perspective shows the influence of many factors such as age, ethnicity, sex, and language structure. There are inevitably, with such a broad topic, many questions that remain unanswered, and many more that remain unasked. It is clear, however, that children, adolescents, and adults face an impressive task as they strive to coordinate their own personal time perspectives with their culture's objectified system of past, present, and future time.

SUMMARY AND CONCLUSIONS

The ability to communicate accurately about nonpresent events, either past or future, develops gradually in children. The major factors that underly the temporal schemas of adults include both conceptual and linguistic distinctions as well as an integration of subjective experience with the linear, objective temporal system of Western culture. An examination of how children master these components of an adult understanding of past–present–future relations has revealed some of the problems as well as some of the patterns in the acquisition process. This summary is intended to highlight some of the major findings and issues affecting the development and elaboration of an objective temporal reference system.

In children's early acquisition of past–present–future relations, a continual interplay of subjective and objective time can be observed. For instance, the earliest use of past verb forms has been found to refer to past events that have some present consequences (Antinucci & Miller, 1976; Bloom, Lifter & Hafitz, 1980). Miller (1978) has called early past reference an expression of "the past-in-the-present," and Berman (1978) has noted that an early use of verbs is rooted in the child's expression of personal needs and feelings.

However, once the conceptual and linguistic systems have been mastered, subjective experience does not fade into the background. Instead, research has found that such factors as social class, age, sex, and ethnicity influence the individual's temporal perspective (Cottle, Howard & Pleck, 1969; Moerk, 1974). Thus, although by adolescence we all possess the same objective system, our individual experiences lead us to different subjective orientations to time and the world.

The conceptual distinctions of significance in children's acquisition of past–present–future relations center around the issue of boundaries. It was easiest for children to grasp that past and future are mutually exclusive categories, and they rarely confused the temporal meaning of past and future verbs (Harner, 1980). However, the same children were less clear about the boundaries of the present–past and the present–future. This difficulty may be understood in terms of the need to coordinate the dual nature of the present as (*a*) a reference point for past and future and (*b*) a category of experience with expandable and contractable boundaries. For very young children the present may be quite broad and inclusive of immediate past and future insofar as these are centered in the child's feelings and desires. As children grow older, they become more familiar with the notion of the present as a reference point in an objective system. Cottle and Pleck (1969) noted that older adolescents see the present as more limited than do younger adolescents.

Language is the medium through which ideas of past and future are communicated, and mastery of the "time language" we have in English is a challenging task. Indeed, the complexity of the verb system results in children's mastering the correct linguistic form for past reference considerably later than they demonstrate an understanding that an event belongs to the conceptual domain of pastness (Kuczaj, 1977). There even appear to be different acquisition patterns for temporally marked verbs (where time is rooted in action) and temporally marked adverbs (where the temporal relation is independent of action) (Harner, 1975; see the section "Order of Emergence and Early Meaning of Temporally Marked Verbs and Adverbs.")

The linguistic system seems to have a major influence on the temporal features of the environment that are expressed. For instance, in one study the aspect of an event (i.e., whether the event was completed with a clear final goal, or whether the action was continuous with no goal achieved) was encoded by children in their descriptions of past actions (Harner, 1981a). However, the same children did not encode aspect in describing identical future situations, perhaps because the linguistic forms for coding aspect are much more complex in future reference; or perhaps because of an asymmetry in their practical experience with the past and future; or perhaps because of the asymmetry in linguistic forms for coding past time and future time.

The final issue to be raised is the asymmetry of past and future in both the domain of practical, personal experience and the domain of linguistic structure. Some of the differences in children's understanding of past and future reference may stem from the relative certainty with which we experience and recall past events and the uncertainty and anticipation we direct towards the future. The verb system parallels this distinction in certain ways. Present and past time are encoded with the inflections s and -ed, respectively (for regular verbs). However, there is no inflection for the future; instead we have a system of modal auxiliaries that express the degree of certainty that a future event will actually occur.

As children slowly master the linguistic and conceptual distinctions and coordinate them with their practical experience of past and future times, they also broaden their understanding of the extent of the past and of the sequencing of events, and they become better able to quantify time and to imagine a novel and distant future. Understanding and communicating clearly about basic past, present, and future relations is an important achievement in itself as well as a foundation for the eventual development of a larger body of temporal knowledge.

ACKNOWLEDGMENT

The author wishes to thank the editor, William J. Friedman, for the suggestions he made about an earlier version of the chapter. The author is also grateful to Charles G. Gross for his comments on the earlier version.

REFERENCES

Ames, L. B. The development of the sense of time in the young child. *Journal of Genetic Psychology*, 1946, *68*, 97–125.

Antinucci, F., & Miller, R. How children talk about what happened. *Journal of Child Language*, 1976, *3*, 167–189.

Berman, R. A. Early verbs: Comments on how and why a child uses his first words. *International Journal of Psycholinguistics*, 1978, *5*, 21–39.

Bloom, L. *Language development: Form and function in emerging grammars*. Cambridge: MIT Press, 1970.

Bloom, L., Lifter, K., & Hafitz, J. Semantics of verbs and the development of verb inflection in child language. *Language*, 1980, *56*, 386–412.

Bortner, R. W., & Hultsch, D. F. Personal time perspective in adulthood. *Developmental Psychology*, 1972, *7*, 98–103.

Bronckart, J. P., & Sinclair, H. Time, tense, aspect. *Cognition*, 1973, *2*, 107–130.

Brown, R., & Fraser, C. Acquisition of syntax. In U. Bellugi & R. Brown (Eds.), *The acquisition of language. Monograph of the Society for Research in Child Development*, 1964, *29*, (1, Serial No. 92).

Bühler, C. *Der menschliche lebenslauf als psychologisches problem*. Leipzig: S. Hirzel, 1933.

Bühler, C. The course of human life as a psychological problem. *Human Development*, 1968, *11*, 184–200.

Bull, W. E. *Time, tense, and the verb*. Berkeley: University of California Press, 1971.

Cazden, C. The acquisition of noun and verb inflections. *Child Development*, 1968, *39*, 433–448.

Clark, E. On the acquisition of the meaning of *before* and *after*. *Journal of Verbal Learning and Verbal Behavior*, 1971, *10*, 266–275.

Comrie, B. *Aspect*. New York: Cambridge University Press, 1976.

Cottle, T., Howard, P., & Pleck, J. Adolescent perception of time: The effect of age, sex, and social class. *Journal of Personality*, 1969, *37*, 636–650.

Cottle, T., & Pleck, J. Linear estimations of temporal extension. *Journal of Projective Techniques and Personality Assessment*, 1969, *33*, 81–93.

Cromer, R. The development of the ability to decenter in time. *British Journal of Psychology*, 1971, *62*, 353–365.

Di Paolo, M., & Smith, C. Cognitive and linguistic factors in language acquisition: The use of temporal and aspectual expressions. In P. French (Ed.), *The Development of Meaning*. The Pedolinguistic Series II, Bunka Hyanon Press, 1978.

Ferreiro, E., & Sinclair, H. Temporal relationships in language. *International Journal of Psychology*, 1971, *6*, 39–47.

Fischhoff, B. Hindsight ≠ foresight: The effect of outcome knowledge on judgment under uncertainty. *Journal of Experimental Psychology: Human Perception and Performance*, 1975, *1*, 288–299.

Fishhoff, B. For those condemned to study the past: Reflections on historical judgment. In R. A.

Shweder & D. W. Fiske (Eds.), *New directions for methodology of behavioral science: Fallible judgment in behavioral research.* San Francisco: Jossey-Bass, 1980.

Fraisse, P. *The psychology of time.* New York: Harper & Row, 1963.

Fraser, C., Bellugi, U., & Brown, R. Control of grammar in imitation, comprehension and production. *Journal of Verbal Learning and Verbal Behavior,* 1963, *2,* 121-135.

Fraser, J. T. *Voices of time.* New York: Braziller, 1969.

Fraser, J. T. *Of time, passion, and knowledge.* New York: Braziller, 1976.

Friedrich, P. On aspect theory and Homeric aspect, Memoir 28. *International Journal of American Linguistics,* 1974, *40,* 1-44.

Gale, R. (Ed.). *The philosophy of time.* New York: Doubleday, 1967.

Harner, L. *Yesterday* and *tomorrow:* Development of early understanding of the terms. *Developmental Psychology,* 1975, *11,* 864-65.

Harner, L. Young children's understanding of past and future reference. *Journal of Psycholinguistic Research,* 1976, *5,* 65-84.

Harner, L. Comprehension of past and future reference revisited. *Journal of Experimental Child Psychology,* 1980, *29,* 170-182.

Harner, L. Children talk about the time and aspect of actions. *Child Development,* 1981, *52,* 498-506. (a)

Harner, L. Immediacy and certainty: Factors in understanding future reference. *Journal of Child Language,* 1981. (b)

Herriot, P. The comprehension of tense by young children. *Child Development,* 1969, *40,* 103-110.

Jesperson, O. *Growth and structure of the English language.* Garden City, N.Y.: Doubleday, 1938.

Kuczaj, S. The acquisition of regular and irregular past tense forms. *Journal of Verbal Learning and Verbal Behavior,* 1977, *16,* 589-600.

Kuczaj, S., & Daly, M. The development of hypothetical reference in the speech of young children. *Journal of Child Language,* 1979, *6,* 563-579.

Lovell, K., & Dixon, E. M. The growth of the control of grammar in imitation, comprehension and production. *Journal of Child Psychology, Psychiatry and Allied Disciplines,* 1967, *8,* 31-39.

Lyons, J. *Introduction to theoretical linguistics.* London: Cambrdige University Press, 1969.

Miller, G. A. Pastness. In G. A. Miller & E. Lennenberg (Eds.), *Psychology and Biology of Language and Thought.* New York: Academic Press, 1978, pp. 167-185.

Moerk, E. Age and epogenic influences on aspirations of minority and majority group children. *Journal of Counseling Psychology,* 1974, *21,* 294-298.

Moerk, E., & Becker, P. Attitudes of high school students toward future marriage and college education. *The Family Coordinator,* 1971, *20,* 67-73.

Palmer, F. R. *The English Verb.* London: Longman, 1974.

Piaget, J. *The construction of reality in the child.* New York: Basic Books, 1954.

Sachs, J. Topic selection in parent-child discourse. *Discourse Processes,* 1979, *2,* 145-153.

Sheehy, G. *Passages.* New York: Dutton, 1974.

Smith, C. The syntax and interpretation of temporal expressions in English. *Linguistics and Philosophy,* 1978, *2,* 43-100.

Smith, C. The acquisition of time talk: Relations between child and adult grammars. *Journal of Child Language,* 1980, *7,* 263-278.

Stern, C., & Stern, W. *Die kindersprache.* Leipzig: Barth, 1907.

Thompson, J. *The rise and fall of Maya civilization.* Norman, Oklahoma: University of Oklahoma Press, 1964.

Werner, H. On early development of expression of time. Unpublished manuscript, Clark University.

Whitrow, G. J. *The natural philosophy of time.* New York: Harper & Row, 1961.

Whorf, B. *Language, thought and reality.* Cambridge: MIT Press, 1962.

Conventional Time Concepts and Children's Structuring of Time

INTRODUCTION

Conventional time systems are among the intellectual tools a culture provides its members, which, like language and technology, allow adaptation to the natural environment and to its own social system. The study of the development of conventional time concepts is the study of an intellectual adaptation that has substantial ecological significance for most of the children whom developmental psychologists study. The development of children's knowledge of time-reckoning systems is also of theoretical interest to students of cognitive development because of the experientially remote referents of these systems. Children must learn to operate upon signifiers whose referents are each temporally extended and that, as a set, are not simultaneously available to perception. In this chapter we will discuss the growth of children's knowledge of conventional time systems, and the contributions that the conceptual features of the systems and representational demands make to the developmental pattern. After considering some of these structure and process issues, we will review previous research and the author's research on children's representation of temporal structure and present a model of the adult representation of conventional time.

Unfortunately, we lack a comprehensive description of the conceptual features

171

The Developmental Psychology of Time

of conventional time systems, just as we lack an adequate theory of the development of knowledge about them. Not only has most of the work on children's understandings of the clock, the calendar, and history been atheoretical, but the researchers have also proceeded as if the nature of the concepts themselves were self-evident. Structural models in other domains, like language or number, have been instrumental in guiding research in these areas, although it is also true that one product of cognitive developmental research is the elucidation of which of the structural distinctions are necessary to describe the child's knowledge. What is needed is a way to characterize the structural richness of conventional time concepts, richness that is also present in the number system and language but absent in a limited system like the alphabet order.

In attempting a preliminary description of the structure of conventional time systems, four features seem to be salient. First, while clock time, days of the week, the annual calendar, and intervals of historical time can be precisely coordinated, it is useful to consider them as a set of interrelated subsystems. At the subsystem level one can consider the significance of specific features such as duration, number of elements, or the arbitrary versus natural grounding of particular cycles or series. The subsystem level is also probably the typical level at which children are taught about conventional time, so it is for researchers to investigate the way in which children learn to coordinate hours with days of the week, days of the week with months, and so on. Second, most individual subsystems incorporate the features of order and recurrence (Friedman, 1977). An adequate developmental description would include the understanding of these structural features and also their disparate nature—the sense in which two Tuesdays or two summers are similar and different.

A third conceptual feature of conventional time systems is their linkage with number concepts. Ordinal numbers are elements in clock time and dates. The cardinal number of hours in a day, days in a week, and months in a year is also the period, and knowledge of the period is prerequisite to a quantitative understanding of recurrence. Duration is expressed in numbers, and many of the operations that apply to numbers apply to quantitative duration as well. It would therefore seem productive for the investigator of conventional time concepts to assess contemporaneous number concepts and the relationship between knowledge of the two domains. This research strategy would clarify both transfer and interference (e.g., 1 o'clock later than 12 o'clock) between number and time, as well as their possible dependence on common cognitive processes.

Finally, conventional time systems can be coordinated with logical time (see Friedman, 1978a), the hypothetical unique ordering of events posited by Newton and investigated developmentally by Piaget (1969) and several of the contributors to this volume. Conventional time provides a precise reference system for describing the order of any two events, describing or deducing a duration, or arranging for some future simultaneity such as a meeting. As in the case of number, the study of the interaction between logical time concepts and conventional time concepts is essential to a full understanding of the latter.

A second foundation for understanding the development of conventional time concepts would be to describe cognitive processes that underlie children's knowledge and problem solving in this area at different ages. Like the model of conceptual features, process models will probably have to be developed and refined through a series of progressive approximations in subsequent research, but many of the following seem to be likely components.

Rote learning of ordered verbal lists, such as the names of the days of the week and months of the year, probably results in what Gelman and Gallistel (1978) call "stably ordered lists," similar to the early representations of counting numbers or the alphabet. Overt or covert recitation of these lists seems to be among the earliest processes the child can apply to certain conventional subsystems, and, as the section, "Nature of Representations" shows, even adults use a similar process in some circumstances. Recitation is an effective way to access the names of all of the set members and the sequential forward order of elements. It may, however, be a less-efficient way of processing transitive relations, backward order, or relations involving recurrence. Recitation of verbal formulae (e.g., "Thirty days hath September . . .") also permits the solution of certain problems involving arbitrary features of the calendar, and these probably change little with development.

Additional memory representations may take the form of associative networks, coding, for example, the characteristics of a month. Associative networks may be well-suited to the storage and accessing of information about points in time, for example, the seasons or weather associated with holidays, but less-suited than verbal lists or images for representing temporal structure. Many of the associations in these networks may be present in quite young children. Still a third form of representation, image codes, may be effective in processing temporal relations not easily accessed in verbal lists, such as transitivity and relative duration of intervals. However, it may not be acquired until a later age than the other two processes. This three-process model will be presented in greater detail under the section, "Models of Symbolic Systems."

An adequate cognitive process analysis would also require considering the superordinate processing level of metacognition—children's knowledge about temporal reasoning and knowledge. One early form is young children's knowledge that adults understand conventional time while they themselves do not. Adults can be used as "temporal orientation devices" to obtain information about the time of an event of interest or the amount of time one will have to wait. Older children display temporal metacognition in their understanding that conventional time measures sometimes conflict with impressions of duration but that the former are really correct. The ability of older children to make an appointment depends upon knowledge of the information necessary to specify a meeting time.

The task of the developmental researcher in this domain, then, is to clarify the conceptual features of the system and to determine the cognitive processes that are employed. Once the features and processes are known, it may then be possible to explain the developmental pattern. These enterprises will require the usual range of research strategies: establishing age norms, experimentally varying task features, relating time of acquisition to that of other abilities, and administering interventions such as training.

Even in the absence of all but the rudiments of such a research program, it may be useful to suggest several hypotheses about the development of children's understanding of conventional time. Most of these predictions can be understood as facets of a more general hypothesis—that there are multiple levels of cognitive adaptation to temporal regularities. The chief limits are presumed to be the difficulty of forming adequate representations of temporally extended elements and the gradual emergence of operations that can be applied to the elements. Naturally, an important source of individual variation will be the age at which children are taught about particular subsystems, and, as Friedman (1978a) has argued, cultural learning may be the main influence on a number of abilities usually acquired after middle childhood, such as appreciating the magnitude of intervals of historical duration.

Three hypotheses apply to children up to about age 6. The first hypothesis is that young children are aware of certain temporal regularities, especially those of relatively short duration (such as daily routines) before they begin to learn conventional time systems. Second, older preschool children learn the names of some of the elements of conventional temporal systems, are aware that these names refer to points in time or duration, and associate these names with their own activities and experiences. Thus far their knowledge of the systems is fragmentary and associative and does not include relational information such as order or recurrence. Though they seldom do, preschool children should be able to learn lists of time names, just as they can memorize counting numbers or the alphabet. But like the alphabet, and unlike counting numbers (see Gelman & Gallistel, 1978), preschool children should be unable to perform operations upon the elements because the verbal list is not linked to actions like counting or to representations based on personal experience. However, a third hypothesis is that preschoolers are able to perform limited operations upon their nonconventional temporal representations; for example, reasoning which one of several daily activities would come first.

Several additional hypotheses reflect the abilities of older children. A fourth hypothesis is that between the ages of 6 and 8 children's range of temporal awareness expands to include patterns as long as a year, and they make finer discriminations in many of the briefer regularities, for example, daily and weekly routines. Concurrently, children learn the order of elements of conventional series like the hours of the day, days of the week, seasons, and usually months of the year, and they will associate many of these elements with personal experiences, natural characteristics, or landmark events. A fifth hypothesis is that children in this age range can perform limited operations upon the system (such as ordering the elements), but cannot yet integrate the features of order and recurrence. Sixth, the various subsystems are initially learned in parallel, and only at a later age, perhaps about 9 years, can children perform operations requiring the coordination of multiple subsystems. Seventh, the conventional time subsystems are not coordinated with logical time until 8 or 9 years, thus limiting the ability of younger children to use conventional time for the measurement of disparate intervals. Eighth, the ability to operate upon the total system (for example, to systematically compare the integrated conventional time system with other possible time systems) is an adolescent achievement.

In the following sections we will consider some of the evidence that bears on the nature of the conventional systems, the related cognitive processes, and the developmental pattern described in these hypotheses.

PREVIOUS RESEARCH

Investigations of children's understanding of conventional time, including historical durations, span the interval since the 1920s and consist of a variety of descriptive approaches taken by psychologists and educational researchers (e.g., Harrison, 1934; Oakden & Sturt, 1922; Springer, 1952). Most of the individual studies have previously been reviewed by Friedman (1978a) and Jahoda (1963) and will only be evaluated briefly and collectively in this section. While the list of the strenths of this literature is shorter than the list of limitations, several of the studies have some utility for the contemporary researcher. The chief value of much of this research is that it provides normative data on the ability of children of different ages to answer a variety of questions concerning clock time, days of the week, seasons, and months. These data suggest fairly consistent developmental trends—from awareness of brief and personally relevant temporal regularities to awareness of the temporally and personally remote. There are even the germs of theories in some of the reports that stress the importance of the child's activity and experience, the role of duration length, or the relation between performance and IQ. Finally, the few instances in which examples of incorrect responses are reported provide at least a glimpse of the processes underlying the children's reasoning.

On the negative side, much of the previous work fails to meet contemporary standards of data presentation and analysis. Among the most frustrating features is the recurrent practice of simply presenting the total score of a heterogeneous set of items. Neither error analysis nor systematic task variation are employed; thus, there is little information about the nature of competence underlying children's performance. This body of research can also be criticized as being atheoretical (Flavell, 1970), though this criticism would probably also apply to most collections of developmental studies with a median publication date of 1946. A final limitation—one shared with many areas of concept development research—is the restriction of scope to Western subjects in spite of substantial and interesting cross-cultural variation in conventional systems (see Jahoda, 1963; Sorokin & Merton, 1937; Zern, 1970). The few available cross-cultural studies have focused primarily on degree of time orientation as assessed by memory for time information (e.g., Price & Tare, 1975).

OPERATIONS AND CONVENTIONAL TIME

In this section we will discuss some of this author's research and related studies that deal with children's abilities to operate first upon the elements of conventional temporal systems and later upon the systems themselves. This work is hardly, as might be hoped, the fruit of a completed research program, but it does suggest several approaches to the study of the conceptual features and cognitive processes that may improve our understanding of the development of conventional time concepts. The first three sections that follow are organized according to types of operations instead of individual studies. The fourth section consists primarily of a more detailed report of a pair of recently completed studies concerning imagery and time concepts. A final section presents evidence concerning children's knowledge about temporal systems as conventions.

Constructing Temporal Order

Children's abilities to order a series of elements has typically been studied using problems of relative size (e.g., Elkind, 1964) or of the temporal order of a brief series of observable events or the events in a story (e.g., Brown, 1976; Piaget, 1969). In the following discussion we will describe children's abilities to operate on representations of more extended temporal relations to produce accurate orders. Some of the representations refer to elements in conventional time systems, while others symbolize natural or social events that are linked to daily or annual cycles. For simplicity of presentation, in this discussion the age of various achievements will be given as the age at which 50% of the children met a given criterion. This is determined by linear interpolation between the proportions and mean ages of adjacent groups.

DAILY CYCLE

Friedman (1976, 1977, 1978b) has provided evidence, consistent with the first and third hypotheses, that children can perform certain operations upon representations of events in a daily cycle before 6 years of age. Using a procedure designed to minimize verbal demands and memory requirements, children between 3- and 10-years-old were presented with four daily activities cards and asked to *"Put them the way you think they go."* The cards depicted a child waking in the morning, working at school, eating dinner, and sleeping at night. The left-to-right convention for placing cards predominated in children's constructions from 4 years onward, showing that by this age children can represent temporal sequences spatially. The ability to produce a correct order of the four cards, allowing any starting point, increased substantially between 3 and 5 years. While the proportion of successful 3-year-olds was at about the level that would be expected by chance responding, 47% of the 4-year-olds produced correct orders, a proportion exceeding chance ($p < .01$ by the binomial test).

This task cannot be accomplished solely by reciting a verbal list. Subjects must (*a*) map the pictorial representations onto personal experience or names for the times of day, (*b*) employ a spatial scheme to represent order, and (*c*) construct a veridical order either by (1) first choosing a starting point and successively selecting a next event in time or (2) relating individual elements to both earlier and later elements. A subsequent test showed that at least 68% of the subjects at each age group from 4 years to 10 years who constructed correct orders were also able to correctly insert two extra daily events into their initial orderings. This indicates that most of the successful children could have met prerequisite (*c*) by process (2).

Presumably, a process analogous to (2) is necessary in length seriation tasks. It is notable, therefore, that children (between 3 and 5 years) showed substantial progress on both the temporal task described above (including the insertion of the extra cards) and a spatial seriation task; and that performance on the two tasks was correlated even when the variance attributable to age was partialled out (partial $r_{(22)} = .50$, $p < .01$; Friedman, 1978b). These findings raise the possibility that some common cognitive process may underlie ordering operations performed on temporal and spatial series. An important point of contrast, however, is that in the daily activities task, children must access temporal information stored in the memory, whereas the seriation task permits overt comparison of stick length.

ANNUAL CYCLE

Similar card arrangement tasks show that 6- to 7-year-old children are able to correctly order representations of holidays, seasonal activities, and natural events associated with the seasons (Friedman, 1976, 1977). At least in the case of the holidays, it appears that this is not initially accomplished by mapping events onto the conventional verbal list of month names. Children did not begin their orders with the holiday that occurs first in the calendar year until 9 years of age, even though 87% of the 8-year-olds were able to order a set of cards naming the months.

Another annual order could apparently be constructed without mapping the elements onto a verbal list of months (Friedman, 1976). In the first part of a task 8- and 10-year-old children were asked to order a set of four cards labeled "school begins," 'winter vacation," "spring vacation," and "school ends." The subjects were significantly more accurate on this part than on a second part in which they were asked to coordinate the same cards with the set naming the months of the year. Error analysis revealed that the 8-year-olds were less likely to match "school begins" with September (33%) than January (40%) and only slightly more likely to match "school ends" with June (40%) than December (33%).

Consistent with the first part of Hypothesis 4, the ability to order the holiday and seasonal sets appeared significantly later than the ability to order the daily activities set. Since these daily and annual tasks were formally identical, it appears that poorer performance on the latter is attributable to the difficulty of forming an adequate mental representation of relationships between such temporally distant elements.

Coordinating Temporal Sets

Just as logical time entails the coordination of events in diverse series, an adequate understanding of conventional time systems requires the coordination of elements of distinct temporal sets. By 7 years children are able to accurately match cards representing four holidays with corresponding cards representing four seasons (Friedman, 1976). The coordination of sets with shorter durations may be possible by even younger children. The season cards are also accurately matched to month cards at 8 years, indicating that by this age the months are understood as more than a verbal list. Children of 8 are able to explain how a hypothetical "North American Indian Calendar" of six seasons (described in terms of natural and agricultural events) would correspond to the traditional four-season system (Friedman, 1979), even though the novel season system begins in late spring. The data presented in the section "Annual Cycle" suggest that the order of months is not the primary code for learning or storing the order of annual events before 9 years, although more evidence is needed to substantiate this point. If this view is correct, then 8–9 years may be the time when an integrated representation of annual events is formed.

Two coordination tasks show that even though most 8-year-olds can easily order the days of the week and months of the year, their ability to operate upon these systems is limited (Friedman, 1976). As was previously shown, the disparate starting and ending points of the school year and the calendar year led to difficulties in coordinating sets of cards representing the two series. In another task 8- and 10-year-old children were asked to match cards naming the days of the week with a set of five cards naming relational days ("day before yesterday," "yesterday," "today," "tomorrow," "day after tomorrow"). It was not until nearly 10 years that subjects could coordinate the sets. The "today" and "tomorrow" cards were correctly matched to the corresponding days of the week by more than 75% of subjects in each group, but the other three relational days were significantly more difficult. The greater difficulty of the latter set may stem from problems in constructing backward orders and forward orders of more than one step from a day other than the conventional first day of the week. The solutions of both the annual and week tasks require constructing orders from points other than the conventional start of the set. This month coordination task, and for most subjects the week coordination task, may also require constructing series that violate the conventional beginning and end of the list. Both processes would have been difficult for the 8-year-olds if their primary mode of representation of the months and days of the week was a verbal list.

Cyclic Recurrence

One of the most important structural features of conventional time systems is their incorporation of astronomical and social cycles. By capitalizing upon cyclic recurrence, the daily, weekly, and annual cycles not only highlight social and natural regularities, but also define units for superordinate systems. In order to understand and eventually coordinate temporal systems, children must develop representations that include information about both the order and recurrence of elements. But cyclic recurrence entails a paradox that might be expected to present problems for the child learning such a system. In contrast to logical time in which any 2 elements can be uniquely ordered, one element in a cycle is both *before* and *after* another. Because of the richer structure and relative infrequency of cyclic systems compared to serial systems, it seems a reasonable prediction that children will initially understand conventional time systems as series and only later conceptualize their recurrent features.

In an attempt to test this predicted sequence, Friedman (1976, 1977) administered a battery of card sorting and judgment tasks to 4- to 10-year-old children. Since most conventional systems have at least seven elements, and the number of elements may increase task difficulty, several measures of the conceptualization of recurrence were first obtained for four element sets. These sets consisted of depictions of four seasonal activities, four natural seasonal scenes (both sets were identified by season name either by the child or experimenter), four daily activities, four holidays, and four stages in the repetitive activity of a laborer (see Friedman, 1977). One measure of the ability to conceptualize recurrence—permutations—was based on success at judging the correctness of rearrangements of the child's spontaneous ordering of the elements. After the child had produced a linear order, the experimenter performed two cyclic permutations and one noncyclic permutation and asked the child whether each order was correct. For each cycle, ABCDAB . . . , the child's arrangement of ABCD would be permuted to BCDA and DABC, which are correct sequences, and ACBD, which is an incorrect sequence. A second measure of recurrence, double sort, was subsequently obtained for the daily activities and seasonal tasks. Subjects were presented with the original set of cards and a duplicate set and asked to arrange the cards to show 2 days/years. Most responses categorized as showing recurrence consisted of continuing in order with each duplicate element placed below its match.

Permutations and double sort appear to tap only partially overlapping concepts and processes. Success on each presupposes the ability to map the pictures onto appropriate representations stored in the memory, to construct their order, and to adopt a linear scheme to represent the order. Double sort also requires at least the knowledge that if one continues in time, the first element succeeds the last element. Permutations make three unique demands. First, the child must not construe an overconstancy (that any reordering would be incorrect) or an overmutability (that any reordering would be correct); second, the child must be willing to accept multiple starting points as veridical; and third, the child must be able to reconstruct relationships of order for new starting points.

The ability to discriminate correct and incorrect orders, permutations, was a significantly later achievement than either producing a correct order or double sort. The latter two did not differ significantly, and most children who could produce a correct ordering of the daily activities and season sets could also continue that order through another period of the cycle. Apparently by the time children can represent the order of elements of these daily and annual cycles, they can also represent the continuity beyond a single period.

Permutations followed ordering by about 2 years for the five stimulus sets, with ages of mastery ranging from about 8 to 8½ years. A disproportionate number of errors on the permutations tasks consisted of judging cyclic permutations to be incorrect. This pattern is consistent with overconstancy, rejection of different starting points, or failure to reconstruct relationships of order. Inspection of the protocols of subjects who failed the permutation index showed two patterns. Many of the subjects accepted or rejected all of the permutations and responded quickly, apparently without carefully examining the arrangements. This pattern is consistent with overconstancy, overmutability, or an unwillingness to perform the task. However, another group of children who failed the permutations measure rejected altered starting points because they felt they were not really *before* other elements. For example, one 5-year-old rejected the permutation "school, dinner, sleeping, waking" saying, "*You don't go to school without sleep.*" Next he rejected "sleeping, waking, school, dinner" by laughing and pointing out, "*You don't go to sleep first!*" These responses reflect difficulty with the paradoxical before and after relationship of two elements in a cycle and, thus, the difficulty in accepting multiple starting points.

The developmental pattern described above is consistent with Hypothesis 5: children can represent both order and forward continuity before they can conjointly incorporate order and recurrence in their judgments. The similar ages of mastery of the five stimulus sets, including the familiar daily activities and the novel laborer sets, suggests that a common cognitive development may underlie successful performance on the permutations tasks.

Evidence concerning the understanding of the recurrence of hours, days of the week, and months of the year is limited. Between 8 and 10 years an increasing number of children use extra first and last elements of days-of-the-week and month sets to indicate backward and forward continuity (Friedman, 1977), perhaps indicating a release from listlike representations of these sets. In the next section we will consider the nature of children's and adults' representations of the order of the months of the year, including the feature of cyclic recurrence.

Nature of Representations

In this section we will discuss research on developmental changes in the representation of a conventional time system, the months of the year. This discussion capitalizes on a distinction between image and verbal representation that is important in contemporary cognitive theories, but the underlying phenomena have received intermittent attention for nearly 100 years. After briefly reviewing theories and research on image representation and its development, we will consider the role that imagery plays in problem-solving tasks involving the months of the year.

MODELS OF SYMBOLIC SYSTEMS

A considerable body of research in cognitive psychology and several current theories incorporate the notion that humans possess two distinct modes of storing and processing information (Kosslyn & Pomerantz, 1977; Paivio, 1971, 1978a; Shepard, 1978a). One mode is characterized by the storage of information in linguisticlike propositions and the sequential access of different items of information. This accessing is thought to be governed largely by a network of associations between semantically related concepts. The other mode involves accessing and operating upon spatiallike representations. These representations are conceived as being isomorphic with pictures in many processing-relevant ways, for example, the simultaneous availability of information from the whole image or several of its parts. Evidence for the dual process model has come from numerous directions, many of them ingenious. It is possible to show, for example, that spatially organized responses like manual pointing interfere with the processing of spatial information more than with verbal processing, whereas a verbal response condition shows the opposite pattern (Brooks, 1968). It has also been demonstrated that the time it takes to mentally scan across an image is dependent upon its subjective size (Kosslyn, Ball & Reiser, 1978).

Paivio (1971, 1978a) and Shepard (1978b) have argued that the imagery code possesses distinct advantages for certain types of processing. Imagery, for example, seems well-suited to conceptualizing object transformations and to simultaneously accessing relational information such as differential size. The verbal code is thought to be superior for accessing and storing abstract information and for processing verbal sequences (Paivio, 1971). Given these characteristics, it is interesting to speculate on which code would be superior for representing the information in conventional time systems. At first appearance, it seems that verbal coding should be better suited to the nonperceptible and ordered nature of time systems. However, temporal systems include substantial relational information (for example, priority and embedding of units within larger units) that might best be processed by having available simultaneously multiple parts of an image. Research to date provides little help in deciding what code is dominant for storing and operating upon conventional time concepts. It may, nonetheless, be useful to consider a model that incorporates the notion of different codes.

In the opening section we suggested three symbolic modes that may be involved in the representation of conventional time systems. Two of these, associational networks and list storage, are subdivisions of the verbal code described above. The third corresponds to the spatiallike imagery code, except that the presumed content is analogous to schematic representations, such as circular diagrams of the cycle of months. In our model of adult knowledge of the months of the year, the three symbolic modes would each store essential information, but individuals would employ the mode best suited to particular processing demands. Some of the strengths and limitations of the codes and means of measuring their use are suggested below.

Much of our knowledge about individual months could be conveniently described by an associational network model (e.g., Collins & Loftus, 1975). Any given month's name would be linked more or less closely with numerous personal or shared concepts or propositions (e.g., my birthday, cold, Halloween, etc.). The advantages of this mode would be the capacity to store and access rich and varied sets of semantic associations, including those with abstract or affective content. A presumed weakness would be the limited or inefficient coding of temporal structure. For example, deciding which of two months is closer in time to January might require a lengthy series of intermediate steps since it is unlikely that all differential temporal distances are stored as associates of January. From a methodological point of view, one could study these associational networks through free association, clustering in free call, priming, or other conventional paradigms.

List storage is not always treated as a distinct verbal code. However, consideration of overlearned verbal chains such as counting numbers or the alphabet (or the temporary chains formed by subjects in serial recall experiments) suggests features of serial order not well-represented by associational network models. Verbal lists seem to play a prominent part in children's learning of conventional time systems and probably continue to enjoy advantages for certain types of processing in adults. For example, a verbal list of the months allows rapid accessing of the conventional starting point, the total set of names and the month immediately following, or a given number of months later than a particular month (except where this exceeds the end of the list). But list storage is probably inefficient when one must access certain other structural features of the calendar. It seems ill-suited for rapidly comparing temporal intervals, for retrieving backward order, or for establishing relationships of continuity, recurrence, or opposition—pairs of months farthest apart in time. The use of verbal lists can be measured by observing overt behavior (such as reciting aloud or lip movement) in younger subjects or subjective reports in older subjects. In addition, the experimenter could show the selective interference, for example, of verbal shadowing (Parkinson, 1972), with solving month order tasks, or a speed advantage for auditory versus visual problem presentation. Other evidence for list storage might take the form of demonstrating faster forward than backward responses when subjects must determine the temporal distance between two months or showing that the greater number of intervening months the subject must count, the longer it will take to solve a problem. Finally, list processing should lead to a faster identification of early elements than of late elements (see Koriat & Fischhoff, 1974, for a test of this prediction for days of the week).

Image representations of temporal systems, according to the model, possess a number of distinct advantages, all of which follow from their capacity to allow temporally extended elements to be simultaneously activated. In essence, a temporal pattern can be "frozen" by a spatial configuration, whether in conventional representations (such as the psychophysiologist's figure of a cortically evoked potential, or the economist's figure of growth in real income over a decade) or in an individually held image representation of temporal systems. By virtue of the simultaneous availability of all parts of the image once it is constructed, processes that are limited in verbal list representations could be accomplished more efficiently. It should be possible, for example, to compare two temporal intervals rapidly, and the speed of response should increase as the difference between the two interval lengths increases. In addition, subjects using images of the organization of the months should be equally fast in judging backward and forward order relations. Certain images (for example circular representations) would seem to be especially well-suited to conceptualizing continuity, recurrence, and opposition. Image representation is probably poorer than verbal list representation for rapidly accessing the names of the total set of months, the month immediately after a given month, or the month that is a specified number of steps after another month. Methods for assessing the use of temporal images include drawings, gestures, or verbal descriptions, and selective disruption by concurrent spatial processing tasks. In addition, spatial analog phenomena, such as the predicted negative relationship between the "discriminability" of two interval lengths and response time, would tend to support image representation.

The model as presented tends to emphasize the distinctness of the three processes. But adults are probably able to integrate information efficiently from more than one code, as, for example, in listing the hot months in order. It may also be misleading to suggest that individuals *possess* a single image representation, a point that will receive additional attention in the section on "Imagery and Verbal Processes in Time Concepts." Finally, while the above model is intended to describe the storage and accessing of the information in temporal systems, the issue of modes of representation of rich systems is a more general one. It may be true, for example, that well-learned verbal formulas (e.g., "Three times three equals nine."), like verbal lists, are employed in some arithmetic operations, whereas imagery (e.g., to find the solution to 9×8, imagine moving 8 steps backward from 80 on a number line) is used in others.

IMAGERY AND ABSTRACTION

Nearly all of the research on visual imagery conducted to date has concerned the previously seen or at least the "seeable." While the range of images studied has been broad enough to include rabbits larger than elephants (Kosslyn, 1975), relatively little attention has been devoted to images of abstractions (see Paivio 1971, 1978a). It is notable, however, that a number of important contributors to science and mathematics emphasize the central role that imagery of the "unseeable" played in their process of discovery (Hadamard, 1935; Shepard, 1978b), and several authors have commented on the potential of imagery to represent temporally extended events (Fraisse, 1964; Shepard, 1978b). In addition, from an evolutionary perspective, new forms of systematic knowledge, such as the awareness of extended temporal patterns, may be processed in modes that have long-standing adaptive value, as spatial analog representation may have had for human hunting and navigation.

The few available studies of temporal imagery used a questionnaire (Guilford,

1926), verbal interrogation (Oswald, 1960), and requested drawings (Werner & Kaplan, 1963). In none of these studies is convergent experimental evidence provided for the use of imagery, though all of them suggest substantial frequency and variety of temporal images. Only Oswald's findings bear directly on the issue of representations of conventional time. Oswald reported that 16% and 11% of his subjects, respectively, claimed that they possessed month forms and week forms. Many of the month forms were circular, and these are easier to elicit, Oswald believes, when an interval rather than a point in time is considered. Unfortunately, Oswald's study fails to demonstrate that imagery plays a specific processing role, and even its estimate of the prevalence of subjective reports may be restricted by the particular questions that the author chose.

Given the few adult studies of temporal imagery available, it is not surprising that there have been no developmental approaches to the problem. However, a number of investigators have either studied children's ability to represent temporal sequences spatially (Goodnow, 1971) or used spatial conventions, such as picture sequences or time lines to measure some aspect of the child's or adolescent's conceptualization of temporal order or duration (e.g., Cohen, 1964; Cottle & Pleck, 1969; and see "Constructing Temporal Order" in this chapter, and Chapters 5, 6, and 8). These studies show that spatial representations of temporal order are understood and constructed by about 4 years and spatial representations of relative temporal intervals can be produced by about 7 years. Thus, we do not know at what age children begin to use imagery to represent temporal order and duration, but at least the overt spatialization of time does not appear to be a late achievement.

IMAGERY DEVELOPMENT

In contrast to the little attention given imagery for abstractions, a considerable amount of research has been conducted on the development of imagery of objects or spatial forms. This literature falls primarily into three categories. The largest number of studies concern the effects of imaginal encoding on associative learning (Reese, 1977). In general, these studies demonstrate the potency of imagery as a mnemonic device, but are less clear in showing either quantitative or qualitative developmental changes (Reese, 1977; Ross & Kerst, 1978). In an ambitious series of studies, Piaget and Inhelder (1971) and their collaborators took a second empirical approach to imagery develoment. They were primarily concerned with children's ability to imaginally reconstruct or anticipate spatial relations during and after physical transformations. Using a variety of stimuli (e.g., rotating rods, bending wire arcs) and response modes (e.g., spontaneous or selected drawings, gestures, verbal descriptions), the authors found developmental increases in the ability to represent transformations between about 5 and 8 years. Piaget and Inhelder concluded that before about 7 or 8 years children's

images are static, unable to represent the results of movements or transformations. Recent studies of children's kinetic representations by Dean (1976, 1979)
have supported Piaget and Inhelder's (1971) developmental trends.

The third category of developmental imagery research includes attempts to
show the presence of perceptionlike imagery effects in children's performances.
For example, Kosslyn (1976) found that first graders, fourth graders, and adults
alike all verified large animal properties (e.g., cats have heads) more quickly
than small animal properties (e.g., cats have claws) even though the small
properties were stronger associates of the animal name. This finding seems most
easily explained by the notion that subjects consult visual images of the animals
and that small features take longer to detect. Marmor (1975, 1977) and Dean and
Harvey (1979) have examined children's performances on mental rotation tasks
in attempts to test for Shepard and Metzler's (1971) linear response time effect in
children. The Marmor studies show the predicted linear relationship between
response time and angular disparity in children as young as 4 years, in apparent
contradiction to Piaget and Inhelder's (1971) conclusion. However, using somewhat different stimuli, Dean and Harvey (1979) found the linear effect in 7- to 9-
and 10- to 14-year-olds groups but not in a group of 4- to 6-year-olds.

Taken together, the three approaches tend to show the presence of imagery-
dependent processing by 7 years or earlier, though several studies indicate qualitative changes in kinetic imagery during the 5- to 8-year age period. In spite of
the considerable empirical attention that children's imagery has received, we are
far from possessing an adequate theory of developmental changes in the nature
and significance of imagery. Bruner (Bruner, Olver & Greenfield, 1966) has
suggested that imagery becomes a less important representational mode during
middle childhood. But this does not appear to be the case, at least for tasks in
which image processes are efficient mediators (e.g., Kosslyn, 1976; Marmor,
1975). Perhaps a more fruitful developmental model can be derived from
Paivio's (1971, p. 27) view that "modes of representation generally evolve
toward more abstract and flexible forms—from concrete to more abstract imagery, overlapping with the emergence of verbal symbolic processes. . . ." In the
next section we will consider two approaches to studying the development of
abstract imagery, in each case concerning the representation of conventional time
systems.

IMAGERY AND VERBAL PROCESSES IN TIME CONCEPTS

We have presented evidence raising the possibility that between 8 and 10 years
of age children shift from a listlike representation of the order of months to more
flexible representation. Not only were 10-year-olds more likely than 8-year-olds
to indicate the continuity of a row of the months beyond its conventional beginning and end points, but they were more successful at coordinating two annual

cycles that have disparate starting points (the school year set and the month set). Assuming the model described under ''Models of Symbolic Systems,'' these age trends may be the result of a shift from only verbal list processing to the availability of both verbal list and image representations of the order of the months. This hypothesis is tested in the following two approaches.

Temporal Problem Solving

Four tasks were designed to demonstrate the distinction between verbal list and image processing and to test the developmental hypothesis previously advanced. In accordance with the model described under ''Models of Symbolic Systems,'' two of the tasks were presumed to be more easily solved by a verbal list process. These involved determining the month that was a set number of forward steps away. The other two were believed to be more amenable to image processing. Both required the comparison of the relative duration of two intervals, in one task going forward in time and in the other going backward in time. The instructions and sample questions from each task follow.

VERBAL LIST TASKS

2-Month Task (2M)
> **Instructions:** *Skip the month that comes after each of these and tell me the next month.*
> **Sample Question:** *Does May or June come 2 months after March?*

4-Month Task (4M)
> **Instructions:** *Skip the 3 months that come after these and tell me the next month.*
> **Sample Question:** *Does October or November come 4 months after July?*

IMAGE TASKS

Forward Task (F)
> **Instructions:** *If you go through the year tell me the month that will come next after these.*
> **Sample Question:** *Does January or September come next after May?*

Backward Task (B)
> **Instructions:** *If you went* backward *through the months of the year, tell me the month that will come next after these. Remember, you will be going to earlier months.*
> **Sample Question:** *Does July or March come next after November?*

The format of the question types was constrained by requirements of the experimental design that all be formally similar and that all withhold the reference month until the last spoken word. The ''distance'' in months to the correct choice was always 2 months for 2M, and 4 months for 4M, F, and B (assuming backward order). The distance to the incorrect choice was always the same as that given in the sample questions.

Subjects who have both image and verbal list processes at their disposal would be expected to use imagery for tasks F and B and to use overt or covert reciting of intervening months for 2M and 4M. This pattern would be consistent with faster response time (RT) on F and B than on 4M, even though the distance to the correct choice is the same in each case. This could be predicted because image processing allows accessing the relative distance of 2 months more rapidly than counting forward 4 months. Alternatively, it could be predicted because there is less interference between rehearsal of the choice months (a verbal process) and the image process used to access their relative distance from the reference month. Subjects who use imagery on F and B should also be accurate on both of these tasks since all parts of the image should be equally accessible and no strong directional effect should be present. Subjects who possess only verbal list processes should show similar RT on F and 4M, and have considerable difficulty with B. Finally, subjects who use a verbal list process on 2M and 4M should take longer on the latter since the correct choice is a greater number of steps away from the reference month. Eight problems of each type were used. The reference months in the problems were randomly selected, with the restriction that two come from each quarter of the calendar year in each task. Groups of 16 third, fifth, and tenth graders and undergraduates, half male and half female, were tested. Pilot testing indicated that in the school sampled, third graders were the first age group in which most children knew the months of the year and their order. The adolescent sample was added after the other three groups were tested and scored in an effort to verify the inferred developmental trends. The order of the tasks was counterbalanced across sex and age groups. For each problem the experimenter noted the answer, the presence or absence of lip movement, and covertly recorded RT. RT was subsequently log transformed to compensate for the obtained positive skew. At the end of each task, subjects were asked how they figured out the answer to that set of problems. Next they were asked if they ''said the months or thought about a picture or did it some other way (order varied).'' Responses were subsequently assigned blind by task, sex, and (for all but the adolescent group) by age into the categories ''image,'' ''reciting,'' ''image and reciting,'' or ''other.'' Responses categorized as ''image'' included referring to an image descriptively or by gesture. Images of continua, cycles, and calendars were included, but references to pictures of events (for example, birthdays) were excluded. The second category included the responses obtained by saying the intervening months to oneself, ''counting,'' or ''reading through the months.''

In light of the uncertain empirical status of temporal imagery, it is important to begin discussion of the results by considering the adult data. Several lines of this evidence clearly supported the distinction between verbal list processing and

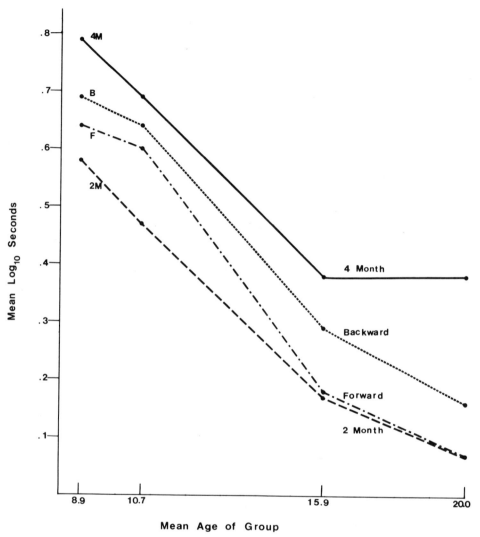

Figure 7.1.   Mean response times for each task by age group.

image processing. First, as Figure 7.1 indicates, adults responded faster on F and B than 4M, planned comparison $F_{(1,42)} = 54.01$, $p < .01$. This is consistent with the prediction that they would use imagery on F and B and list processing on 4M. Mean RT on 4M was substantially slower than on 2M, consistent with the predicted distance effect when a verbal list process is used. Second, subjects were very accurate on both F and B (Table 7.1), and task was not a significant

TABLE 7.1
Mean Proportion Correct for Each Task by Age Group

Mean age of group	N	Task				Mean	Level of significance of task effect by repeated measures ANOVA
		2M	4M	F	B		
8.9	16	.56	.47	.55	.42	.50	n.s.[a]
10.7	16	.81	.57	.77	.49	.66	.01
15.9	15	.78	.77	.89	.83	.82	n.s.
20.0	16	.90	.94	.97	.95	.94	n.s.
	Mean	.76	.69	.79	.67		

[a] Nonsignificant.

source of variance for this age group. F had a mean RT shorter than B by only .4 sec, nonorthogonal comparison $F_{(1,42)} = 4.73$, $p < .05$. By contrast, a separate adult group specifically instructed to recite 4 months forward and 4 months backward from reference months showed a directional difference of 1.8 sec, $t_{(3)} = 2.74$, $p < .05$, 1-tailed test. The lack of a directional effect on accuracy and the relatively slight directional effect on RT is consistent with the use of imagery on F and B.

A third line of support for the process distinction comes from the adults' reported methods of solving the tasks. Table 7.2 presents the number of subjects in each age group who reported imagery or reciting as their method of solution on a given task. These frequencies include subjects who spontaneously reported imagery or reciting and those whose spontaneous reports fell in the "other" category but who met the "imagery" or "reciting" criteria in their response to the probe question. Methods classified as imagery typically involved descriptions of the relative placement of reference and choice months on a circle or continuum, frequently accompanied by gestures. The adult subjects (last line in each of the small tables in Table 7.2) show a strong tendency to report reciting on 2M and 4M but to report imagery on F and B. Indeed, the 100% rate for the B task provides reason to doubt the generality of Oswald's (1960) conclusion about the rarity of temporal imagery! In his defense, however, many of these subjects claimed to have been unaware of their use of such images before the testing session.

Three individual difference analyses also supported the distinction between verbal list and image processing. First, intertask RT correlations showed significant 2M–4M and F–B correlations and no significant cross set correlations. The correlation between RT for 2M and 4M is .89, corrected for attenuation, $p < .01$, suggesting a strong speed-of-reciting factor. The correlation of F and B is .52, corrected, $p < .05$, suggesting a moderate speed-of-image-processing factor.

Second, while the 2M and F RT's were not significantly correlated overall, the correlations of the 6 S's who reported imagery or imagery plus counting on 2M were significant, $r = .73$, $p < .05$. Finally, while adult males and females were very accurate on all tasks and sex was not a significant source of variance for proportion correct, sex differences in RT are consistent with the common finding of female superiority on verbal tasks and male superiority on spatial tasks (Maccoby & Jacklin, 1974; McGee, 1979). A significant sex × task interaction, $F_{(3,42)} = 5.92$, $p < .01$, and a significant planned comparison $F_{(1,42)} = 15.80$, $p < .01$, supported this pattern. Paivio (1978b) recently used individual difference data in a similar way to support a verbal and image processing distinction.

Given this evidence for the two-process distinction in adults, we can examine the developmental data for information on when each process is acquired. We predicted that 8-year-olds would have only verbal list processes available, and that about 2 years later verbal list or image processes could be used as appropriate for a given task. Since the third graders in this school population were the first to

TABLE 7.2
Frequency of Reported Method by Age and Chi-square Statistics for Each Task

	2-month			4-month	
	Reported method			Reported method	
Age group	Imagery	Reciting	Age group	Imagery	Reciting
9	0	13	9	0	11
11	0	11	11	0	12
16	2	11	16	0	14
20	3	10	20	0	14
$\chi^2_{(3)} = 5.56$, n.s.[a]			$\chi^2_{(3)} = 0.00$, n.s.		

	Forward			Backward	
	Reported method			Reported method	
Age group	Imagery	Reciting	Age group	Imagery	Reciting
9	2	11	9	3	11
11	2	12	11	2	9
16	8	6	16	8	5
20	13	2	20	16	0
$\chi^2_{(3)} = 21.50$ $p < .001$			$\chi^2_{(3)} = 25.58$, $p < .001$		

[a] Nonsignificant.

predominantly claim that they knew the months of the year, we assumed that the shift would occur between grades 3 and 5 in our sample. The results suggest that verbal list processing is present from third grade onward. However, the use of image processing, at least on these tasks, appears to be a later development than predicted.

The developmental pattern was investigated by performing ANOVAs on the RT and proportion correct (PC) data with the factors sex, age, and task. PC for each task is the proportion correct out of eight problems. Age and task were significant main effects for both PC (Table 7.1) and RT (Figure 7.1), $p < .01$. The sex main effects were not significant, and the only significant interaction involving sex is attributable to the adult RT effect previously discussed. The age $\times$ task interaction for PC, $F_{(9,165)} = 2.42$, $p < .05$, and for RT, $F_{(9,165)} = 1.84$, $p < .10$, were examined through separate task ANOVAs at each age, with the following exception. A theoretically interesting component of the age $\times$ task interaction in RT was age change in the *difference* between 4M RT and F RT. Image processing, when available, was expected to lead to substantially faster RT's on F than 4M, even though the distance to the correct choice was the same for both tasks. A separate interaction test showed that the difference was greater (and thus the two-process distinction was more strongly supported) for 16-year-olds and adults than for the younger subjects, $F_{(3,55)} = 5.10$, $p < .01$ (see Figure 7.1).

Three lines of evidence support the conclusion that verbal list processing is used by 9 years of age, although initially with little success on these tasks. First, the distance effect—that 2M RT is shorter than 4M RT—is strong and reliable (by Tukey tests) at each age level (see Figure 7.1). This is consistent with the expectation that it takes longer to recite 4 months than 2 months. Second, as Table 7.2 indicates, "reciting" is the predominant reported method on 2M and 4M for each age group from 9 years onward. Finally, the mean number of problems on which lip movement was observed was significantly greater than zero for the third and fifth graders in each task, $t_{(15)}$'s > 3.49, p's $< .01$.

In spite of the fact that nearly all of the third and fifth graders claimed to know the months of the year, their performance was surprisingly poor on one or both of the verbal list tasks. Third graders performed at about chance level on both 2M and 4M, and the fifth graders' PC on 4M did not significantly exceed the 50% chance level. The high error rates can be attributed either to a limited ability to operate upon the verbal lists or to special problems introduced by the processing demands of these tasks. According to the first interpretation, when children initially learn the list of months, they may still be unable to perform unusual operations such as starting in the middle of the list or moving forward a fixed number of steps. The latter would be consistent with Bradley's (1947) finding that it was not until 12 years that 75% of children could name the seventh month. A second interpretation is that rehearsal of the choice months (or the question itself) may interfere with the verbal list process of reciting intervening months and thus cause high error rates. Indirect evidence for this interpretation comes from comments that a number of adult subjects made when describing their method of solution for 2M and 4M. Several pointed out that in order to avoid confusion, they deliberately ignored the choice months as the question was read and simply began reciting forward from the reference month. Since younger subjects never reported this approach, the age differences in accuracy may be attributed in part to strategy differences. A related interference problem specific to 4M was the necessity for skipping over a choice month to get to the correct answer. This may account for the fifth graders' more accurate performance on F than 4M, planned comparison $F_{(1,42)} = 5.73$, $p < .05$. In 4M the wrong choice always came right before the correct month, whereas in F it came 4 months after the correct choice.

The second main developmental conclusion is that image processing did not predominate on F and B until a later age than predicted. Three criteria for the use of image processing were applied to the third, fifth, and tenth graders: (1) shorter RT's on F and B than 4M, (2) PC on F and B that are equal and significantly greater than chance, and (3) half or more of the subjects reporting imagery in solving the tasks (see Figure 7.1, Tables 7.1 and 7.2). The first two criteria were tested by planned comparisons and t-tests against chance level performance, and the third was tested by the binomial test.

The third graders met only one of the three criteria. F and B RT's were shorter than 4M RT, nonorthogonal planned comparison $t_{(42)} = 2.77$, $p < .01$. It is not clear why the 9-year-olds responded more rapidly on F and B than 4M. However, since accuracy was at about chance level for each task, it is possible that many 9-year-olds simply "gave up" sooner on F and B problems. In any case, 9-year-olds failed to meet criterion 2, since neither F nor B was solved at greater than chance level. Criterion 3 was not met since significantly fewer than half of this group reported imagery on either F or B. None of the subjects who reported imagery on F or B showed PC significantly greater than the .5 chance level.

The fifth graders failed all three criteria for imagery. B and F did not have significantly shorter RT's than 4M; F was significantly more accurate than B, planned comparison $F_{(1,42)} = 11.23$, $p < .01$; and significantly fewer than half of the subjects reported imagery on F or B. One fifth grader apparentely was using image processes similar to the adults on both F and B. She reported picturing a calendar in her mind and going either forward or backward through the months. Her responses were very fast and perfectly accurate.

By about 16 years it appears that most subjects spontaneously employ image processes in solving the imagery tasks. All three of the criteria were met by the tenth-grade group. F and B had significantly shorter RT's than 4M, nonorthogonal planned comparison $F_{(1,39)} = 18.00$, $p < .01$. F and B PC significantly exceeded .5, and the difference between the two was small and nonsignificant.

Half of the subjects in this group reported imagery on F and B. Analyses by reported method showed that subjects reporting imagery on F were more accurate on this task than subjects reporting reciting, and that subjects reporting imagery on B responded more quickly and more accurately than reciters. Only the last difference reached conventional significance levels, $F_{(1,11)} = 6.49$, $p < .03$.

The data presented in this section support the distinction between verbal list and image processing of month-order information. The results also suggest that there are age differences in the spontaneous use of the two processes. It appears that children initially learn the order as a verbal list, usually by 8 or 9 years, but that they may be unable to use verbal list processes in other than routine ways. In contrast, it appears that the nonroutine use of month order, for example, in coordinating school events with months (see "Coordinating Temporal Sets"), is possible at about this age when *overt* spatialization is possible. By about 11 years, verbal list processes can be used to solve certain interval problems, but it appears that most children of this age do not use image processes on certain tasks that are approached by most 16-year-olds and adults in this way. In the next section we will consider an alternative line of evidence concerning developmental trends in image representation of the order of months of the year.

Drawings of a Temporal System

In an effort to obtain convergent information about developmental trends in temporal imagery, we asked two samples of children and adolescents to make drawings of a year. Our chief interest was in tapping habitual modes of conceptualizing the organization of the months. Sample 1 consisted of 72 children ranging in age from 7 to 16 years. Subjects were initially asked to select their preferred card out of four figural representations of the order of the months and to explain the relative advantages and disadvantages of each card. The cards had line drawings of a circle, square, horizontal line, or zig-zag with the month names printed next to tick marks on the lines. Next, subjects were asked if they could make a better picture. It was presumed that the card choice task would serve to orient children to figural ways of representing the year and that the drawings would correspond to their introspections.

The subjects used in the preceding temporal problem-solving study served as subjects in Sample 2. Following the four main tasks, subjects were asked what they think of when thinking about the months of the year. Next they were instructed to "*draw a picture of a year with all of the months on it.*" Finally, half or more of the subjects in each group were asked if the drawings they produced were the way they "really thought about a year." Seventy-five percent of the adults, 94% of the 16-year-olds, and 89–100% of the subjects in the other two groups who were asked the question responded affirmatively. Only the drawing responses of each sample will be discussed.

Drawings by the subjects in each study were quite varied, but only four subjects claimed that they did not know how to respond. Responses were categorized as (*a*) pictorial, consisting primarily of one or more realistic depictions; (*b*) arrangements of month names, usually in a column, or one or more rows; or (*c*) diagrammatic, including mainly linear or circular line drawings with the position of the months indicated. In both samples pictorial drawings predominated in the youngest age group and decreased in relative frequency with age. Name arrangements and diagrams increased in relative frequency with age. About one-third of the responses at each age from 10 years and older in Sample 1 and 16 years and older in Sample 2 consisted of closed forms, such as circles or rectangles.

Since a number of drawings categorized above as "pictorial" actually involved the orderly arrangement of small depictions corresponding to each month, the following dichotomy was used for a second analysis. A "spatially organized" category included diagrams, regular arrangements of month names, and pictorial responses in which scenes corresponding to each month were arranged in an orderly way. The remaining responses were grouped in a new "pictorial" category. Table 7.3 shows the frequency of each category for each study. By about 9–10 years spatially organized representations are predominant.

TABLE 7.3
Frequency of Response Types for Each Age Group and Chi-square Statistics

Study 1				
	Mean age of group			
Response category	7.2	9.7	11.4	13.8	16.2
Pictorial	10	4	1	2	1
Spatially organized	5	10	13	15	11

$$\chi^2_{(4)} = 19.73, \, p < .001$$

Study 2			
	Mean age of group			
Response category	8.9	10.7	15.9	20.0
Pictorial	9	5	4	1
Spatially organized	5	9	12	15

$$\chi^2_{(3)} = 12.12, \, p < .01$$

Within the limits of introspective evidence (and to the extent that the drawings correspond to children's introspections), these data suggest that images of the organization of the months are common by about 10 years. Clearly, a larger proportion of the children and adolescents in the second study would be credited with images of the months using the spontaneous drawing method than using the measures of the problem-solving tasks. One interpretation of the age disparity is that early images may serve to orient a child to the overall organization of months, but cannot initially be used with the flexibility required to solve interval problems such as those of the F and B tasks. Furthermore, this sort of problem solving may depend on not one but several image types, flexibly employed as a problem demands. For example, several adult subjects reported using a linear image when all of the months of a problem were within a single calendar year, but shifting to a circular representation when a problem required going forward or backward over the December–January boundary. If this interpretation is correct, it may be that the main developmental differences in temporal imagery after about 10 years reside not in the *possession* of images but in the ability to *construct* them for a particular purpose. This emphasis on the constructive and flexible nature of temporal imagery is consonant with Fraisse's (1964) discussion of the limits of any single temporal representation, and with Kosslyn's (1975) position that images are constructed, not simply stored and accessed. The presumed trend of increasing flexibility with age is consistent with Paivio's (1971, p. 27) view of the nature of imagery development.

Our conclusions about the development of temporal imagery must necessarily be restricted to the one case studied—images of the organization of months. It is possible that image processing may be applied to other briefer conventional systems, for example, hours of the day or days of the week, at an earlier age. In addition, the role of image processing in the logical time tasks studied by Piaget (1969) and several of the contributors to this volume warrants attention. In light of the common finding in this literature that spatial cues interfere with time judgments and some suggestive evidence (Friedman, 1979) that verbal presentation of analogous problems leads to unexpectedly high levels of performance in 7-year-olds, it seems a reasonable hypothesis that image representation (or inappropriate forms of image representation) may limit the performance of preschool children on many of these tasks.

Knowledge about Temporal Systems

Adults' understandings of conventional time includes knowledge beyond the structural features of temporal systems. We are also aware that time is independent of any particular set of human activities, systems, or devices used for marking its passage. We know that conventional systems are composed, in part, of arbitrary units and that other systems for reckoning the passage of time are possible. It seems extremely unlikely that children are aware of these distinctions while they are in the process of learning the elements and basic structure of the systems, just as early language learners are unaware of the arbitrary nature of symbols (Piaget, 1929).

The development of children's knowledge of the distinction between arbitrary and natural aspects of time was first investigated by Michaud (1949; summarized in Fraisse, 1964). Michaud interviewed nearly 1800 children between 10 and 15 years of age and asked them to explain the effects upon their age of turning the clock forward 1 hour in the spring. The first line of Table 7.4 lists the percentage of children at each age classified as recognizing the independence of clock time and natural processes (Fraisse, 1964, p. 279). Before age 13 most children

TABLE 7.4

Percentage of Subjects Distinguishing between Natural and Arbitrary Features of Conventional Systems

Task	Age										Significance level of age effect by χ^2
	7	8	9	10	11	12	13	14	15	16	
Michaud, 1949											
Daylight saving time											
1. Judgment and explanation				20	30	39	48	57	59		.001[a]
Friedman, 1979											
Daylight saving time											
2. Judgment	40		57		85		94			83	.02
3. Judgment and explanation	7		31		69		81			56	.01
Time zone											
4. Judgment	40		50		92		100			83	.01
5. Judgment and explanation	13		23		46		91			66	.01
Metric day											
6. Consistent system	13		21		38		59			50	.06
7. Day length unchanged	14		29		31		65			67	.03
Metric week											
8. Consistent system	7		31		62		94			75	.001
9. Day length unchanged	7		31		69		88			75	.001
Indian calendar											
10. Accept correctness	7		21		69		65			83	.001

[a] Estimated from data presented in Fraisse (1963) using 2 response categories.

reported either (*a*) that the change caused them to grow older or (*b*) that people did not grow older in as brief a time as 1 hour.

Friedman (1979) attempted to replicate this pattern using verbal methods, as did Michaud, but with convergent evidence from several different tasks. Seventy-two children between 7 and 16 years of age were tested on a series of tasks designed to tap their understanding of the distinction between natural and arbitrary features of time and time systems. One task incorporated Michaud's procedure with two modifications. First, before the main question, subjects were asked whether they grew older as each hour passed. If they said no, the experimenter explained that people are always getting a little older as each hour passes. This intervention was intended to reduce the frequency of the ambiguous failure category (*b*). Second, in an effort to obtain a conservative test of Michaud's age pattern, both affirmative and negative answers to the main question were met with countersuggestions. To receive credit by the *judgment* criterion, children had to consistently assert that their ages would remain unchanged by the clock change. To receive credit by the *judgment-plus-explanation* criterion they also had to justify their responses. Most acceptable justifications involved stating that only the clock was affected, that biological processes were unaffected, or that age cannot be changed. Lines 2 and 3 of Table 7.4 show the proportion of children at each age meeting these criteria. By 9 years most children believed that their age was unaffected by the clock change (nearly identical proportions were found for a similar item involving turning the clock back in the fall). Adequate justifications were given by 11 years—at least 2 years earlier than Michaud's subjects.

A second task assessed knowledge of age constancy during a hypothetical jet flight to an earlier time zone. As Lines 4 and 5 of Table 7.4 show, the age patterns are quite similar to those for the daylight saving time question.

A third series of questions required children to consider the consequences of a hypothetical shift to "metric time." In the metric day subtask it was explained that "*people got together and decided on a new system with 10 'metric hours' per day and 100 'metric minutes' per hour. Of course that wouldn't change the way the earth moved.*" The latter sentence was included to reduce confusion, eveident in a pilot study, about the consequences of a conventional change. Subjects were then asked to explain how the system would work and to judge whether hours, minutes, and days would be shorter, the same, or longer. Line 6 of Table 7.4 shows the proportion of subjects at each age who held either days, hours, or minutes constant and correctly judged the implications for the other quantities. Only the adolescent subjects were able to accomplish this, perhaps because proportionality is a prerequisite concept (see Inhelder & Piaget, 1958). The age trends in the ability to construct consistent systems on this and the next subtask may also be taken as tentative support for Hypothesis 8—that operating upon integrated temporal systems is an adolescent achievement. Of main interest here is the age pattern for holding day length constant. since day length is a natural duration but its subdivision are arbitrary. As Line 7 of Table 7.4 indicates, day length was not preserved by the majority of subjects until between 11 and 13 years.

In the similar metric week subtask, subjects were asked to pretend that *"people decided to make weeks 10 days long,"* and were reminded that the earth's movement would not be affected. Producing consistent systems proved to be easier in this subtask than in the previous one (Line 8, Table 7.4), probably because only two interval lengths had to be coordinated. In addition, day length, which unlike week length is a natural duration (theological considerations aside), was preserved by most 11-year-olds (Line 9, Table 7.4). The earlier preservation of day length in the metric week than in the metric day subtasks may be attributable to the greater complexity of the latter. Alternatively, week length may be subjectively more arbitrary than minute or hour length for many of these subjects.

Finally, a part of the "Indian Calendar" coordination task described under "Coordinating Temporal Sets" was designed to test children's knowledge of the fact that the number of seasonal divisions of the yearly cycle is arbitrary. After coordinating the two compatible sets and answering questions about their similarities and differences, subjects were asked whether the novel calendar was correct or not. Subjects who answered affirmatively were given a countersuggestion indicating the different starting point, number of seasons, and seasons' names. Line 10 of Table 7.4 shows the proportion of subjects at each age consistently claiming that the novel calendar is correct. This criterion was met by most 11-year-olds.

If we adopt the judgment-plus-explanation criterion for the first two tasks, the developmental patterns in the Friedman (1979) data (Table 7.4) indicate that by about 11 years children are aware of the distinction between arbitrary and natural temporal features. They can (*a*) explain that clock changes do not influence natural processes; (*b*) preserve day length when constructing a novel week system; and (*c*) accept the validity of a novel calendar that begins at a different time and has more seasons than the conventional four-season system but that retains the natural year length. Day length was not preserved in the metric day subtask until slightly later, perhaps because of the greater complexity of the task or because of the greater subjective "naturalness" perceived in the duration of minutes or hours than of weeks. These data suggest that children are aware of the arbitrary nature of many temporal conventions at somewhat earlier ages than indicated in Michaud's study, but probably not before 9–11 years. It is not possible to explain the sample differences, but possible contributors include procedural, educational, and cultural differences.

CONVENTIONAL TIME CONCEPTS
AND COGNITIVE DEVELOPMENT

Developmental Explanations

Adequate developmental explanations are surprisingly rare in cognitive developmental research, even in relatively well-studied areas (*e.g.,* see Winer, 1980); indeed, there is little agreement as to what form an adequate explanation would take (*e.g.,* Keating, 1979; Piaget, 1970; Sternberg, 1979). Nonetheless it may be useful to consider the evidence presented as it relates to the explanatory goals suggested in the first section of the chapter. These goals are (*a*) describing the conceptual structure of conventional time concepts, (*b*) determining the processes that children of different ages employ when reasoning about the systems, and (*c*) identifying the factors responsible for the developmental changes.

Several tentative conclusions can be drawn about the conceptual structure of temporal systems. First, knowledge of conventional systems must be distinguished from knowledge of the temporal regularities to which they correspond. The card arrangement tasks described earlier indicate that young children are able to construct representations of daily and annual orders of events before they have mastered clock time or the calendar. Thus, there seem to be multiple levels of conceptualization of these temporal regularities. A second structural distinction is between the ordinal nature and cyclic nature of temporal cycles. A study presented in the section on "Cyclic Recurrence" showed that children can construct the order of elements of several temporal cycles before they are able to discriminate correct from incorrect permutations. In addition, the ordinal–cyclical dichotomy is supported by the reports of several adult subjects in the temporal problem-solving study that they switched between images of continua and images of circles in accordance with the demands of individual problems. The adolescent and adult data of the temporal problem-solving study also suggested the utility of a third distinction, between the features of serial order and relative order of the months of the year. Tasks that required subjects to determine the month that was a specified number of units forward were approached in a different way than tasks that required subjects to determine which of the two months occurs next in either forward or backward order. Finally, the studies discussed in the section "Knowledge about Temporal Systems," support a structural distinction between natural and arbitrary units of duration, one that becomes important by about 11 years.

The studies presented under "Operations and Conventional Time" also provide some indication of developmental changes in the availability of representational modes and in the operations that can be performed on the elements of temporal systems. By 4 years old children are able to construct the order of daily events when overt spatialization—arranging cards—is possible (see also Brown, 1976), although the form of memory representation that underlies these constructions is unknown. Previous research on conventional time concepts (see Friedman, 1978a) shows that 6- to 8-year-olds are usually able to recite the days of the week, seasons, and months in order—a performance that probably depends upon verbal list processes. Further information about age changes in representational modes comes from the studies on imagery and verbal processes reported earlier. By 9 or 10 years of age most subjects reported possessing spatially organized images of the set of months, but it was apparently not until about 16 years that this mode of representation was used in the problem-solving tasks.

A number of findings suggested age changes in the availability of mental operations. At about 4 years children begin constructing the temporal order of small numbers of daily events, an achievement apparently related to early spatial seriation. The acceptance of multiple starting points and the reconstruction of temporal order after cyclic permutations (''Cyclic Recurrence'') at about 8 years may be evidence of the availability of a second type of operation at this age. The ''metric time'' tasks showed that children have difficulty constructing nonconventional but consistent alternatives to conventional time systems before about 11–13 years. The study provided no direct evidence as to the nature of the underlying operations, but reasoning about pairs of proportional relations may have been involved. Finally, the results of the temporal imagery studies raise the possibility that flexible construction of abstract images is an operation not present until mid-adolescence.

The third explanatory goal, accounting for developmental change, must be approached even more tentatively. The common distinction between specific cultural experiences and relatively autonomous and general cognitive developmental processes may be helpful in thinking about age changes in conventional time concepts, though the two certainly interact. There is no direct evidence concerning the influence of specific experiences on conventional time concept development. The few intervention studies available (K. Friedman & Marti, 1945; Pistor, 1940) are of limited value because the training programs are inadequately specified and the criterial measures are too general. Children obviously learn the systems used in their own cultures, but there is reason to doubt that the conventional systems are the first codes used to represent temporal regularities. A presently unavailable but promising sort of evidence for the cultural learning issue might come from observational studies of parents teaching their preschool and school-age children about time systems. In addition to examining the information exchanged it would be valuable to have an estimate of the sheer amount of parental energy that goes into the enterprise.

Evidence for cognitive developmental contributions, though indirect, comes from several sources. First, there seems to be considerable regularity in ages of acquisition, often when no common educational experience is apparent. Two examples are the onset of certain temporal ordering operations at about 4–5 years, and the mastery of the permutations measure of conceptualizing cyclic recurrence at about 8 years. A second sort of evidence, also cited by Fraisse (1964), is the consistent positive relationship found between performance on tests of conventional time concepts and I.Q. (Buck, 1946; K. Friedman, 1944; Harrison, 1934). Third, it seems likely that the construction and use of temporal images by mid-adolescents is rooted in a kind of ''natural selection'' of higher information modes of processing rather than in specific educational experiences. Temporal images reported by adults are quite idiosyncratic in their specifics, but encode essential structural features of the systems they represent.

Admittedly, each of these conclusions about structure, representational modes, operations, and developmental change must be stated in a rather weak form. One can hope, however, that these sorts of distinctions will allow research on conventional time concepts to progress beyond superficial descriptions of performance on complex tasks.

The Problem of Representation

Studies of the development of conventional time concepts and the conceptualization of temporal regularities occupy a special niche in cognitive developmental research because of the representational requirements of conceptualizing temporally extended elements. In most of the familiar paradigms (for example, concrete operational tasks), representational demands are limited by the direct presentation of the materials about which the child must reason. When we require children to solve problems involving days of the week or months of the year, the completeness and structural properties of their representations may impose upper bounds on their performances.

The area of children's conceptualization of temporal regularities has some interesting parallels with another representational achievement—the development of cognitive maps (Hardwick, McIntyre & Pick, 1976; Siegel & White, 1975). Both pose important questions concerning children's capacities to organize sequentially acquired information into structured representations. Isolated, static percepts are inadequate for capturing the richness of structure of either familiar spatial environments or daily routines. Hardwick et al. suggest that young children's cognitive maps may really be a set of isolated ''perspective maps,'' each associated with a particular point of view. Only later are the perspective maps supplemented by ''general level representations'' that allow the coordination of a larger set of spatial relations than can be perceived from any one viewpoint. Hazen, Lockman and Pick (1978) provide evidence that young children can learn specified routes through a novel spatial layout at an earlier age than they can abstract the overall layout. If we pursue the analogy between cognitive maps and temporal representations, we might predict that early "temporal maps" consist largely of remembered actions, perhaps poorly coordinated. At a later age children may develop general level temporal representations with greater independence from particular content. These general level temporal representations might serve to coordinate small unit representations, just as general level spatial representations may serve to coordinate the information of many different viewpoints. Of course, in the case of temporal regularities, the culture provides ready-made frameworks in the form of conventional time systems. These may both provide supportive symbolic media and serve to increase the salience of the temporal regularities themselves. Thus, an important problem for understanding representational development in general is the effect of idiosyncratic, possibly action-oriented representations of temporal regularities compared to convention-influenced representations in learning to reason about time.

To take the cognitive map analogy a step farther, there may be important similarities between embedding subordinate and superordinate conventional time systems and embedding hierarchical spatial frameworks. From a functional point of view, rather than *possessing* a general representation of the relations among times of day, days of the week, months, and so on, or one's house, neighborhood, and town, older children and adults may *construct* integrated representations as needed to solve particular problems. Perhaps the capacity to construct multilevel spatial representations and the ability to embed temporal systems are related developmental achievements. Finally, it is possible that the imagery findings discussed earlier have implications for the development of spatial concepts. In our study, flexible construction of temporal images appeared to be uncommon before mid-adolescence. Hardwick *et al.* found that cognitive maps could be accurately rotated by adult but not by fifth-grade subjects. This interesting finding raises the possibility that some common image process underlies the development of both the temporal and spatial abilities.

DIRECTIONS FOR FUTURE WORK

We have observed repeatedly in this chapter the limited amount of information available concerning the conceptual structure of conventional time systems and age changes in the processes used to represent and operate upon the systems. We have also noted that a variety of research strategies (including varying task features, correlating performance on multiple tasks, and administering interventions) will have to be applied to the numerous temporal systems that have been inadequately studied. In addition, there are several problems worthy of study that concern the application of temporal knowledge to everyday problem solving.

One such area concerns the role that conventional time concepts play in episodic memory (Tulving, 1972). While information is not stored in memory in a time-ordered format, adults are able to reconstruct sequences and durations by linking events to conventional markers (e.g., Lindsay & Norman, 1972, p. 379). Indeed, our rich knowledge of conventional time systems allows us to detect patterns in our lives (e.g., vacations each summer) and to capitalize on these patterns when recalling events. If knowledge of conventional time plays an important role in adult memory, it may also account for some of the differences in the long-term memory capabilities of children of different ages. It would, therefore, seem productive to study children's memories of life events as a developmental phenomenon, to concurrently assess their knowledge of conventional time systems, and perhaps to evaluate the contribution that time marking makes to encoding and recall. For example, progress in understanding conventional time systems may lead to the reorganization of previously encoded information or facilitate new means of accessing temporally related information.

Another approach to conventional time concepts might follow a recent trend in cognitive psychology (e.g., Harris, 1980) of studying ecologically relevant cognition. For example, one research program might collect adults' reports of how they solve common temporal problems and then study the processes used by children of different ages to solve similar problems. Examples that may be salient for adults would be planning a schedule, remembering periodic events (e.g., birthdays, watering the flowers), or estimating the time that some activity will take. Developmental analyses of age changes in these activities may provide information on the nature of temporal metacognition and perhaps suggest educational interventions.

SUMMARY AND CONCLUSION

Conventional time systems raise a number of interesting developmental issues because of their ecological significance, rich structures, and special representational demands. However, the literature in this area is extremely limited. Notably lacking are adequate conceptual analyses of the time systems, cognitive process analyses of children's changing abilities, and theories to explain the developmental pattern. In this chapter we have attempted to describe some of the structural features that influence the pattern of acquisition and have suggested a model for processing modes that are applied to conventional time systems at different ages. Eight hypotheses about the developmental pattern were advanced, and most of them receive support from past research or from the studies summarized in this chapter. Evidence was presented that children can represent the order of daily activities by about 4 years and certain annual regularities by about 6–7 years. The cyclic structural properties of order and recurrence appear to be difficult for children to integrate before 8–9 years, and certain types of problems involving the coordination of disparate temporal series are also mastered at about this age. Other evidence indicated that the distinction between natural and arbitrary durations in conventional time systems is expressed in children's explanations by 11 years and in their judgments by 9 years.

The processing mode that received the greatest attention in this chapter was image representation of temporal structure. There has been little past research on abstract image representation, but the adult data presented here suggest that imagery may play an important role in certain types of temporal problem solving. The developmental data indicate that the flexible use of images of the orgnization of months in problem solving may be uncommon before mid-adolescence, but children's drawings reflect the *possession* of images by 9 or 10 years.

We concluded, albeit tentatively, that the pattern of development of children's conventional time concepts can be understood as the learning and construction of representations, the acquisition of operations, and a shift in representational modes and the flexibility with which they can be used. There is no shortage of issues for future research in this area, and the potential benefits seem to warrant the effort. Chief among these benefits is the possibility of understanding better the nature of human knowledge of richly structured systems.

ACKNOWLEDGMENTS

I am grateful to Frank Laycock and Robert Becklen for their comments on an earlier draft of this chapter.

REFERENCES

Bradley, N. C. The growth of the knowledge of time in children of school age. *British Journal of Psychology*, 1947, *38*, 67–78.

Brooks, L. R. Spatial and verbal components of the act of recall. *Canadian Journal of Psychology*, 1968, *22*, 349–368.

Brown, A. L. The construction of temporal succession by preoperational children (Vol. 10). In A. D. Pick (Ed.), *Minnesota Symposia on Child Psychology*. Minneapolis: University of Minnesota Press, 1976.

Bruner, J. S., Olver, R. R., & Greenfield, P. M. *Studies in cognitive growth*. New York: Wiley, 1966.

Buck, J. N. The time appreciation test. *Journal of Applied Psychology*, 1946, *30*, 388–398.

Cohen, J. Psychological time. *Scientific American*, 1964, *211*(5), 116–124.

Collins, A. M., & Loftus, E. F. A spreading activation theory of semantic processing. *Psychological Review*, 1975, *82*(6), 407–428.

Cottle, T. J., & Pleck, J. H. Linear estimations of temporal extension: The effect of age, sex, and social class. *Journal of Projective Techniques and Personality Assessment*, 1969, *33*, 81–93.

Dean, A. L. The structure of imagery. *Child Development*, 1976, *47*, 949–958.

Dean, A. L. Patterns of change in relations between children's anticipatory imagery and operative thought. *Developmental Psychology*, 1979, *15*, 153–163.

Dean, A. L., & Harvey, W. O. An information processing analysis of a Piagetian imagery task. *Developmental Psychology*, 1979, *15*, 474–475.

Elkind, D. Discrimination, seriation and numeration of size and dimensional differences in young children: Piaget replication study VI. *Journal of Genetic Psychology*, 1964, *104*, 275–296.

Flavell, J. H. *Concept development*. In P. H. Mussen (Ed.), *Carmichael's manual of child psychology* (3rd ed.) (Vol. 1). New York: Wiley, 1970.

Fraisse, P. *The psychology of time*. London: Eyre & Spottiswoode, 1964.

Friedman, K. C. Time concepts of junior and senior high school pupils and of adults. *School Review*, 1944, *52*, 233–238.

Friedman, K. C., & Marti, V. A. A time comprehension test. *Journal of Educational Research*, 1945, *39*, 62–68.

Friedman, W. *The development of children's understanding of temporal cycles*. Unpublished doctoral dissertation, University of Rochester, 1976.

Friedman, W. J. The development of children's understanding of cyclic aspects of time. *Child Development*, 1977, *48*, 1593–1599.

Friedman, W. J. Development of time concepts in children. In H. W. Reese and L. P. Lipsitt (Eds.), *Advances in child development and behavior* (Vol. 12). New York: Academic Press, 1978. (a)

Friedman, W. J. *The development of relational understandings of temporal and spatial prepositions*. Unpublished manuscript, Oberlin College, 1978. (b)

Friedman, W. J. *The development of temporal reasoning from childhood to adolescence*. Paper presented at the biennial meeting of the Society for Research in Child Development, San Francisco, March 1979.

Galton, F. *Inquiries into human faculty and its development*. New York: Macmillan, 1883.

Gelman, R., & Gallistel, C. R. *The child's understanding of number*. Cambridge, Mass.: Harvard University Press, 1978.

Goodnow, J. J. Matching auditory and visual series: Modality problem or translation problem. *Child Development*, 1971, *42*, 1187–1201.

Guilford, J. P. Spatial symbols in the apprehension of time. *American Journal of Psychology*, 1926, *37*, 420–423.

Hadamard, J. *An essay on the psychology of invention in the mathematical field*. Princeton, N.J.: Princeton University Press, 1945.

Hardwick, D. A., McIntire, C. W., & Pick, H. L. The content and manipulation of cognitive maps in children and adults. *Monographs of the Society for Research in Child Development*, 1976, *41*, (3, Serial No. 166).

Harris, J. E. Memory aids people use: Two interview studies. *Memory and Cognition*, 1980, *8*, 31–38.

Harrison, M. The nature and development of concepts of time among young children. *Elementary School Journal*, 1934, *34*, 507–514.

Hazen, N. L., Lockman, J. J., & Pick, H. L. The development of children's representations of large scale environments. *Child Development*, 1978, *49*, 623–636.

Inhelder, B., & Piaget, J. *The growth of logical thinking from childhood to adolescence*. New York: Basic Books, 1958.

Jahoda, G. Children's concepts of time and history. *Educational Review*, 1963, *15*, 87–104.

Keating, D. P. Toward a multivariate theory of intelligence. In D. Kuhn (Ed.), *Intellectual Development Beyond Childhood*. San Francisco: Jossey-Bass, 1979.

Koriat, A., & Fishhoff, B. What day is today? An inquiry into the process of time orientation. *Memory and Cognition*, 1974, *2*, 201–205.

Kosslyn, S. M. Information representation in visual images. *Cognitive Psychology*, 1975, *7*, 341–370.

Kosslyn, S. M. Using imagery to retrieve semantic information: A developmental study. *Child Development*, 1976, *47*, 434-444.

Kosslyn, S. M., Ball, T. M., & Reiser, B. J. Visual images preserve metric spatial information: Evidence from studies of image scanning. *Journal of Experimental Psychology: Human Perception and Performance*, 1978, *4*, 47-60.

Kosslyn, S. M., & Pomerantz, J. R. Imagery, propositions, and the form of internal representations. *Cognitive Psychology*, 1977, *9*, 52-76.

Lindsay, P. H., & Norman, D. A. *Human information processing: An introduction to psychology.* New York: Academic Press, 1972.

Maccoby, E. M., & Jacklin, C. N. *The psychology of sex differences.* Stanford, Cal.: Stanford University Press, 1974.

Marmor, G. Development of kinetic images: When does the child first represent movement in mental images? *Cognitive Psychology*, 1975, *7*, 548-559.

Marmor, G. S. Mental rotation and number conservation: Are they related? *Developmental Psychology*, 1977, *13*, 320-325.

McGee, M. G. Human spatial abilities: Psychometric studies and environmental, genetic, hormonal, and neurological influences. *Psychological Bulletin*, 1979, *86*, 889-918.

Neimark, E. D. Longitudinal development of formal operations thought. *Genetic Psychology Monographs*, 1975, *91*, 171-225.

Oakden, E. C., & Sturt, M. The development of the knowledge of time in children. *British Journal of Psychology*, 1922, *12*, 309-336.

Oswald, I. Number-forms and kindred visual images. *Journal of General Psychology*, 1960, *63*, 81-88.

Paivio, A. *Imagery and verbal processes.* New York: Holt, Rinehart & Winston, 1971.

Paivio, A. Dual coding: Theoretical issues and empirical evidence. In J. C. Scandura & C. J. Brainerd (Eds.), *Structural/Process models of complex human behavior.* Alphen aan den Rijn. The Netherlands: Sijthoff & Noordhoff, 1978. (a)

Paivio, A. Comparison of mental clocks. *Journal of Experimental Psychology: Human Perception and Performance*, 1978, *4*, 61-71. (b)

Parkinson, S. R. Short-term memory while shadowing: Multiple-item recall of visually and aurally presented letters. *Journal of Experimental Psychology*, 1972, *92*, 256-265.

Piaget, J. *The child's conception of the world.* London: Routledge & Kegan Paul, 1929.

Piaget, J. *Structuralism.* New York: Basic Books, 1970.

Piaget, J. *The child's conception of time.* London: Routledge-Kegan Paul, 1969.

Piaget, J., & Inhelder, B. *Mental imagery in the child.* New York: Basic Books, 1971.

Pistor, F. How time concepts are acquired by children. *Educational Method*, 1940, *20*, 107-112.

Price, J. R., & Tare, W. A cross-cultural study of recall of time-related and non-time-related verbal material. *International Journal of Psychology*, 1975, *10*, 247-254.

Reese, H. W. Imagery and associative memory. In R. V. Kail & J. W. Hagen (Eds.), *Perspectives on the development of memory and cognition.* Hillsdale, N.J.: Erlbaum, 1977.

Ross, B. M., & Kerst, S. M. Developmental memory theories: Baldwin and Piaget. In H. W. Reese & L. P. Lipsitt (Eds.), *Advances in child development and behavior* (Vol. 12). New York: Academic Press, 1978.

Shepard, R. N. The mental image. *American Psychologist*, 1978, *33*, 125-137. (a)

Shepard, R. N. Externalization of mental images and the act of creation. In B. S. Randhawa & W. E. Coffman (Eds.), *Visual learning, thinking and communication.* New York: Academic Press, 1978. (b)

Shepard, R. N., & Metzler, J. Mental rotation of three-dimensional objects. *Science*, 1971, *171*, 701-703.

Siegel, A. W., & White, S. H. The development of spatial representations of large-scale environ-
    ments. In H. W. Reese (Ed.), *Advances in Child Development and Behavior* (Vol. 10). New
    York: Academic Press, 1975.

Sorokin, P. A., & Merton, R. K. Social time: A methodological and functional analysis. *American
    Journal of Sociology,* 1937, *42,* 615–629.

Springer, D. Development in young children of an understanding of time and the clock. *Journal of
    Genetic Psychology,* 1952, *80,* 83–96.

Sternberg, R. J. *The development of human intelligence.* (Tech. Rep. No. 4, Cognitive Development
    Series). Yale University, Department of Psychology, 1979.

Tulving, E. Episodic and semantic memory. In E. Tulving & W. Donaldson (Eds.), *Organization
    and memory.* New York: Academic Press, 1972.

Werner, H., & Kaplan, B. *Symbol formation.* New York: Wiley, 1963.

Winer, G. Class-inclusion reasoning in children: A review of the empirical literature. *Child De-
    velopment,* 1980, *51,* 309–328.

Zern, D. The influence of certain child-rearing factors upon the development of a structured and
    salient sense of time. *Genetic Psychology Monographs,* 1970, *81,* 197–254.

Merry Bullock
Rochel Gelman
Renée Baillargeon

The Development of Causal Reasoning[1]

For the world mankind has hacked out of chaos—all science, art, religion, and indeed civilization itself—depends for its existence on the basic limiting principles: that no effect can precede its cause, that effects must be physically related to causes, that cause and effect if separated in space must also be separated in time, and that mind cannot operate independently of brain.

John Gardner, *The Resurrection*[2]

INTRODUCTION

Our understanding of the physical world and, in particular, of the changes—the displacements and the transformations—that take place within it, rests in large part on our ability to group temporally successive occurrences into coherent units. The world does not appear to us as an ever-changing stream of coincidental, arbitrary occurrences. To the contrary, our perceptions, memories, and descriptions all tend to be of events occurring in organized patterns (cf. Mandler, 1980; Neisser, 1976; Schank & Abelson, 1977) over specific time courses (Gibson, 1980).

How do we establish the boundaries of events? It is clear that the perception of discrete, temporally bounded events requires "bracketing" simultaneous and/or successive occurrences together. A fundamental basis for this partitioning is provided by our tendency to perceive or infer cause–effect relations.

[1]This work was supported by NIMH predoctoral fellowship 1-F31-HD-05588 and SSHRC general grant to UBC, 66-3157 to M. Bullock; NICHHD grant No. HD-10965 and NSF grants No. BNS 770327 and 80-40573 to R. Gelman; and Quebec Department of Education grant to R. Baillargeon.

[2]Reprinted from *The Resurrection,* copyright 1966 by John Gardner, Reprinted with permission of the author.

209

Consider the act of cutting bread. This could be described simply as two interlocking sequences of knife movements and bread movements, occurring over time. However, because we regard the parting of the bread to be *caused by* the knife's action, we perceive not a succession of separate, coincidental movements, but one event, a knife cutting bread. This example illustrates two points. First, by imposing a causal connection, we efficiently collapse a series of temporally successive motions into a single event. Second, by this bracketing into causal events, we not only separate meaningful, coherent patterns from all that goes on around us, but also impart structure to the world. When we attribute the parting of the bread to the knife's action, we relate actions to results, transformations to outcomes, and thus construct our own physical reality.

A tendency to relate events causally underlies much of the learning during development, especially concerning the physical world. We learn how the objects around us characteristically work, and we use this knowledge to predict, influence, and eventually explain those actions. We learn what transformations can be applied to what objects, with what likely outcomes, and again use this knowledge to bring about desired ends or avoid undesirable ones. We could describe this learning by saying that we discover relations between objects or occurrences in time. In this sense, our understanding of events would be derived from a representation of the temporal sequencing of particular instances. However, the notion that we frame events in terms of causal relations implies that our representations of temporal sequences are mediated by an understanding of cause–effect relations. That is, the "limiting principles" specified by John Gardner in the epigram may influence how the temporal flow of occurrences is parsed, interpreted, and understood.

In this chapter we will consider how children apply causal understanding to physical events in time. We will address two related questions: (*a*) How does a causal framework operate? (*b*) How does it develop? Since models in developmental psychology must ultimately make reference to how we as adults operate in the world, we begin with a model of adult causal thinking—one that we believe captures the ways in which adults reason about everyday events. After we review the extant literature in light of this model, we present recent experimental evidence that suggests that children as young as 3 years of age relate physical events in much the same manner as adults. In addition to an analysis of the nature of causal understanding, the studies we report address the general methodological issues of assessing the thinking of young preschoolers.

A Characterization of Causal Reasoning

We present below a "common-sense" model of the organization that seems to underlie our everyday ideas about cause and effect. We believe the adult's understanding of causal events is constrained by a small set of assumptions, or principles, which not only define what could constitute a causal event, but delimit as well the type of information adults look for or consider when making causal attributions. Although there may be overlap in application in this model, we distinguish conceptually between *principles* underlying the definition of cause and effect, *stimulus information* used in making causal attributions, and the role of general *knowledge* about objects in causal attributions and causal explanations.

CAUSAL PRINCIPLES

At least three separate principles underlie an adult's definition of cause–effect relations. A first principle is *Determinism*. Adults typically assume that physical events are caused, so they are reluctant, if not unwilling, to allow causeless occurrences. Imagine, for instance, a window shattering. We are likely to believe someone or something caused the window to break, even if we cannot identify who or what it was. We might be forced, in other words, to confess ignorance of the precise *identity* of the cause of the shattering, but we are not likely to doubt that it exists.

A second principle, that of *Priority*, concerns the temporal ordering of causes and effects. For adults, the causal relation is always unidirectional: causes precede or are coincidental with their effects. In our example of a window shattering, adults would consider *only* events that occurred prior to the breakage when searching for a possible cause. Events that followed would simply not be admitted as candidate causes.

We include a third principle, *Mechanism*, as central to the psychological definition of cause–effect relations. Adults typically assume that causes bring about their effects by transfer of causal impetus, effected directly (e.g., two billiard balls colliding), or through a chain of intermediary events (e.g., starting the engine of a car). This assumption leads adults to look for antecedents that they know, or at least suspect, *could* have produced the phenomenon to be explained. Thus, in the case of the shattered window, we would search for objects (e.g., a bullet, a boomerang, a chair) whose impact we knew might have broken the glass; conversely, we would ignore objects (e.g., a feather, a sponge, a pin) whose lesser impact would surely have left the window intact. It is important to note that this attitude can lead to the selection of real or imagined events, including supernatural ones.

The adult's assumption and use of the principles of determinism, priority, and mechanism need not imply that the world operates according to these or even similar principles. The veracity of a determined, temporally bound, mechanistic universe is an issue debated by both philosophers and physicists. Still, we claim that these principles are an essential part of an adult's *causal theory* or *causal attitude,* and as such contribute to the structuring and interpretation of events.

While the principles of determinism, priority, and mechanism constrain causal attributions, they do not in themselves specify the causes of events. The choice of which of a set of possible causes led to a particular outcome must ultimately depend on what an individual understands about the events involved. This may include a general knowledge of the kinds of transformations that occur in the physical world, as well as specific information about the particular events. The role of knowledge will be considered in a later section. We turn now to the role of stimulus information.

THE ROLE OF STIMULUS CUES IN
THE SELECTION OF CAUSES

The ways in which causal judgments are affected by stimulus cues can be illustrated most clearly in a case where adults do not have complete knowledge of the phenomenon to be explained.

Say we are shown a large covered box, told it contains a bell, and asked to decide which of three marbles made the bell ring. The first marble is dropped through a hole in the top of the box, a few seconds go by, and then the remaining two marbles are dropped, one through the hole, the other next to the box. A second or two later the bell rings. Our most likely answer in this situation is to say the second marble dropped inside the box was the cause. This marble was dropped immediately prior to the bell's sound, and it went inside the box, making physical contact between marble and bell possible. Now it could easily turn out that the first marble dropped was in fact responsible for the ringing of the bell—if, for example, some complex, slow-moving mechanism had been activated which resulted, many seconds later, in the bell ringing. Clearly, the probability of a *correct* causal attribution is lower when only temporal and spatial cues are available. Still, a reliance on the cues of temporal and spatial contiguity serves as an excellent rule of thumb since in many causal sequences causes *are* found to be temporally and spatially contiguous to their effects. Given this, it comes as no surprise that temporal and spatial contiguity have been shown to be particularly important for generating "causal perceptions" in adults. Michotte (1963) and others (Gruber, Fink & Damm, 1957; Olum, 1957) demonstrated that adults will have a strong, direct impression of a causal connection between events when these cues are provided, even when they know the connection is in fact illusory.

Adults do not, however, rely on temporal and spatial cues only when they lack knowledge relevant to a particular situation, or when confronted with schematic sequences such as those devised by Michotte (1963; Bassili, 1976; Olum, 1957). Adults also use information about relative contiguity to decide among different potential causes. If two rocks were thrown at our window, one after the other, but both before the window shattered, we would probably consider as cause the one that arrived at the window just before it broke. In other words, given two plausible causes (either rock could have broken the window), we would select the one immediately prior to the effect as the cause. It is important to realize that our use of temporal contiguity may be mediated by our general knowledge of rocks and windows (i.e., windows shatter immediately upon impact). Had we been told that the particular window in question shattered no sooner than three seconds after impact, we might have chosen differently. Similarly, spatial contiguity may help decide between two plausible causes. We will be most likely to pick the one closer in space to an effect, unless we know of some reason why this cue might be misleading (magnetic or electrical phenomena come to mind here). The use of spatial and temporal information is in accordance with the principles previously outlined. The assumptions of priority and mechanism allow us to use the temporal and spatial relations among events to decide among possible causes.[3]

Another source of information about possible causes comes from the contingency relations between events. Covariation of one event with another, or the marked regularity with which events co-occur, is likely to lead us to suspect a causal connection (see the literature on attribution theory, especially Kelley, 1973; Nisbett & Ross, 1979, for more detailed discussions of covariation and sufficiency arguments). Covariation and contingency information are important for causal attributions made over a number of experiences. However, they neither speak to how we form a causal impression in the single case, nor to how we learn about causal transformations in general. We will return to the use of contingency information in our concluding discussion when we consider the role of necessary and sufficient conditions in providing explanations for events.

THE ROLE OF KNOWLEDGE IN THE SELECTION OF CAUSES

An adult's choice of a cause is constrained by the principles which mediate the interpretation of stimulus information. Further, it is influenced by two sources of knowledge. One is specific and concerns the types of events involved; the other is more general and concerns an understanding of transformations over time.

To illustrate the role of specific knowledge, the choice of a cause for our familiar broken window will depend in part on such things as knowledge of the brittleness of glass, the force of impact, and so on. If this knowledge is incomplete, the range of possible causes will be restricted. An individual who did not

---

[3]We are ignoring, for this discussion, instances that may be labeled "over-determined," and are assuming a choice of one cause. There are of course exceptions to this. Say two bombs hit a target within seconds of each other. Either alone could have caused the resulting explosion, thus both could be causes, and the *relative* temporal or spatial information is not relevant. In other words, both are sufficient causes, and it is likely that we would say that both bombs were causes. However, in many everyday events with these same properties, we do tend to identify single causes, even at the expense of oversimplifying the matter.

know that sound waves exert force would most likely (and perhaps mistakenly) reject the notion that a sonic boom or Ella Fitzgerald's voice could ever be responsible. Similarly, if asked whether an ''irredentist'' was the cause, we would be uncertain until we knew what an ''irredentist'' was, or at least what *type* of thing it was. The nature and extent of one's knowledge about the physical world thus plays a central role in determining which antecedents one will allow to play a causal role.

Related to our tendency to bracket events in terms of causal relations is a more general ability to track objects through time and over transformations. Framing events in causal terms imposes a unidirectional relation over time. This relation may be described in terms of cause and effect, or in terms of a transformation that has changed the state of some object or event. The unidirectionality of causal sequences implies that the transformations they embody are also unidirectional. For example, while a rock's action may transform a window, the window's shattering does not cause the rock to move. To understand events in this way, one needs to be able to relate object states to each other, infer the connecting transformations, and distinguish the direction of transformations.

CAUSAL UNDERSTANDING AND CAUSAL EXPLANATIONS

It is necessary at this point to distinguish two senses of causal knowledge. In one sense, knowledge can be explicit, accessible, and articulable. In this case, we gauge how someone understands an event by what he or she says about it. The person who declares ''causes precede effects,'' for example, has an explicit knowledge of at least one of the defining criteria of cause.

In a second sense, an individual may be said to possess knowledge about an event when she or he treats it in a principled, consistent manner. This more tacit knowledge can be detected through its systematic influence on behavior. It need not be accessible to conscious reflection and may not be articulated in causal explanations. We need not, for example, be able to articulate the fact that priority is a causal principle to only pick prior events as causes.

The relation of causal explanations to the senses of understanding just outlined is not direct. We may possess principles defining cause and effect, we may use stimulus information in a particular way, we may be able to relate object states and transformations in time; yet, explanations require something more: we must understand *what* an explanation entails. While statements given in answer to ''Why did it happen?'' may range from a restatement of the phenomenon (''*It fell*''), to identification of a salient feature of the event (''*It wasn't nailed in too well*''), to complex chains of interpolated causal mediation (''*The picture fell off the wall because vibrations from the jack hammer sent shock waves through the foundation, up the walls, across the beams, and caused the wire to jiggle and break*''), in general we accept as more adequate those explanations that make reference to some implied or demonstrated mechanism, indicating *how* a cause brought about its effect rather than the fact that it did so. We might expect, then, that the quality of explanations will depend on our interpretation of the question asked, the ease with which we can postulate the nature of a mechanism, and the extent to which we understand that explaining is different from restating an event.

Developmental Evidence

In distinguishing causal principles, information about the stimulus environment, and general knowledge, we have implied that the principles are fundamental to the structuring of causal reasoning, constraining the uses of stimulus information and general knowledge. The ontological questions then are: How have the principles arisen, and do they change over development? We may conceptualize at least three distinct models that address these issues.

A first model, one most directly related to the empiricist philosophical approach (cf. Hume, 1748/1955), postulates that the principles underlying adult causal thinking are abstractions from repeated experience with the world. This model could take different positions on how the principles are abstracted, from simple associations (cf. Kendler & Kendler, 1975) to the detection of event invariances (cf. Gibson, 1966), but it would claim that the principles underlying adults' causal reasoning are derived from, not responsible for, the structuring of events.

A second approach, one more related to a structuralist philosophical stance (cf. Kant, 1787/1965), reverses the relation between stimulus information and principles, and postulates that the principles reflect a prior organization that the mind imposes on experience. This second approach provides two models. In one, the organization that the mind imposes on experience is seen to change with development; thus, children's thinking should be characterized by a different set of principles than adults'. In the other model, the organization underlying causal thinking may remain constant throughout development, but may be only imperfectly reflected in children's reasoning because of performance limitations.

Developmental researchers have not, by and large, explicitly acknowledged these models. However, the extant literature may be roughly divided into those studies that have focused on the use of stimulus informaiton, and those that focused on characterizing underlying principles or organizaiton, allowing us to categorize them along the empiricist and structuralist lines. We shall categorize our brief review of the literature accordingly. First, we consider those studies that address the issue of the use of stimulus information: What cues do children notice? How is stimulus information combined? and How is children's use of information limited or different from adults'?

EMPIRICIST STUDIES

While it is generally agreed that even young children use temporal information, specifically temporal contiguity (e.g., Kuhn & Phelps, 1976; Shultz &
Mendelson, 1975; Siegler & Liebert, 1974; Wilde & Coker, 1978), there is
disagreement over whether children are limited to the use of *only* temporal
contiguity. For example, both Shultz and Mendelson (1975) and Kuhn and
Phelps (1976) presented evidence suggesting that initially children were as likely
to pick subsequent events as antecedent events when asked for the cause of a
particular occurrence. This research suggested that while contiguity information
was used, children did not understand the unidirectional nature of the cause–
effect relation. Kun (1978), however, has shown that preschoolers *will* use order
information when judging picture sequences of activities. Similarly, others have
argued that even very young children's representations of events include order of
occurrence (e.g., Brown, 1975; Copple & Coon, 1977; Mandler, 1980).[4]

Spatial cues also affect children's attributions under some circumstances.
Mendelson and Shultz (1976), for example, reported that preschoolers were more
likely to pick a temporally contiguous but inconsistent event as cause over a
consistent, noncontiguous event unless there was a spatial connection (or contiguity) between antecedent and effect. Similarly, Lesser (1977) and Koslowski
(1976) both reported that preschoolers were *less* likely to pick a spatially removed event as cause. Although these studies are primarily suggestive about the
role of spatial information, they do indicate that spatial information may, in some
circumstances, be used in causal judgments. Wilde and Coker (1978) found that
children as young as 3 required spatial contiguity between cause and effect for
events that involved motion or hitting (such as moving blocks).

Children's use of stimulus information other than contiguity, particularly the
covariation of events, seems to be affected by both the complexity of the events
and the child's prior knowledge. Preschoolers (3–4 years of age will select, as
cause, an antecedent that consistently co-occurs with an event over another
antecedent that occurs less regularly (Shultz & Mendelson, 1975; Wilde &
Coker, 1978). However, the influence of covariation information is more limited
in younger children's attributions, especially if they must extract it over a time
delay or if it contrasts with contiguity information (Siegler, 1975; Wilde &
Coker, 1978). Siegler presented children aged 5–9 with a choice between a
temporally contiguous but inconsistent cause (a computer whose lights flashed on
and off), and a cause that regularly preceded the effect by 5 seconds (the insertion

---

[4]The researchers claimed they were investigating order cues. However, in terms of our model, it is
possible that children's responses were constrained by the priority principle. thus making the use of
order cues a matter of course. This argument may also be applied to the cue of spatial contact versus
the principle of mechanism.

of a card into a sorter). Older children picked the regular event as cause; younger children were more likely to pick the contiguous event.

Wilde and Coker (1978) have similarly reported that while all their 4- to 8-year-old subjects used temporal and spatial contiguity cues, only the older (6 and 8 years old) children's attributions used covariation information when it contrasted with contiguity information.

Several investigators have suggested that children's use of stimulus information is influenced by their familiarity with or general knowledge about the events they witness. Ausubel and Schiff (1954), for instance, had children learn to predict which side of a teeter-totter would fall when its supporting pins were removed. In one series of trials, children learned that the longest side of the teeter-totter would always fall (''relevant'' condition). In another series of trials, they learned that the side supporting a red block would always fall (the ''irrelevant'' condition). Ausubel and Schiff found that kindergarteners required the same number of trials to learn either relationship, while sixth graders required significantly more trials to learn the irrelevant relationship than the relevant relationship. The authors suggested that the older children's greater experience with teeter-totters might have facilitated their learning the relevant relationship, as well as inhibited their learning the irrelevant relationship.

In general, investigators looking at the use of stimulus information have argued that the preschooler's appreciation of cause–effect relations is incomplete relative to older children's or adults'. Preschoolers rely more on temporal contiguity, even when additional information such as regularity or covariation is available. The differences between older and younger children are not, though, usually ascribed to reasoning or inference processes per se, but to other processes such as memory (Shultz & Mendelson, 1975), perceptual distractibility (Siegler, 1975), differential weighting (Wilde & Coker, 1978), or familiarity with the events (Berzonsky, 1971; Ausubel & Schiff, 1954).

While studies in the empiricist tradition provide a good deal of valuable information concerning the cues children can and do use, they do not, in our opinion, provide a complete account of children's causal understanding. Attributions in these studies were undoubtedly influenced by the stimulus information. However, the very fact that children used some, but not all, of the available stimulus information suggests that some organization guided the use of stimulus cues. In other words, children's attributions may have been directed by hypotheses about ways in which events could be causally related. This suggests that a characterization of causal reasoning that stresses the *interpretation* of physical situations, rather than the use of kinds of stimulus information, might provide a richer, more satisfactory account of children's understanding.

In offering this criticism of the empiricist approach, we do not mean to deny the role of stimulus cues in children's causal reasoning, but only to suggest that the interpretation of such cues may be constrained by children's assumptions about the nature of cause–effect relations. We would further argue that studies focusing on stimulus information may be tacitly testing principle use. Those children who pay attention to order cues may do so because of a principle of priority; similarly, those whose responses vary with spatial contiguity cues may be following a principle of mechanism that directs them to look for possible contact. Differences between younger and older children's attributions might then be interpreted to reflect younger children's inabilities to formulate satisfactory hypotheses concerning the way in which specific causes might be connected to their effects, due either to their limited physical knowledge or to their failure to use underlying adult causal principles. This final suggestion leads us to the structuralist approaches to causal understanding.

STRUCTURALIST STUDIES

A second line of research has focused less qn children's use of particular stimulus information, and more on the issue of principle development. In contrast to characterizing developmental differences in terms of changes in the ability to extract causal relations from stimulus arrays, this view asks about children's criteria for defining events as causal.

Such a focus underlies the work by Piaget (1930, 1974), who claims that children's use of stimulus information is different from adults' because they interpret it according to different criteria or principles. He and his collaborators asked children to explain a variety of natural phenomena (e.g., the cycle of the moon, the floating of boats) and mechanical events (e.g., bicycles and steam engines). Analyses of the children's explanations led Piaget to characterize the preschool child's thought as *precausal*. Young children appeared to be fundamentally indifferent to causal mechanisms. Unlike older children, they never concerned themselves with the question of *how* a cause could actually bring about an effect, but took co-occurrence in time or space as sufficient indication of a causal relation. Young children also appeared indifferent to the temporal direction in which causal events occurred, taking the first or the second of two successive events as cause of the other. Finally, children did not restrict the types of events that could be causally related, attributing nonphysical causes to physical events. This is because the preschooler's approach to reality is profoundly subjective: the physical and psychological realms of their everyday experiences are not yet fully differentiated, and children do not distinguish physical, psychological, and supernatural events as being of different types. Thus, children often attributed the results of their actions to their own wishes and feelings, or explained the displacements and transformations of inanimate objects in terms of properties and motivations more appropriately reserved to sentient beings.

According to Piaget, then, the structure of the young child's thought is qualitatively different from that of an older child or adult. While there is empirical support for Piaget's observations (e.g., Dennis & Russell, 1940; Laurendau & Pinard, 1962), his conclusions may be questioned on both theoretical and methodological grounds.

First, the standard Piaget used in evaluating his subjects's explanations may have been too stringent. Only those children who offered correct explanations were classed as demonstrating "truly causal" understanding. It is not clear, though, that adults would always be granted "truly causal" understanding given these criteria. It is not uncommon to hear mention of psychological causes (*"My car died"*), omission of mechanism (*"The moon affects my mood"*), or causation by an aspect of the event (*"The cup broke because it's fragile"*). It is unlikely that adults who give these sorts of explanations lack principles of causation such as mechanism, although it is difficult to tell from their explanations. Moreover, without precise knowledge of elementary physics, explanations will be less precise and, according to the Piagetian position, less advanced developmentally.

Investigators have also questioned Piaget's conclusions because of the nature of the phenomena Piaget asked his subjects to explain. Most of his questions concerned events with which young children have little direct contact (e.g., the moon, steam engines). Yet, many investigators have noted that the quality of children's explanations is directly related to their familiarity with the target events (e.g., Berzonsky, 1971; Huang, 1943; Mogar, 1960; Nass, 1956). Finally, Piaget's conclusions that preschoolers' thoughts are precausal are based almost exclusively on explanation data. Harkening back to our earlier discussion of kinds of knowledge, the ability to provide an explanation for an event may require far more than an understanding of how the event is produced. Whichever criterion one uses to classify children's explanations, there always remains the distinct possibility that children's poor explanations reflect their limited verbal skills, and/or an inadequate understanding of what constitutes a good or satisfactory explanation.

All of this suggests that Piaget's account of the development of causal reasoning may be inaccurate: his criteria for mature causal reasoning may be too stringent and, given the added requirement of articulated explanations, may assess more than causal thinking.[5] Nonetheless, the Piagetian position is important because of the focus on the underlying organization of causal understanding.

---

[5]Of course, Piaget's treatment of causality in the infant derived from behavioral, not explanation, data. However, in the Piagetian account, causal reasoning depends on representational abilities denied to the infant, so the issues of underlying definitional principles would not be relevant during the sensorimotor period.

Let us assume for a moment that when children reason about causes and effects, they do *not* abide by the same principles as adults. How then do they later come to recognize and use these principles? Piaget argued that the young child starts off with incorrect beliefs and, over development, comes to construct the correct adultlike beliefs. Alternatively, it could be that the young child makes *no* specific assumptions about the nature or status of cause–effect realtions, and adopts the adult's beliefs one by one, at successive points in development. (Koslowski, 1976, makes this argument with respect to the belief in mechanism.) In any event, whether one believes children proceed from an absence of beliefs or change erroneous ones, they are postulated to reason about causal events in a mode qualitatively distinct from adults.

Alternatively, adults and children might share the same reasoning principles and thus have the same implicit causal theory. This does not deny that young children perform less well than older children in causal tasks, but it interprets those failures differently. Huang (1943), for instance, collected explanations for various phenomena from children aged 5–10 years and college students. He concluded that children's and adults' explanations differed only in sophistication and particular content, not in form, and suggested that specific knowledge plays a large role in causal explanations. Perhaps it is not the principles that change with development, but rather the ability to apply these principles to a broad range of events, and to access them to mediate the content of explanations.

The conceptual differences between this alternative and the preceding one lie in the question of whether or not there is a qualitative shift in the structure of causal reasoning over development, and in the role granted to specific experience. Thus, when attempting to distinguish betweeen these two alternatives, the empirical task becomes one of asking *whether* preschoolers' causal judgments seem constrained (as are adults') by particular underlying causal principles, and *how* the nature and extent of specific knowledge affects causal attributions.

If young children reason about events according to a tacit definition of cause–effect relations similar to the adult's, we should find that they assume events obey the principles of determinism, priority, and mechanism, they should use spatial and temporal information in particular ways, and relate object states across transformations. However, since the extent of any specific knowledge base changes ontogenetically, the content and sophistication of causal *explanations* should demonstrate the most obvious change—not only in form, but in accuracy as well.

The remainder of this chapter will discuss research work that led us to favor the alternative that children and adults share the same causal reasoning principles. In our empirical work we have focused on tacit knowledge rather than explicit explanations, and we have considered reasoning about a limited class of events: those that involved inanimate objects (e.g., physical events), were discrete, temporally bounded sequences, and that afforded clearly separable cause–effect components.

In exploring the structure of children's thinking about physical causality, we addressed two related developmental questions: (*a*) Do preschoolers show evidence of reasoning about causal matters according to the same principles as adults? (*b*) What role *does* factual information play in children's causal attributions, and how is this reflected in their judgments and explanations of events?

EMPIRICAL STUDIES

We have attempted to test the issues raised in the last section by examining causal understanding in preschool-aged children. There are, of course, substantial methodological problems in studying thinking in very young subjects. For one thing, it is not always easy to decide whether a child's inferior performance on a particular task should be ascribed to poor verbal skills, task difficulty, motivational deficits, or truly deficient reasoning. Until the first three factors have been ruled out, one cannot draw definite conclusions about the status of the child's understanding.

In our research we have attempted to rely less on explanations than on other responses, such as predictions, judgments, and direct manipulations. We, like others (e.g., Brainerd, 1977; Donaldson, 1978), take the position that the underlying structure of a child's knowledge may not be reflected in that child's verbalizations. Those investigators who have characterized preschoolers as "precausal," most notably Piaget, have done so primarily on the basis of explanation data. In general, children's explanations *are* different from older children's and adults'. When asked to talk about events, children do seem to violate the principles of determinism, priority, and mechanism. Since it is not clear how to interpret these data, we structured our tasks so that children's predictions and judgments could serve as the primary data base.

Task difficulty and motivational variables were also taken into account. In some studies children were shown novel, although very simple, event sequences; in others we used relatively complex event sequences, but allowed children to become familiar with them before being tested. Serious efforts were made to construct events that would be attractive to young children and that could actively involve the subject in the procedures.

In general, our tasks involved presenting children with event sequences that could be interpreted in different ways, depending on the presence or absence of a set of underlying principles defining cause and effect. By careful analysis of judgments, predictions, and attributions, we hoped to infer the reasoning that guided children's responses. For example, if the choice of an event as cause carries with it the belief that there must be some connection between cause and effect (the mechanism principle), sequences in which antecedent and end components have no obvious means of contact should elicit different reactions than sequences in which a plausible connection is available. Similarly, if temporal order determines causal direction, then only antecedent events should be chosen as causes.

The studies reported in the following sections provide converging evidence on preschoolers' causal reasoning abilities. In some cases, we compare responses within one study; in others, we compare responses across experiments. This method is not direct: There are considerable inferential leaps from a description of what children do and say in different tasks to a description of their causal understanding. Still, in the course of this chapter we hope the reader will come to agree that these leaps are warranted, and that it is indeed possible to tap young children's knowledge about causal relations in the physical world.

The order in which the studies are reported traces the different questions we have raised concerning causal understanding: (*a*) Do children's attributions reflect underlying principles that define cause–effect relations? (*b*) How is stimulus information used in causal judgments? (*c*) How does knowledge of specific events or general transformations influence causal judgments?

Causal Principles

To find out if in fact children's reasoning is based on tacit causal principles, we designed studies that made it possible for children to behave in one way if their judgments were mediated by a principle, and to behave in another way if they were not. In this manner, we could see if situations informed by a principle made a difference.

PRIORITY

Bullock and Gelman (1979) investigated 3-, 4-, and 5-year-olds' use of the priority principle to identify the cause of an event. Subjects were shown a sequence of three events (X–Y–X'), and were asked whether the first (X) or the last (X') event was responsible for the occurrence of the intermediate event (Y). The first and last events were physically identical: each consisted of a ball rolling down a runway. The intermediate event was a jack-in-the-box popping up. The apparatus, pictured in the top half of Figure 8.1, consisted of two mirror-image ball-runway boxes, placed on either side of a jack-in-the-box. The ball events were produced by dropping a ball in a hole in the top of each runway box; the

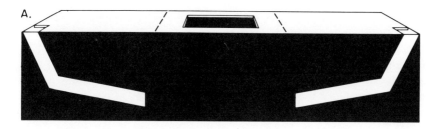

Figure 8.1. Apparatus for priority study. A. Configuration for initial demonstrations. B. Configuration for "separated" control conditions. Reprinted with permission from *Child Development*, 1979, *50*, 89–96.

runways gave the appearance of disappearing into the jack box. Children saw three demonstration sequences (the location of X or X', that is, to the right or left of the jack, was counterbalanced across subjects). They were asked which ball had made the jack come up. Bullock and Gelman reasoned that children who were truly indifferent to the order of cause and effect would choose at random between the first and last events; by contrast, children who assumed that causes can only precede their effects in time would consistently select the first, antecedent event as cause. They found that 75%, 87%, and 100%, respectively, of the 48 3-, 4-, and 5-year-olds tested consistently chose the first event as the cause of the jack popping up.

This result suggested that children as young as 3 years of age shared the adult's assumption of priority. To assure that it was order per se that directed the subjects' choices, Bullock and Gelman included two control manipulations at the end of their procedure. The two manipulations were always introduced in the same order. The first one controlled for differential attention to the X over X' event by presenting both components separately with the jack. When then shown the initial X-Y-X' sequence again, a choice of X over X'—coming after direct experience with each component—would provide stronger evidence of the use of the priority principle.

The second control manipulation pitted the priority principle against a cue of spatial contiguity. Lesser (1977) and others (e.g., Koslowski & Snipper, 1977) have suggested that children are generally reluctant to choose an unconnected event over a spatially contiguous one as the cause of an effect. A violation of spatial contact, but not priority, would thus present children with a potential conflict. Faced with such a situation, adults rank temporal order above spatial contiguity and pick the first event because the assumption of priority precludes a cause ever following its effect in time.

At the start of the second manipulation, the X-runway box was moved 2 in away from the jack-in-the-box, resulting in the configuration shown in the bottom half of Figure 8.1. Children were shown two kinds of sequences: X(separated)–Y–X' and X'–Y–X(separated). The children again were asked which event was responsible for the jack's coming up. A choice of X in the first case, but not the second, would indicate that the children relied on the principle of priority, even when it conflicted with the spatial cue. Such a choice would go a long way towards indicating that children not only shared adults' assumption of priority, but recognized the inviolable character of this principle, and interpreted temporal and spatial information accordingly.

Table 8.1 summarizes children's choices across all experimental conditions. Regardless of the location (left or right) of the first event or the spatial gap, children consistently selected the prior event as the cause.

TABLE 8.1

Percentage of Children Who Chose on the Basis of Temporal Order During Experimental Trials in Priority Study (Bullock and Gelman)[a]

	Age		
Type of demonstration trial	3 years	4 years	5 years
1. Initial demonstration	75	87.5	100
2. Judgment after seeing that both X and X' could be causes	87.5	100	100
3. Judgment when first event is separated (X–Y–X')	87.5	100	87.5
4. Judgment when previously second event is first (X'–Y–X)[b]	75	93.8	100

[a] Adapted, with permission, from *Child Development*, 1979, *50*, 89–96.

[b] An order-based choice is to pick X' in this condition.

Bullock and Gelman also analyzed children's explanations of their judgments. They found that only the older children verbalized the basis of their choice: 63% of the 5-year-olds and 43% of the 4-year-olds mentioned temporal order. In contrast, most of the younger subjects either gave no explanation or mentioned (without giving any justification for doing so) some portion or other of the sequence (e.g., "*Ball went*"). Still, the 3-year-olds consistently selected the temporally prior event as cause, strongly suggesting that they believed that causes must precede their effects. That they were unable to articulate the principle that guided their choices (i.e., priority) in no way precludes the possibility of such a principle being available and operative. Rather, it suggests that children's abilities to use a particular principle may long precede their articulation of that use. The existence of such a delay is not surprising given what we know of the development of metaconceptual abilities (e.g., Flavell, 1979).

MECHANISM

Two studies addressed the principle of mechanism. One, the Jack-in-the-box study, compared children's attributions and explanations when a plausible connection between cause and effect was or was not available. The second, the Fred-the-rabbit study, collected children's descriptions of a chain of cause–effect events and their predictions of what would happen when the sequence was modified.

The Jack-in-the-Box Study

Bullock (1979) conducted two experiments that provide information about preschoolers' tendencies to consider the need for a mechanism linking cause and effect events. She utilized variations in a simple event sequence.

Imagine the following: You see a long box. Across its opaque face are two parallel, horizontal windows, sloping downward and covering the left ⅔ of the box. While you watch this box you see two things occur simultaneously: a ball rolls across one of the windows and a light "rolls" across the other window. Both ball and light pass out of sight simultaneously, and a second or two later a jack-in-the-box jumps up from the area of the box to the right of the runways. On the basis of temporal and spatial information, both events are potential causes for the jack's jumping. However, most adults and 3- to 5-year-old subjects in a pilot test (Bullock, 1976) reported that the ball was the cause; it made the jack jump by hitting or releasing it. Subjects focused on the ball rather than light in their attributions, presumably because rolling and hitting can produce movement in another object through impact, while illumination cannot. Thus it seemed that

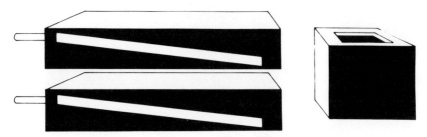

Figure 8.2. Components of the Jack-in-the-Box apparatus.

event type and possible mechanism were matched. However, subjects may have chosen the ball rather than light because they classed illumination as effect, not cause, or because the ball and jack made noise while the lights did not. To analyze *what* information subjects used and whether choosing the ball reflected an underlying principle of mechanism, Bullock repeated this procedure as a *standard sequence* and compared responses with another *unconnected sequence* in which the stimulus cues did not provide a choice consistent with a principled assumption of mechanism. The apparatus for these studies is illustrated in Figure 8.2. It consisted of three component boxes, each made of wood with a shiny black front (see Bullock, 1979, for a complete description). One of the boxes contained a jack-in-the-box (more precisely, a Snoopy-in-the-box) that was operated by a remote control, silent radio transmitter. The other two component boxes had clear windows across their faces. Behind one window was an inclined runway down which a ball could roll and fall silently out at the rear of the boxes. A series of small lights was mounted behind the other window; when the lights were flashed in succession they created the impression of a traveling light.[6] Each box additionally had a colored handle mounted on the side next to the window. The handles could be deflected by pushing down on them; they returned automatically to a horizontal position. The ball and light boxes were stacked one on top of the other (the order varied), and were the same height as the jack-in-the-box.

Although the apparatus consisted of component pieces, each of which was operated independently, it could be assembled so that it appeared to be one box. If the ball or light movement was begun as a handle was deflected, it looked as though the handle had released the action; when the ball and lights preceded the jack, it looked as though they, not a hidden switch, produced the jack's jumping. The events were carefully timed to support the impression of a unified sequence.

[6]This is the *phi phenomenon*. Since it is not clear that the children in Bullock's studies actually saw the lights as one traveling light rather than a series of sequential lights, we refer to it as a traveling series of lights.

The ball and light events took 2 sec, there was a 1-sec lag, then the jack popped up.

In the comparison or *unconnected* experiment, there was a 6-in gap between the end of the runways and the beginning of the jack so that now the ball and light seemingly disappeared just before the open space between the unconnected pieces of the apparatus. Again, after a pause, the jack popped up.

When adults watched the *standard* demonstration, they selected the rolling ball as the causal event. However, when they watched the *unconnected* demonstration, they either rejected both antecedent events as plausible causes or chose the light event. Such choices reflect a concern with mechanism. In the *standard* demonstration the rolling ball disappeared into a spatially contiguous box; hence, its action served as an intermediary (e.g., hitting a lever or spring that released the jack). The light was an unlikely prop in such a mechanical device; hence, despite the fact that it shared the same temporal and spatial characteristics, namely, the outcome event, it was not as plausible a cause as the rolling ball. In the *unconnected* experiment, there was no spatial contiguity between the antecedent and outcome events. Thus, the ball could not in any visible way make contact with the jack-in-the-box. Indeed, neither could the light. However, adults do have considerable experience with electrical phenomena, which often appear to act at a distance and without any obvious spatial contiguity (e.g., light switches and ceiling fixtures; garage door openers, etc.). Thus, the adult who takes mechanisms into account might choose the light. He or she would be unlikely to pick the ball. Bullock reasoned that similar differences in preschoolers' causal attributions to the *standard* and *unconnected* demonstrations would reveal a sensitivity to mechanisms as well as concerns about the plausibility of one mechanism over another.

Sixty 3-, 4-, and 5-year-olds participated in the *standard* and *unconnected* experiments. Independent groups of 10 children from each age level served as subjects. Bullock used hand puppets to tell the children about the events they were to see, and to ask probe questions.

In both experiments, children saw the *standard* or *unconnected* demonstrations after they had become familiar with the runway portion of the apparatus. When a child entered the experimental room, he or she saw only the ball and light boxes, stacked one on top of the other (the box on the top or bottom was counterbalanced across subjects). The child was asked to push one of the two runway handles to "see what happens," and then to push the other. Children were asked to describe each of the runway events to be sure they could label the ball and light movements. The child was then told to "*Make the ball go*" or "*Make the light go*" at least three times. This phase ended with the puppet's asking the child whether he or she liked to see the ball or lights better. (There was no significant bias across children, although 3-year-olds showed a slight preference for the light event.)

Phase 2 of both experiments began when the puppet told the child there was another part to the game and the child's job was to carefully watch everything that happened. The puppet then disappeared "for a nap" and the experimenter brought out the jack-box and either joined it (*standard* experiment) or placed it 6 in away from the ball and light boxes (*unconnected* experiment). Children in both experiments watched three identical demonstration trials: the ball and light began together in time, took 2 sec to travel down their respective runways, disappeared, there was a 1-sec lag, then the jack popped up. During these demonstration trials the handles were not used, although they were in place. To begin each trial the experimenter began the ball action from the rear of the apparatus, out of view of the child; the light event was yoked to the ball's action through an electrical circuit completed through the ball runway. The sequence was completed when the experimenter stepped on the hidden remote control for the jack-in-the-box, allowing it to spring up. After the demonstration trials, the puppet reappeared while the jack was visible and asked the child what had happened. Since all the children provided at least the information that the jack had come up (e.g., "Snoppy came," "it popped," etc.), children were asked how this had occurred, that is, for a causal attribution. Additionally, children were asked to explain *how* the ball, lights, or other stated cause made the jack come up. Following their verbal judgments and explanations, the jack-box was closed and children were asked if there was something they could do to make the jack come up again. Most children spontaneously pulled a handle; if they did not, the experimenter suggested it. The child's handle choice was noted.

By and large children in the standard experiment responded as adults did and picked the ball as the cause of the jack's action both in their verbal judgments and actions. Since handle choices and verbal choices were highly similar, we report only the judgment data. Table 8.2A lists the choices of the 30 3- to 5-year-olds in the standard experiment. From these data we can see that children (*a*) pick an antecedent as the cause of a particular event and (*b*) distinguish between the two types of antecedents.[7]

Bullock coded the childrens' explanations of their choices into three major categories on the basis of scoring systems used in the literature (e.g., Berzonsky, 1971; Laurendau & Pinard, 1962). The categories were *nonnaturalistic* (including no answers, animistic, or magical explanations), *phenomenistic* (merely restated the events seen without connecting them causally), and *mechanistic* (described the events and stated, or inferred, a causal connection). While there

---

[7]Only three children's verbal choices fell into the "other" category: They said that "wires" or "buttons" had made the jack pop up.

TABLE 8.2
Percentage of Children Making each Causal Choice for the Jack-in-the-Box Mechanism Experiments (Bullock)

| | A. Standard experiment | | |
| | | Age | |
Choice	3 years	4 years	5 years
Ball	70	90	70
Light	20	10	10
Other	10	0	20

| | B. Unconnected experiment | | |
| | | Age | |
Choice	3 years	4 years	5 years
Ball	70	10	40
Light	20	60	60
Other	10	30	0

were no age differences in children's choices, the explanations were a different matter. Only the older children's explanations fell into the most advanced category: 90% of the 5-year-olds, 50% of the 4-year-olds, and 10% of the 3-year-olds gave mechanistic explanations. The remaining children tended to give phenomenistic explanations, merely describing the events seen. Interestingly, Bullock found few nonnaturalistic or animistic explanations (two 3-year-olds, one 4-year-old), a finding consistent with other investigations of children's explanations for simple or familiar events (cf. Berzonsky, 1971; Deutsche, 1943; Huang, 1943).

The judgment choices of the 30 children who participated in the unconnected experiment are shown in Table 8.2B. While 3-year-olds tended to pick the ball as cause (as did the children who saw the standard events), 4- and 5-year-olds did not. A comparison of choices in this experiment with those in the standard experiment reveals that the two 3-year-old groups are indistinguishable, while older children responded differently ($\chi^2 = 9.7$, $p < .01$ for the 4-year-olds, and $\chi^2 = 4.2$, $p < .05$ for the 5-year-olds), with most 4-year-olds picking the light and 5-year-olds divided in their choices.

The explanation data suggest that the older children not only noticed the spatial gap, but used it in deciding which antecedent was the cause. Consider first the 5-year-olds: *all* who chose the ball as cause *also* postulated ways that this could have occurred. Their speculations included "very fast" balls, a pathway under the table, or invisible tubes: all implied mechanisms. Those 5-year-old children who picked the light tended to refer to some property of lights that would account for their causal impact, including *"the power of the lights"* or *"electricity can go over."* The 4-year-olds, the majority of whom chose the lights, also mentioned connections, although they were less explicit about the mechanism. By contrast, the explanations of 3-year-olds made no mention of intermediary events or connections. Further, when directly asked whether the ball needed to make contact with the jack, only one 3-year-old agreed that it did.

As a check on her interpretation of children's responses, Bullock recoded each child's protocol for some expression of concern with the implications of the spatial gap. She counted expressions of surprise during the demonstration trials (e.g., *"How did* that *happen?"*) or mention of a connection in either the choice or explanation trials. While 90% of the 5-year-olds and 70% of the 4-year-olds commented on the lack of spatial contact, only 20% of the 3-year-olds did so ($\chi^2_{(2)} = 10.83$, $p < .01$).

Since the 4- and 5-year-old children in both experiments behaved as adults did when confronted with the same demonstrations, it seems fair to conclude that these children did make inferences about mechanisms that can or cannot mediate cause–effect sequences. What can we make of the 3-year-olds' results? In the unconnected experiment, 3-year-olds revealed a remarkable indifference to matters of mechanism; they apparently believed that metal balls can act at a distance. One could conclude that 3-year-olds' understandings do not reflect a use of the principle of mechanism. Alternatively, one could argue that the children knew even less about electrical events than they did about rolling balls and hence had a limited knowledge base from which to make an informed decision. Experiments by Baillargeon and Gelman lead us to prefer the latter interpretation.

Fred-the-Rabbit Experiments

The preceding study suggested that some children's lack of concern about mechanism arose because they lacked specific knowledge about events, not because they lacked principles by which to reason. One way to test this question is to provide children with information about a causal mechanism and see whether they use this information to judge or explain events.

Baillargeon and Gelman (1980) conducted an experiment in which they varied what information 4- and 5-year-olds had about the intermediary parts of a sequence of events. They asked whether those children who knew the precise nature of the intermediary steps would use this information to explain the outcome of the sequence, and to predict how modifications of the sequence affected the outcome. If they did, it would suggest that children's alleged indifference to causal mechanism resides in their ignorance of what a particular mechanism might be, rather than a belief that mechanisms are irrelevant.

Children were asked to describe the workings of the three-step sequence illustrated in Figure 8.3. The sequence included an *initial event* (an orange rod was pushed through a post), a *final event* (Fred-the-rabbit fell into his bed), and a series of *intermediary events* (the rod knocked down the first of five standing wooden blocks; each block fell upon the next in a dominolike fashion; the fifth block fell on a small lever which pushed the rabbit off a platform).

Sixty-four 4- and 5-year-olds participated in the study. Sixteen children of each age were randomly assigned to one of two conditions that varied the amount of information they had about the apparatus. Children in the *complete information* condition saw the entire apparatus during pretest demonstration trials. The experimenter pointed to each part, labeled it, and invited children to demonstrate the sequence. After the demonstration trials, a screen was put up that blocked from view the middle portion (blocks and lever) of the apparatus. All that the children could see was the rod and post to the left and Fred standing on the platform to the right.

Children in the *partial information* condition were never shown the middle portion of the apparatus; the screen was already in place when they walked into the experimental room. During pretest trials, the experimenter demonstrated the sequence by pushing the rod through the post. Since the screen was in place the children could see only the initial and final events; however, they could hear the blocks as they fell.

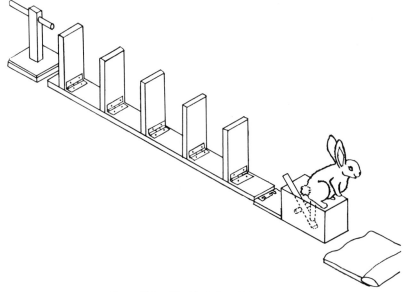

Figure 8.3. The Fred-the-rabbit apparatus.

After the pretest trials, children in both conditions were treated identically. In a first phase, the experimenter asked children to predict whether the rabbit would fall when she pushed the long orange rod through the post, and then to describe what had happened when the rabbit did fall. Not surprisingly, all children in the *complete information* condition correctly predicted that the rabbit would fall, and all but three were able to provide "integrated" descriptions of the event after the rabbit had fallen. A description was judged to be integrated if (*a*) all the component events comprising the sequence were mentioned; and (*b*) each event was indicated to be the effect of the event that preceded it and the cause of the one that followed it. Children in the *partial information* condition also correctly predicted that the rabbit would fall, although, of course, fewer of their descriptions of the sequence were rated as integrated. Still, 69% of the 16 5-year-olds correctly included the information that something must have connected the rod's action to the rabbit's. In contrast, the majority of the 4-year-olds answered that the rod had somehow pushed the rabbit off his box—an unlikely story since the rabbit stood more than 3 ft away from the post! Moreover, the children could hear the falling blocks.

In Phase 2, the experimenter introduced two modifications of the initial event, in random order. One modification was to substitute another orange rod that was too short to reach the first block when pushed through the post. The other modification involved substituting a long multicolored rod for the orange one. The first modification was labeled *relevant* since it should affect the outcome of the sequence (Fred should not fall); the second change was labeled *irrelevant* since it should not change the usual outcome (Fred should still fall into his bed).

Children were asked to predict whether Fred would or would not fall for each modification. Following each prediction, the experimenter demonstrated the sequence. Regardless of the modification type, though, the rabbit did not fall after either modification (the experimenter surreptitiously prevented the multicolored rod from hitting the first block). In both cases, children were asked to explain why the rabbit had not fallen. Two questions were of interest: Would children predict differently following relevant and irrelevant changes? Secondly, would explanations for the rabbit's failure to fall depend on children's prior information concerning the apparatus?

The results from the Phase 2 modification trials indicated that while children's predictions did *not* differ by information condition (half the children predicted Fred would not fall with the short rod; only one child predicted he would fall with the multicolored rod), their explanations for why the rabbit had not, in fact, fallen did differ.

All but two children in the *complete information* condition offered the correct explanation for why Fred failed to fall with the short rod. This is especially interesting when one considers that about half the children in this condition were incorrect in their predictions. After the rabbit failed to fall, these children revised their earlier judgments and correctly pinpointed rod length as the reason for the rabbit's not falling.

In contrast, when Fred did not fall following the irrelevant modification, children attributed the outcome to something other than the substituted rod. Twenty-one of the 32 *complete information* children said the experimenter had done something (e.g., moved the post away, put the blocks down, taken some blocks away) to prevent the rabbit's falling. An additional 8 children claimed the multicolored rod had somehow not pushed the blocks down.

These results suggest that children can and do use their knowledge of inter-mediary events in a causal sequence to reason about the sequence. Children in the *complete information* condition attributed an outcome to a modification *only* when their understanding of the sequence led them to infer that this modification effectively prevented the intermediary events from occurring. When the modification was *not* relevant to the sequence of events, children resisted at-tributing the outcome to it. It is notable that while children in the *partial infor-mation* condition performed less well, most of those children who *did* postulate some mechanism during the first phase also referred to hypothesized inter-mediary events in their explanations of the outcomes of the two modifications. This suggests that children's explanations are limited by their knowledge about *what* could connect cause and effect, not by a fundamental belief that such a connection is unnecessary.

Given that 4- and 5-year-olds could, if informed, explain modifications in a way that implied an understanding of mechanism, Baillargeon, Gelman, and Meck (1981) conducted a follow-up study that included even younger children. Twenty 3- and 4-year-olds were asked to predict the effects of a series of modifications to the rabbit apparatus after they had seen the complete event sequence in pretest trials. The children in this study were not asked to explain or describe the events, but merely to predict whether or not modifications would disrupt the expected sequence.

As in the earlier study, Baillargeon *et al.* included two types of modification: *relevant* modifications, which would disrupt the sequence; and *irrelevant* ones which would not. Modifications involved either the initial event (rod or post) or the intermediary events (blocks or platform). Children were asked to make 23 predictions. If they were truly indifferent to mechanism, they should not predict differently depending on whether the modification was relevant or irrelevant. Alternatively, predicting that the rabbit *would* fall after irrelevant changes, and *would not* fall after relevant changes would be evidence that children took mechanism information into account when reasoning about events.

The relevant changes to the initial part of the sequence included using a rod of soft, flexible material, a rod with a stopper that prevented it from going through the post and contacting the first block, a rod too short to hit the first block, or moving the supporting post so the rod could not contact the blocks. Relevant

TABLE 8.3
Mean Percentage of Correct Predictions Following Modifications to an Event Sequence
(Baillargeon, Gelman & Meck)

		Source of modification	
Modification type	Age	Initial event	Intermediary event
Relevant	3 years	81	78
	4 years	87	85
Irrelevant	3 years	88	96
	4 years	100	100

changes to the intermediary part of the sequence included putting the blocks
down or moving the platform to one side of the blocks so the last block could not
hit the lever. Irrelevant changes of the initial compdnent included changing the
color of the rod or the substance of the rod (from wood to glass), or moving the
post position without affecting its function. Irrelevant changes of the intermediary components included putting a cloth around one block or putting a
screen in front of the blocks.

Children were first asked about modifications to the initial event, then about
those concerning the middle events. Within these categories, the presentation of
particular modifications was random. For all changes children were asked to
predict whether or not the rabbit would fall. Feedback was not provided.

Children's performance over the 23 predictions is shown in Table 8.3. The
range of correct predictions was 78–91% and 70–100% for the 3- and 4-
year-olds, respectively. Children's accuracy did not depend on whether the
change was to the initial or intermediate part of the apparatus. Although there
was a slight bias toward more accurate predictions for irrelevant changes, (i.e.,
children were more likely to accurately predict that a modification would not
disrupt the sequence), all predictions were significantly above chance level
(binomial test, all p values $< .005$).

Baillargeon et al.'s prediction data demonstrate that children as young as 3
years can use information about connecting mechanisms to reason about event
sequences. The 3-year-olds' superior performances in this experiment, compared
with the 3-year-olds in Bullock's unconnected experiment (see "The Jack-in-
the-Box Study"), are likely due to the availability of specific information in
Baillargeon et al.'s study. It seems that knowledge of actual mechanisms influences the child's willingness to refer to intermediary events in explaining occurrences. Thus, even 3-year-olds are sensitive to questions of mechanism in some
situations.

DETERMINISM—A CONTROL CONDITION

To assess the assumption of determinism essentially requires asking if there exist any conditions under which a child believes that events may not be caused. While it would be impossible to investigate this question for all possible events, a belief in determinism may be demonstrated if a child resists attributing an event to "itself," or actively searches for a cause for a seemingly causeless event.

Bullock (1979) conducted a control study for the jack-in-the-box experiment to test the determinism assumption. Bullock provided a seemingly uncaused event, but questioned children about it in a way that would allow them to attribute the cause to some plausible, but inappropriate, event, or to say that the event needed no cause. The procedure for this study was identical to that described for the Jack-in-the-box study. In the first phase children became familiar with the runway portion of the jack-in-the-box apparatus and learned to push handles to make the ball and light events occur. The jack-in-the-box portion of the apparatus was attached to the runways, and children watched demonstration trials during a second phase. In the previously described jack-in-the-box study, ball and light action preceded the jack; children attributed the jack's jumping to these antecedents. In this study the runway events did *not* occur during the demonstration phase: the jack simply jumped up. After watching demonstration trials, children were asked for a causal judgment, that is, how the jack had come up. If a child claimed ignorance or surprise, the experimenter probed him or her in a way to allow animistic (*"It wanted to"*) or inappropriate (e.g., *"The ball* (or light) *did it"*) causes. The experimenter asked the child if the jack had come up by itself, or if not, what had been the cause. Of interest in this study was whether children would resist the opportunity to say that the event occurred on its own or was the effect of the ball or light—the only other salient occurrences in the experimental setting.

Thirty 3-, 4-, and 5-year-olds participated in this study. When asked what made the jack pop up after the demonstration trials, only five children (three of these 3-year-olds) mentioned the ball or light. The other children either accused the experimenter of playing a trick, complained that there was no way of determining the cause, or claimed that something—though they knew not what—was the cause. Thus, children indicated that they believed some causal event was required.

Children's explanations were instructive. In contrast to subjects in the earlier jack-in-the-box mechanism experiment, children in this study neither referred to the ball and light events nor put the impetus for the causal action in the jack itself. Rather, most children tried to specify the nature of the cause that was responsible for the event they had witnessed. Consistent with the other studies reported thus far, the older children were better at this than the younger. While only 40% of the

3-year-olds speculated about what the cause could be, 70% and 90% of the 4- and 5-year-olds did. They said that wires, buttons, or switches were the cause, indicating not only a belief that there must be some cause, but also suggesting its identity.

Following completion of the explanation phase of this study, 20 of the 30 subjects saw one additional trial where the ball and light *did* occur. All children, when asked, now attributed the cause of the jack's action to one of the two antecedents; 65% of them additionally showed signs of relief or amusement.

In sum, responses to this condition offer support for at least a weak assumption of determinism: children claimed that what appeared to be an uncaused event required some explanation, even if they could not specify the details. This finding was consistent with earlier (Bullock & Gelman, 1979; Gelman, 1977) "magic studies" in which children reacted with surprise and amazement to surreptitious alterations in object arrays, and often searched for the cause of the change.

The Use of Stimulus Information

In outlining the model of causal thinking, we distinguished between the use of causal principles and the use of specific information from events to arrive at a causal attribution (see "A Characterization of Causal Reasoning"). In many of the studies reported here causes were spatially and temporally contiguous to their effects, providing a good deal of redundant information about the events. Hence, these studies do not allow us to ask about the relative contributions of stimulus information (especially temporal and spatial contiguity) to causal attributions in the particular case.

There are two exceptions to the generalization about redundant temporal and spatial information. First, children in Bullock's unconnected experiment were shown events that were temporally but not spatially contiguous. The 4- and 5-year-olds in that study paid attention to the spatial gap and selected causal events that might rectify the situation so that spatial and temporal contiguity cues applied (e.g., they suggested tubes under the table for the ball, or that an object really had made spatial contact, etc.). Three-year-olds, though, seemed perfectly content to select the steel ball as cause and did not mention the lack of spatial contact. This result suggests that the youngest children relied on temporal priority alone.

A second exception occurred at the end of the Bullock and Gelman study on priority (see "Causal Principles"). Here, temporal and spatial information was inconsistent so that the event that preceded an effect was not spatially contiguous to it, while an event that followed the effect was. Again, 4- and 5-year-olds were surprised at this and tended to invent mechanisms that would preserve both temporal and spatial contiguity; and, again the 3-year-olds seemed to base their judgments on temporal information only.

It is just this sort of lack of interest in spatial contact information that has led children to be characterized as "precausal." However, the Baillargeon et al. studies reported here suggest that 3-year-olds were not oblivious to mechanism information under some conditions. One alternative interpretation, then, is that under conditions of ignorance about *possible* or likely mechanisms, younger children's choices are guided more heavily by the priority assumption, suggesting they will *overlook* cues from the stimulus environment. Further, children may need to learn the relation between spatial cues and the mechanism principle; after all, there are many spatially unconnected events that are causally related (light switches and illumination, TV controls, commands and answers, and so on).

One way to assess the role of stimulus information in causal attributions, though, is to ask whether children, like adults, use *relative* contiguity to choose between two or more plausible causes, and whether temporal or spatial information is weighted more heavily. Bullock and Baillargeon (1981) focused on asking whether children's causal judgments would vary with relative temporal or spatial contiguity.

The apparatus for this study used the same components as the Bullock and Gelman (1979) study on priority (see Figure 8.1). That is, a ball event could occur in either of two boxes adjoining a jack-in-the-box. Here, though, both ball events occurred before the jack jumped under all conditions. What varied was the *relative* temporal or spatial contiguity relation of each of the ball events to the jack, that is, the timing of the balls or the placement of the ball boxes.

The design for this study included the four conditions outlined in Table 8.4. In all cases the possible causes *preceded* the effect. In Conditions 1 and 2, either temporal contiguity or spatial contiguity varied alone. In Conditions 3 and 4, both temporal and spatial proximity varied so that the cues were either consistent (one event was closer in time and in space) or inconsistent (one event was closer in time, one in space). By comparing children's choices within each condition, and across the four conditions, Bullock and Baillargeon assessed how particular information was weighted in determining a cause.

Seventy-two children (24 3-, 4-, and 5-year-olds) saw the four conditions. For half the subjects the spatially proximate box was connected to the jack, and the other box was 6 in away. For the other half of the subjects, the boxes were always separate, one at 2 in and one at 6 in. Children saw six trials for each condition; on each trial they were asked to judge which ball event had made the jack pop up. On two of the six trials children were asked to explain their choices. Conditions 1 and 2 were always presented first, in counterbalanced order. Trials for Conditions 3 and 4 were mixed and presented in random order.

Responses were coded separately for each of the four conditions. The pattern

TABLE 8.4
The Four Conditions Varying Stimulus Information
(Bullock and Baillargeon)

Condition	Spatial configurations					Temporal sequences
1. Relative temporal contiguity (TC) Varies alone	1^a	2	3			1-2-3 or 2-1-3
2. Relative spatial contiguity[b] (SC) Varies alone	or	$\dfrac{1}{1}$	3	3	$\dfrac{2}{2}$	1, 2 simultaneous, followed by 3
3. Consistent Temporal and spatial contiguity	or	$\dfrac{1}{1}$	3	3	$\dfrac{2}{2}$	$\dfrac{2\text{-}1\text{-}3}{1\text{-}2\text{-}3}$
4. Inconsistent Temporal and spatial contiguity	or	$\dfrac{1}{1}$	3	3	$\dfrac{2}{2}$	$\dfrac{1\text{-}2\text{-}3}{2\text{-}1\text{-}3}$

[a] The numbers refer to the components of the apparatus: "1" and "2" represent the runway boxes; "3" represents the jack-in-the-box.

[b] In conditions 2, 3, and 4, two configurations were used over the trials. In condition 2, the timing remained constant with the two configurations; in conditions 3 and 4, the timing changed to allow spatial and temporal cues to be consistent or inconsistent.

of choices for each set of six trials was classified as consistent with one cue if at least five of the choices used information determined by that cue, and as "indifferent" if not. For example, a child in Condition 2 would be classed as using the cue of spatial contiguity only if he or she chose the closer event on five or six of the trials. If he or she chose the closer event two, three, or four times, the choices would be classed as "indifferent." Choosing the more distant event five or six times would be classed as a negative use of the spatial cue.

Table 8.5 summarizes the pattern of choices for the three age groups and a subsequently tested group of adults. Since there were no differences between the three groups of children depending on whether they saw the connected or close configurations, this factor is collapsed for this presentation. The results for Condition 1, where relative temporal continguity varied alone, were surprising. Those theories that posit that the preschooler is "precausal," limited to or primarily reliant on temporal cues alone, would predict that children's choices in this situation would favor the event that was more contiguous temporally. This should have been the most straightforward of all conditions. However, children's choices indicated that, far from *relying* on temporal contiguity, they did not even use it (except, of course, that both antecedents were near to the effect in time in an absolute sense). By and large children picked the first event in the sequence as cause, or were indifferent. The 5-year-olds were more consistent in their choices than were the younger children—a trend that was mirrored in the other conditions. This finding led Bullock and Baillargeon to test an adult group as a check on their intuition that adults *would* pick a temporally more contiguous event as cause. The 12 adults, whose choices are indicated in Table 8.5, were more likely as a group to pick the more contiguous event, although there was not unanimous agreement. Those adults who picked the first event, though, also mentioned that they supposed some mechanism was slowly linking the first event to the effect, and there was not enough time for the second event to get to the jack. In contrast, the children picked the first event and said they picked it *because* it was first, a dubious justification, although one that is consistent with a use of the priority principle.

Conditions 2, 3, and 4 each involved spatial proximity information, either alone (Condition 2) or in combination with temporal cues (Conditions 3 and 4). For all subjects, of all ages, the configuration with the greatest relative *spatial* proximity between cause and effect was picked over the other configuration regardless of the temporal cue. While over half the 3- and 4-year-olds chose

TABLE 8.5
Percentage of Subjects Classified as Choosing by Stimulus Cue or as Indifferent
(Bullock and Baillargeon)

Condition		Cue Classification		
1. TC varies alone		TC	First	Indifferent
	3 years	4	16	79
	4 years	4	42	54
	5 years	13	50	38
	Adults	58	33	8
2. SC varies alone		SC	−SC	Indifferent
	3 years	42	4	54
	4 years	63	0	38
	5 years	75	0	25
	Adults	100	0	0
3. TC/SC consistent		SC/TC	First	Indifferent
	3 years	17	4	79
	4 years	58	4	38
	5 years	63	13	25
	Adults	100	0	0
4. TC/SC inconsistent		TC	SC/First	Indifferent
	3 years	4	25	71
	4 years	0	46	54
	5 years	0	75	25
	Adults	25	58	17

inconsistently enough to be labeled "indifferent" in their choices, those who did choose consistently opted for relative spatial proximity.

The age trends in this study deserve additional note. While younger children were primarily indifferent (or variable) in their choices, a common finding for young subjects, there is some indication that this was due to the complexity of the situation, not the absence of any criteria underlying their choices. First, 3-year-olds were *least* indifferent for the condition where spatial cues varied alone (Condition 2), suggesting mediation by a mechanism principle, as long as other information was held constant and only one cue varied. Secondly, the overall age trends showed that children became more consistent in their choices and more similar to adults' very consistent (with the exception of Condition 1) choices. It is interesting to note that children did not pick causes incompatible with the principles of priority or mechanism (the *inconsistent* antecedent in Condition 3 or the spatially removed box in Conditions 2, 3, or 4). This suggests that what changes with development is the knowledge of how to weight stimulus information in relation to the principles defining causal events.

The results from Condition 1, in which children picked the first event, suggests one area where adults' and children's criteria may differ in terms of weight given to contiguity information. It may be that children's definitions of causal events were such that they took the *first* salient occurrence as cause, and not the more contiguous one (either one is consistent with a priority principle). This question will be addressed in future studies that vary the temporal spacing between events even more, in an effort to see when children deny that the first event is the cause and pick a more contiguous one.

Knowledge about Transformations and Objects

The ability to make causal inferences or to explain events relies in part on general knowledge about transformations and possible outcomes with respect to object states. This idea is a central component of those theories that describe the structure of representation, be it in terms of schemata (e.g., Piaget, 1974; Premack, 1976), scripts (e.g., Schank & Abelson, 1977), or schematic organization (Mandler, 1978). Our expectations about event outcomes—the way we parse occurrences—and our verbal explanations of events probably all make use of the notion that causation involves a transformation over time. In keeping with our earlier discussion, we may distinguish between the ability to comment upon the nature of transformations, and the use of this knowledge to trace changes in objects over time.

Consider, again, a rock shattering a window. When we understand this event, we may reason about it using temporal and spatial information to determine what is effect and what is cause. However, another way that we may reason about the event is in terms of the transformation that changes the window from one state to another. The object of the transformation, the window, had a beginning and an end state (whole and broken) that were related in time by a transformation, breaking. Furthermore, the transformation was instantiated by an instrument, a rock.

The young child's understanding of the relationships that hold between components of an event, object states, and the transformations that link them, has not received much direct investigation. Yet, assumptions about just this sort of knowledge figure in theories of linguistic competence, conceptual organization, and causal and temporal reasoning. On the one hand, young children are granted tacit knowledge of the semantic categories that components of events fit into, for example, agent, object, location, and instrument (see Ammon & Slobin, 1979; Bowerman, 1978; Clark & Clark, 1977). Similarly, they are granted sensorimotor schemes for organizing objects and actions (Piaget, 1954). On the other hand, children of the same ages are characterized as unable to *reason* about the relation of causes and consequences and as unconcerned about the specific nature of a transformation that might connect two states of an object (Piaget, 1974).

The results presented in the preceding sections suggest that even very young preschoolers may reason about cause–effect relations according to the same basic principles as adults, even though they do not give all stimulus information the same weight or explain events with adultlike sophistication. A study by Gelman, Bullock, and Meck (1980) indicates that young preschoolers are also capable of relating object states through appropriate transformations.

Gelman *et al*. (1980) investigated children's understandings of transformations and object states by asking 3- and 4-year-olds to fill in missing elements in three-item picture stories. Each completed sequence consisted of an object, an instrument, and the same object in another state. Figure 8.4 illustrates some of the complete stories. Note that some sequences depicted everyday events, others "bizarre" events, such as sewing a cut banana together or drawing on fruit. The latter type of sequences were included to control the possibility that when children had to fill in a missing slot, they did it simply on the basis of everyday memories.

Following pretraining trials to teach a left–right "reading" of the sequences, children were shown test sequences with either the first, second, or third positions empty. The task was to pick one of three choice cards to fill in the missing slot, and to tell the story depicted by the three cards. Examples of trial sequences with each position blank and the three choice cards are shown in Figure 8.5. Test sequences included two broad categories of transformations. One type altered an object from a standard, or canonical, form, (e.g., wetting, breaking, cutting, and so on). A second type restored objects to a more canonical form (e.g., drying, fixing, erasing, and so on).

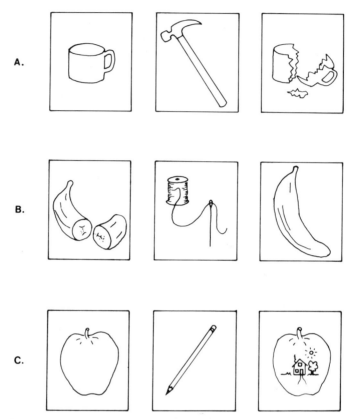

Figure 8.4. Three examples of story sequences. Reprinted with permission from *Child Development, 1980, 51,* 691–699.

Gelman *et al.* used these story sequences to test children's understanding of causal transformations by asking whether children could reason from two of the elements in the story to the (missing) third. That is, could they infer the instrument that related two object states, predict the result of a transformation given an object and instrument, and retrieve the initial state of an object, given an instrument and final state?

Forty-eight 3- and 4-year-olds participated in the study. Half the children saw sequences that altered objects (the *canonical condition*) and half saw sequences in which an altered object was restored (the *noncanonical condition*).

Children did very well at filling in the missing items in the story sequences. Twenty-one of the 24 3-year-olds and all the 4-year-olds reliably chose the correct picture across the 12 trials, as illustrated in Table 8.6. There are several noteworthy trends in these data. First, the older children made few errors overall, regardless of type of transformation or familiarity of sequence. When they did err, it tended to be in retrieving the initial state of the event sequence. While the 3-year-olds' responses also showed no difference depending on common or unusual sequences, they, unlike the older children, were influenced by whether the transformation altered or restored an object. The younger children who saw noncanonical (or restoring) transformations tended to make more errors, suggesting it was easier for them to reason about sequences in which an object is changed away from its standard state. Finally, all children found it relatively easier to fill in the instrument slots than the object slots.

The differences in error scores between canonical and noncanonical altera-

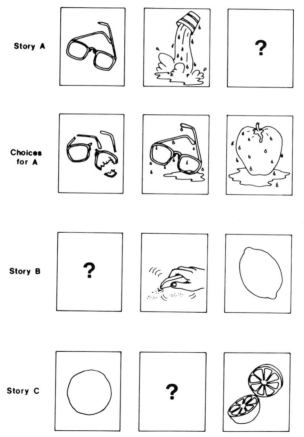

Figure 8.5 Examples of test sequences for the picture card studies. The correct answer for Story B is a lemon with a drawing on it; the correct answer for Story C is a knife. Reprinted with permission from *Child Development*, 1980, *51*, 691–699.

TABLE 8.6
Percentage of Children Who Made at Least 75% Correct Choices on Each Story Position (Gelman, Bullock & Meck)[a]

| | A. Canonical stories | | |
| | Position of missing item | | |
Age	1	2	3
3 years	66	91.7	83.3
4 years	91.7	100	100

| | B. Noncanonical stories | | |
| | Position of missing item | | |
Age	1	2	3
3 years	58.3	75	58.3
4 years	100	100	100

[a] Modified with permission from *Child Development*, 1980, *51*, 691–699.

tions, shown only by 3-year-olds, were reflected in all children's verbal descriptions of their completed sequences. The content of children's descriptions were categorized for how "complete" they were. A *complete story* was one in which a child mentioned both object states and the transformation that related them, supplying the action implied by the picture sequence (e.g., *"There was that cup and the hammer broke it"*). *Less-complete stories* described just the action of the instrument (*"It broke it"*) or listed the picture components (*"cup, hammer, cup"*). The older children told more complete stories than the younger ones did: on the average, 80% of the 4-year-olds' stories were complete; 41% of the 3-year-olds' were. However, stories of children in both age groups were more complete when they involved the canonical sequences than the noncanonical (44% versus 37% for the 3-year-olds; 89% versus 71% for the 4-year-olds). There were no differences in stories depending on position of the missing items.

In sum, although the youngest subjects made more errors, they still did very well. All children were able to predict or retrieve the missing object states and infer a transformation that linked object states through time. This is true for transformations that both were and were not likely to be a part of the children's everyday experiences.

Linking object states through transformations—an ability even 3-year-olds possess—is one aspect of the kind of general knowledge that would allow one to use causal principles to reason about and explain events. In one sense, though, applying this knowledge implies a further ability: that one can think of cause and effect as *related,* through a transformation, in a coherent unit. This suggests that one not only has some schema, script, plan, or structure that frames the relation, but that one can also operate within those event representations. Thus, using one's knowledge is more than just relating events in time; it includes relating them in a larger context.

Piaget's theory of cognitive change emphasizes that the child only gradually develops structures that make it possible for him or her to escape the unidirectional nature of experience, and to think of transformations as related and reversible (e.g., addition and subtraction may be applied to any set of objects and may operate within a relational system). Preschool thought is characterized by Piaget (1974; 1976) as irreversible, implying that younger children are more constrained by the actual sequencing of events in time when they reason about those events. In the case of causal thinking, the preschooler is similarly presumed unable to consider together reversible or reciprocal transformations on objects. It is possible that this restriction is indeed a deficit in the child's reasoning; however, it is also possible that children's explanations and judgments about causal events most often are unidirectional in character because causal events *do* take place through time and are not, in reality, reversible (much to a preschooler's chagrin, broken dishes are irreparable, eaten cookies are gone, and dirty clothes stay dirty). A second study by Gelman *et al.* (1980) addressed this issue.

In the context of the preceding picture card study, the question of reversibility of causal thinking may be specified as follows. A child might be able to relate cause and effect in a specific instance, for example, seeing that hammering will produce a broken bowl or that gluing will fix it. However, he or she should have difficulty in thinking of the two actions, hammering and gluing, as a pair that reverse the effects of each other. To do this requires more than filling in implied actions or instruments; it involves separating the transformations on objects from their particular reference frame, and freeing them from temporally unidirectional occurrences.

To test whether preschoolers could treat transformations in such a general sense, Gelman *et al.* ran a second study, using a slight modification of the picture card procedure. Again, children were presented with the card sequences, but in each case the middle instrument card was the missing item. Children were asked to choose from four alternatives. As before, the choices included an appropriate instrument for reading the sequence from left to right. Additionally, there was an appropriate instrument card for reading the sequence in the reverse order, from right to left. On each trial, a child was asked first to choose an instrument that would complete a left–right reading of the story, then to pick a second instrument for a right–left reading. Thus, children were asked to think of the same object pair (e.g., blank and marked paper, broken and fixed cup, wet and dry dog) in two different ways.

Forty-eight 3- and 4-year-olds participated in the second picture card study. Overall, children's first choices were not as accurate as those of children who participated in the first study. Three-year-olds were correct on 49% of the trials, and 4-year-olds on 75%. However, most errors consisted of picking a card appropriate for what was a "reversed" reading of the sequence, that is a right–left reading. If a child was allowed to respond in his or her preferred direction, 80% and 90% of the 3- and 4-year-olds' initial choices were correct, a figure consistent with the instrument choices for the first study. Fifty-eight percent of the 3-year-olds and 83% of the 4-year-olds then reliably picked a *second* accurate instrument card, demonstrating that they could interpret the object transformation in two reciprocal ways. Those 3-year-olds who did not do this included all the children younger than the median age of the 3-year-old group, suggesting that still younger children might have difficulty with reciprocal transformations.

The results from the second study suggest that while young preschoolers can represent events in a general enough manner to be able to abstract object states and transformations, this is neither easy nor automatic. The younger 3-year-olds were not able to "reverse," although they could infer what action linked object states in a single case. This suggests that the developmental changes in general reasoning abilities may be more profitably conceived as advances in the flexibility and generality of representation, rather than as changes in the form of representation.

Explanations and Judgments

In all the studies reported, the procedures required explanations as well as judgments, predictions, or attributions. Across studies, two consistent findings recurred. First, children's explanations for events improved with age, even where there were no age differences in judgments or predictions, such as in the jack-in-the-box standard experiment or the priority experiment. Secondly, children's explanations for events did not seem to reflect the same level of causal reasoning as did their judgments or predictions. The evidence we interpreted as indicating reasoning by causal principles came from children's judgments or predictions; it did not come from their explanations. These results are, of course, not a surprise to anyone working with preschool-aged children. Children are more likely to demonstrate their reasoning in actions and simple choices than in explanations.

The question we wish to address in this section is what the differences between pictures of preschoolers' thinking gleaned from explanations and those from judgments might mean for the study and interpretation of the development of causal reasoning. On the one hand, we have implied that judgments and explanations arise from the same underlying knowledge—the causal principles. We have also argued that the production of explanations may require more than an explicit understanding of the rules or principles that guide causal understanding, and thus may not allow valid assessment of the thinking of the young preschooler. Indeed, there is evidence that children as old as 7 years may judge and justify their judgments according to different criteria (Klayman, 1976).

One could conclude from this that the way to study thinking in young children is to ignore everything they say and become more and more clever in devising nonverbal tests. This approach certainly has merit; it may even be necessary as a means of gaining an initial assessment of the extent of a young child's knowledge. However, the children in the studies we reported did provide explanations and their explanations changed in consistent ways. A full account of causal reasoning must address the issues of how explanations are related to causal judgments and how they change with age.

These are two issues embedded in the above questions. One is to ask whether, or in what ways, children's explanations were "deficient." The second is to ask what sorts of knowledge one must draw on to provide an adequate explanation.

Across the studies, the coding systems used for judging explanations included some specific criteria: explanations were judged as being "better" when they included information about possible mechanisms or intermediary events. In most conditions, this information was not directly seen, but was inferred from the events that were seen. Indeed, it is a concern with mechanism—or the "hows" of causal action—that allows one to distinguish causal from coincidental events. According to Piaget (1974), it is the lack of an assumption of mechanism that allows a child to violate constraints of temporal order, to posit animistic causes, and so on.

We found that the older children were more likely to provide information about inferred mechanisms in their explanations. However, although the younger children's explanations did not often include mechanism information, they were constrained in certain ways. We did not, in any of the studies, find much evidence for the many categories of explanation Piaget (1930) claimed were rampant in precausal thought (e.g., animism, dynamism, etc.). The children in the studies talked about the events they saw. They did not endow the toys with human qualities, although the tasks were structured so that they could have. The experimenters talked about the rabbit "going to sleep" or the jack "jumping." Indeed, the fact that the puppets used in some studies "talked" should have suggested to children that it was acceptable to endow inanimate objects (such as the apparatuses) with human qualities.

Across the studies, the most general change in explanations with age was an increase in the amount of information included in an explanation and the extent to which elements of the events were related to each other, including unseen intermediary events. The youngest children (3-year-olds) tended to "explain" by restating only some portion of the events seen; many of the youngest children said an event occurred because "it did," merely affirming the event. In contrast, the older children not only stated what happened, but often included an inference linking the events together in time. We should note that the 5-year-olds' responses were remarkably similar to those of adult colleagues who were asked to view, judge, and explain the same sequences.

Certain conditions in the different studies seemed more conducive than others to the production of "good" explanations. Explanations were more integrated, more complete, or more mechanistic in those cases where children either had ready information about possible mechanisms or when they were asked to explain an outcome that was unexpected. To illustrate: children in the Baillargeon *et al.* study showed that when information was available, connections would be mentioned in descriptions and explanations; when it was not, some children could fill in the information, but many did not. This suggests that children may be reluctant to talk about events when they can only speculate as to their content.

The effects of unexpected outcomes is illustrated in the jack-in-the-box studies. Children were more likely to talk of mechanisms when some violation of an unexpected outcome occurred. The proportion of mechanistic explanations was greater for children who saw the unconnected demonstrations than for those who saw the connected trials. Similarly, in the priority study, 4- and 5-year-olds were more likely to be surprised and talk of connections when the unconnected ball preceded the jack's action. These results are consistent with other studies. Berzonsky (1971) reported that children were better able to explain how or why something broke than how it worked. While the same information was relevant in either case, explaining how something worked required choosing which of the many aspects of an event was crucial; explaining how it broke required pinpointing only a single element. This suggests that children's explanations will depend on the complexity of events and on a child's ability to use particular pieces of information, and to gauge the relative importance of one cue over another.

Another reason children's explanations may have been more descriptive than inferential (with respect to mechanism) is that the direct information about the actual events that children saw may be more salient and therefore more easily articulated. That is, children may have had more ready access to the stimulus information than to the principles that guided their attention to these cues. This implies that children's explanations should improve as they become better able to access their implicit causal theories. Given the difficulties preschoolers have in articulating much of anything about their internal mental worlds (cf. Flavell, 1980), it is not surprising that their explanations were less telling of their reasoning abilities than their judgments.

A final issue concerning explanations and judgments focuses on the nature of the explanations themselves. It may be that children have to learn exactly what an acceptable explanation is; thus, their understanding of requests to "explain" may develop with age. In most accounts of causal explanation, it is assumed that there is a taxonomy of explanation type, arranged from less to more adequate. The better types are those that more closely approximate the ideal of scientific explanation. This includes providing not only the sufficient conditions for an event's occurrence, but the necessary ones as well. Thus, for example, an explanation of why a picture fell from the wall that included information about why one picture fell and another did not would be considered better than an explanation that described merely how the one picture fell.

It may be, though, that this criterion for a mature explanation is a special case, not adhered to in everyday adult explanations. That is, the model of a "good" explanation adopted by the sciences (and by scientists studying causal explanations) may not reflect the ordinary adult's criteria. Depending on the extent of knowledge about a phenomenon, descriptions often suffice as well as statements about necessary and/or sufficient conditions. We would agree, for instance, that to say an apple falls to the ground because of gravity is an adequate explanation. Similarly, to explain the action of an internal combusion engine by describing its components is adequate for most purposes. Finally, to return once more to our irreplaceable, shattered window, we could explain its breaking by referring to a property of glass (it was brittle) or of the cause (the rock was hard). In short, it may not be necessary in everyday explanations to outline the necessary or sufficient causes for an event. Indeed, some current analyses of causal explanations suggest that a *request* for an explanation is a tacit command for information about the unexpected or unusual aspects of a situation (Kahneman, 1980). Thus, the answer *"Because it was brittle"* may be a perfectly reasonable answer to the question *"Why did the window break?"* if there was no reason to expect the window to be bulletproof. Note that such an explanation from a child might be classified as precausal since it refers to a property of an event as causing the event.

Such a characterization of everyday adult explanations would suggest that children's explanations might differ because they know less about the world and, presumably, have a less clear idea about the usual. Without an articulable understanding of the usual, one would have greater difficulty picking out *which* aspects of a situation to include as content for an explanation. This idea could be tested by asking whether children's explanations are more sophisticated when they are asked to explain why familiar events do not occur than when they do. To the extent that they understand the *expected* event, its nonoccurrence might allow them easier access to the basis of their expectations. Similarly, if it is the case that explaining an event involves an ability to reflect upon and articulate one's implicit causal theory, it should be possible to highlight the underlying bases of judgments by showing children events in which the stimulus information predicted by the principles was not available. If these manipulations lead children to explain events in a more "mechanistic" manner, it would suggest that the preschooler's problems in explaining are not so much a failure to *have* causal knowledge as a disinclination to use that knowledge in explaining.

A final way in which children's abilities to explain may depend on more than causal understanding concerns the task of explaining. Psycholinguistic work on children's knowledge of conversational constraints (e.g., Clark & Clark, 1977; Gelman & Shatz, 1977) reminds us that even young preschoolers are sensitive to conversational demands. For instance, one rule that guides adult conversation is "tell only new information." Children who are sensitive to this rule may refrain from fully explaining an event to an adult who also witnessed it. Lloyd and Donaldson (1976) for instance, suggest that if one wants a preschooler to reveal the best of his or her competence, the child should be put in the position of offering information, not merely answering questions.

Similarly, children may be sensitive to the form of the questions they are asked (cf. Nass, 1956). For example, "why" suggests a request for a reason for an event; "how" suggests a mechanism. It may be that children's explanations vary with whether they are asked why or how. A current study by M. Bullock (1981) is designed to test these intuitions. Children are asked to explain several events ranging from simple, mechanical sequences to more complex chains of occurrences. They are queried under one of four conditions, varying who asks the questions and how they are phrased. The question is asked by either an experimenter, who has also witnessed the events, or by a puppet adjunct, who has not witnessed the events. The questioner asked "how" an event occurred or "why" it did so. Preliminary results are straightforward: children's explanations are most likely to be mechanistic, physically oriented, and more complete when questioned by someone who has not seen the event and when asked how something occurred rather than why. Children's sensitivity to these fairly subtle manipulations should caution against interpreting deficient explanation data to reflect deficient reasoning abilities.

SUMMARY AND CONCLUSIONS

We began this chapter with a set of related questions: How are causal events understood and how does this understanding develop? In the course of our investigations, we have begun to fill out a framework that breaks causal reasoning into a hierarchy of components (the principles, knowledge, and use of stimulus information), and that allows us to ask which, if any, of the components change with development.

In this final section we hope to accomplish three things: summarize why we believe that children's understanding of events uses the same implicit principles as adults'; suggest ways in which empirical investigations need to expand on our knowledge of children's thinking; and speak more generally to the questions of causal reasoning across time and space.

We have suggested that causal reasoning is directed by adherence to the principles of determinism, priority, and mechanism, and that children as young as 3 years possess these principles. This means that the development of causal understanding is more a process of learning where, when, and how to apply the rules of reasoning rather than figuring out what those rules might be. We find support for this notion in several areas.

First, 4- and 5-year-olds consistently chose causes on the basis of information consistent with such principles, and did not choose events that would be inconsistent with the principles. Furthermore, older children, for the most part, articulated the bases of their choices, at least when they explained simple or unexpected events or events about which they were knowledgeable. While the 3-year-olds were not as consistent in their choices and did not explain well, even they showed evidence of reasoning according to the principles in some situations. In the determinism study, the priority study, the rabbit prediction studies, and the picture card study, the 3-year-olds' choices—though not as robust as those of older children—were consistent with the use of underlying causal principles. Unless one provides a simple situation, ample experience with it, and unambiguous response instructions, then, the abilities of the youngest children are not as likely to be evident in their performance.

There is one important point to be made here. We are not implying that preschoolers' causal thinking is identical to adults'. Certainly, there are pervasive and consistent differences. However, we do want to argue that the differences that exist arise not because the child and adult think about things in fundamentally different ways, but because the child's thought is more constrained by context, complexity, and verbal demands, limiting the scope and flexibility with which the child can apply his or her knowledge.

In the introductory sections we outlined three models of how causal principles might arise. Our data now allow us to choose among these models. Neither the empiricist approach nor a structuralist view that denies adult principles to preschoolers can account for responses mediated by the principles of determinism, priority, or mechanism.

Two cases may serve as illustrations of the unambiguous use of principles. First, the Fred-the-rabbit prediction studies offer support for an ability that is not demonstrated by explanations or judgments. Had children not been sensitive to issues of mechanism, they would not have predicted as well as they did, and they would not have differentiated between those modifications that would and would not alter an outcome. Predicting, in contrast to explaining or making a choice between alternatives, may be a simpler task in that one does not need to articulate the basis of a judgment or to consider and choose between alternatives.

Secondly, the studies on the relative use of spatial and temporal information revealed that children's choices between temporal contiguity cues were mixed, or indifferent. We would argue that in this case their indifference arose because all the choices they were given were consistent with the defining principles of priority and mechanism. Given that, they genuinely had no basis for a differential judgment. This suggests that what may change with development is the use of stimulus information. Children may need to learn that among those events that obey the causal principles, there are variations in direct spatial and temporal properties that provide the means for choosing a cause. This suggests that learning about specific events or types of events will contribute to children's increasing accuracy in choosing a *correct* cause.

The series of studies we have reported here demonstrate an approach that involves analyzing a content area (causal reasoning) into its constituent components, asking whether children's performances reflect an understanding of the components to differing degrees, and asking what does and does not change with development. In arguing that preschoolers show a remarkable competence in reasoning about causal matters, we have also pointed out some areas in which they do *not* show adultlike competence. Notably, their explanations, use of stimulus information, and willingness to speculate about events for which they have scanty particular knowledge all stand in contrast to their robust reasoning according to underlying principles. This suggests that future research should concentrate on three areas: children's understanding of explanations and explaining; children's use of particular stimulus information; and finally, children's abilities to *integrate* the different aspects of causal thinking into a coherent, articulable system.

ACKNOWLEDGMENTS

We thank the children, parents, and staff of the following: Alma Y Day Care, Broadway West Day Care, Beach Day Care, Cedar Cottage Neighborhood Services, and Rainbow's End Day Care, Kits Area Child Care, and False Creek Child Care Society, all of Vancouver; Chestnut House, YM/YWHA Preschool, and Penn Day Care of Philadelphia.

REFERENCES

Ammon, M. S., & Slobin, D. A cross-linguistic study of the processing of causative sentences. *Cognition,* 1979, *1,* 3–17.

Ausubel, D. M., & Schiff, H. M. The effect of incidental and experimentally induced experience on the learning of relevant and irrelevant causal relationships by children. *Journal of Genetic Psychology,* 1954, *84,* 109–123.

Baillargeon, R., & Gelman, R. *Young children's understanding of simple causal sequences: Predictions and explanations.* Presented at the meetings of the American Psychological Association, Montreal, 1980.

Baillargeon, R., Gelman, R., & Meck, E. *Are preschoolers truly indifferent to causal mechanism?* Paper presented at the biennial meeting of the Society for Research in Child Development, Boston, April 1981.

Bassili, J. Temporal and spatial contiguity in the perception of social events. *Journal of Personality and Social Psychology,* 1976, *33*(6), 680–685.

Berzonsky, M. The role of familiarity in children's explanations of physical causality. *Child Development*, 1971, *42*, 705–712.

Bowerman, M. *Reorganizational processes in lexical and semantic development*. Paper presented at a workshop-conference on "The State of the Art" in language acquisition, University of Pennsylvania, May 19–22, 1978.

Brainerd, C. Cognitive development and concept learning: An interpretative review. *Psychological Bulletin*, 1977, *84*, 919–939.

Brown, A. L. Recognition, reconstruction and recall of narrative sequences by preoperational children. *Child Development*, 1975, *46*, 156–166.

Bullock, M. *Aspects of the young child's theory of causation*. Unpublished doctoral dissertation, University of Pennsylvania, 1979.

Bullock, M. *Puppet play: Children's interpretation of causal questions*. University of British Columbia, 1981.

Bullock, M., & Baillargeon, R. *Relative temporal and spatial contiguity in causal judgments*. Unpublished manuscript, University of British Columbia, 1981.

Bullock, M., & Gelman, R. Numerical reasoning in young children: The ordering principle. *Child Development*, 1977, *48*, 427–434.

Bullock, M., & Gelman, R. Children's assumptions about cause and effect: Temporal ordering. *Child Development*, 1979, *50*, 89–96.

Clark, H., & Clark, E. *Psychology and language*. New York: Harcourt Brace Jovanovich, 1977.

Copple, C., & Coon, R. The role of causality in encoding and remembering events as a function of age. *Journal of Genetic Psychology*, 1977, *130*, 129–136.

Dennis, W., & Russell, R. W. Piaget's questions applied to Zuni children. *Child Development*, 1940, *11*, 181–187.

Deutsche, J. M. The development of children's concepts of causal relations. In R. Barker, J. Kounin, & H. Wrights (Eds.), *Child behavior and development*. New York: McGraw-Hill, 1943.

Donaldson, M. *Children's minds*. New York: Norton, 1978.

Flavell, J. *Metacognitive development*. Paper presented at the NATO Advanced Study Institute on Structural/Process Theories of complex human behavior. Banff, Alberta, Canada, June 20–30, 1977.

Gardner, J. *The resurrection*. New York: Ballantine, 1966.

Gelman, R. How young children reason about small numbers. In N. J. Castellan, D. B. Pisoni, & G. R. Potts (Eds.), *Cognitive theory* (Vol. 2). Hillsdale, N.J.: Erlbaum, 1977.

Gelman, R. Cognitive development. *Annual Review of Psychology*, 1978, *29*, 297–332.

Gelman, R., Bullock, M., & Meck, E. Preschoolers' understanding of simple object transformations. *Child Development*, 1980, *51*, 691–699.

Gelman, R., & Shatz, M. Appropriate speech adjustments: The operation of conversational constraints on talk to two-year-olds. In M. Lewis and L. A. Rosenblum (Eds.), *Interaction, conversation, and the development of languae*. New York: Wiley, 1977.

Gibson, E. J. *Development of knowledge about intermodal unity: Two views*. Paper presented at the Jean Piaget Society Annual Symposium, Philadelphia, May 29–31, 1980.

Gibson, J. J. *The sense considered as perceptual systems*. Boston: Houghton-Mifflin, 1966.

Gruber, H., Fink, C., & Damm, V. Effects of experience on perception. *Journal of Experimental Psychology*, 1957, *53*, 89–93.

Huang, I. Children's conception of physical causality: A critical summary. *Journal of Genetic Psychology*, 1943, *64*, 71–121.

Hume, D. *An inquiry concerning human understanding*. New York: Bobbs-Merrill, 1955. (Originally published, 1748).

Kahneman, D. Personal communication, 1980.

Kant, I. *Critique of pure reason* (N. K. Smith, trans.). New York: St. Martin's Press, 1965.

Kelly, H. The process of causal attribution. *American Psychologist*, 1973, *28*, 107–128.

Kendler, H., & Kendler, T. From discrimination learning to cognitive development: A neobehavioristic odyssey. In W. K. Este (Ed.), *Handbook of learning and cognitive processes*. Hillsdale, N.J.: Erlbaum, 1975.

Klayman, J. *Judgment and justification in concept development: The case of animism*. Paper presetned at the biennial meeting of the Society for Research in Child Development, San Francisco, May 1979.

Koslowski, B. *Learning about an instance of causation*. Unpublished manuscript, Cornell University, 1976.

Koslowski, B., & Snipper, A. *Learning about an instance of non-mechanical causality*. Unpublished manuscript, Cornell University, 1977.

Kuhn, D., & Phelps, H. The development of children's comprehension of causal direction. *Child Development*, 1976, *47*, 248-251.

Kun, A. Evidence for preschooler's understanding of causal direction in extended causal sequences. *Child Development*, 1978, *49*, 218-222.

Laurendau, M., & Pinard, A. *Causal thinking in the child*. New York: International Universities Press, 1962.

Lesser, H. The growth of perceived causality. *Journal of Genetic Psychology*, 1977, *130*, 143-152.

Lloyd, P., & Donaldson, M. On a method of eliciting true-false judgments from young children. *Journal of Child Language*, 1976, *3*, 411-416.

Mandler, J. Categorical and schematic organization in memory. In C. R. Puff (Ed.), *Memory, organization and structure*. New York: Academic Press, 1978.

Mandler, J. *The construction of knowledge in the child*. Paper presented at the Jean Piaget Society Annual Symposium, Philadelphia, May 29-31, 1980.

Mendelson, R., & Shultz, T. Covariation and temporal contiguity as principles of causal inference in young children. *Journal of Experimental Child Psychology*, 1976, *22*, 408-412.

Michotte, I. *The perception of causality*. New York: Basic Books, 1963.

Mogar, M. Children's causal reasoning about natural phenomena. *Child Development*, 1960, *31*, 59-65.

Nass, M. L. The effects of three variables on children's concepts of physical causality. *Journal of Abnormal Social Psychology*, 1956, *53*, 191-196.

Neisser, U. *Cognition and Reality*. San Francisco: Freeman, 1976.

Nisbett, R., & Ross, L. *Human inference: strategies and shortcomings of social judgment*. Englewood Cliffs, N.J.: Prentice-Hall, 1979.

Olum, V. Developmental differences in the perception of causality. *American Journal of Psychology*, 1956, *69*, 417-423.

Piaget, J. *The child's conception of physical causality*. London: Rutledge & Kegan Paul, 1930.

Piaget, J. *The construction of reality in the child*. New York: Basic Books, 1954.

Piaget, J. *Understanding causality*. New York: Norton, 1974.

Piaget, J. *The grasp of consciousness*. Cambridge, Mass.: Harvard University Press, 1976.

Premack, D. *Intelligence in ape and man*. New York: Wiley, 1976.

Schank, R. A., & Abelson, R. *Scripts, plans, goals and understanding*. Hillsdale, N.J.: Erlbaum, 1977.

Shultz, T., & Mendelson, R. The use of covariation as a principle of causal analysis. *Child Development*, 1975, *46*, 394-399.

Siegler, R. Defining the locus of developmental differences in children's causal reasoning. *Journal of Experimental Child Psychology*, 1975, *20*, 512-525.

Siegler, R., & Liebert, R. Effects of contiguity, regularity and age on children's causal inferences. *Developmental Psychology*, 1974, *10*, 574-579.

Wilde, J., & Coker, P. *Probability, spatial contact and temporal contiguity as principles of causal inference*. Unpublished manuscript, Claremont Graduate School, 1978.

Nancy L. Stein
Christine G. Glenn

Children's Concept of Time:
The Development of a Story Schema[1]

INTRODUCTION

In the last few years, several attempts have been made to initiate more systematic investigations of language comprehension beyond the level of the word or single sentence. An area of particular interest has focused on the young child's ability to comprehend and tell stories. Stories are an important form of discourse because they often reflect and transmit the most central components of a society's value system, as well as reflecting problem-solving strategies that can be used in everyday social interaction. The story is also the most common form of discourse found in elementary school basal reading series. Thus, increasing our understanding of the difficulties children experience during the comprehension process will enable us to create better instructional strategies.

One recent approach to the study of story comprehension has been the development and expansion of text analysis systems as these systems relate to

[1]The writing and research reported in this chapter was supported by National Institute of Education grants NIE-G-77-0018 and NIE-G-79-0125 to Tom Trabasso. In addition, the authors were supported in part by the National Institute of Education under contract No. HEW-NIE-400-76-0116 to the Center for the Study of Reading, University of Illinois.

255

memory for texts. By combining aspects of linguistic text analyses, similar in spirit to Propp's (1958) morphology of Russian folktales, with broad theoretical assumptions about the nature of memory in general, several investigators have constructed a set of working hypotheses about the structure of story knowledge and the way in which the organization of this knowledge might affect comprehension. The strength of most of these approaches is that they include a description of the invariant features found in many different types of stories, as well as a description of the nature and function of a story schema that is used to facilitate memory for stories (Johnson & Mandler, 1980; Mandler & Johnson, 1977; Rumelhart, 1975, 1977; Stein, 1979; Stein & Glenn, 1979; Thorndyke, 1977).

In order to facilitate an understanding of these approaches, we will outline the basic assumptions underlying the construction of a story grammar, and then illustrate how a comprehender uses a story schema to break down incoming story information and construct a coherent representation of the text. The Stein and Glenn grammar (1979) will be used. However, there are grammars other than the Stein and Glenn grammar. In discussing studies carried out on children's comprehension of stories, an attempt will be made to integrate findings from all gramatical studies, especially those of Mandler and Johnson (1977).

STORY GRAMMARS AND STORY SCHEMAS

A basic assumption underlying the Stein and Glenn (1979) grammar is that some type of schematic knowledge is used to guide the encoding and retrieval of story information. This knowledge may be acquired in two ways: by listening to or reading stories, and by participating in and developing an understanding of everyday social interaction. As comprehenders become more exposed to the variations in story structure and to different social situations, their schematic knowledge is gradually thought to correspond to the structural descriptions given in the story grammar.

One of the assumed functions of the story schema is to guide a listener or reader in breaking down story information into its component parts. This occurs because the schema specifies the types of information that should occur in a story and the types of logical relations that should link the components of a story. Thus, a story schema guides the listener in determining what parts of the story have not been included and in determining when a story has deviated from the normal temporal sequence of events. One implication is that when the text structure violates the expected story sequence, the resulting representation will tend to correspond more to the expected story sequence than to the original text sequence.

Most investigators interested in story structures have argued that story knowledge is organized either in the form of rewrite rules containing knowledge about the generic structure of stories (Johnson & Mandler, 1980; Mandler, 1978; Mandler & Johnson, 1977; Rumelhart, 1975; Stein, 1978, 1979; Stein & Glenn, 1979; Thorndyke, 1977; Thorndyke & Yekovitch, 1980), or as goal-directed, problem-solving episodes (Black & Bower, 1980; Rumelhart, 1977). Although these approaches differ in emphasis, the description of a simple story schema is highly similar. The schema can be described as a hierarchical network of story categories and logical relationships connecting these categories. *Categories* represent the different types of information that recur in most stories. The *logical relations* connecting the categories specify the degree to which information in one category influences the occurrences of events in subsequent categories.

The initial division in the story structure consists of two parts: the *setting* category plus the *episode*. The episode is the basic higher-order unit of analysis in a story and contains a sequence of five different categories. Each category contains specific types of information and serves a different function in the schema. Table 9.1 contains a description of each of the categories in a simple narrative, the logical relations connecting each category to the adjacent one, and an example of a story broken down into each of the basic categories. The categories described correspond to those used by Stein and Glenn (1979) and bear a close resemblance to categories in other grammars previously cited.

As Table 9.1 indicates, the story begins with the introduction of the protagonist and usually contains one or more statements about the physical, social, or temporal environment in which the remainder of the story occurs. The setting is not considered a part of the episode, as it is not usually directly related to the subsequent sequence of events described in the episode. However, the setting information allows for interpretation of subsequent events. Thus, information in the setting category may constrain the possible events that can occur in the episode.

The episode consists of five different categories. The *initiating event* (IE), the category beginning the episode, contains information that marks some type of change in the protagonist's environment. Its major function is to evoke a desire in the protagonist to achieve some sort of goal (or change of state). The goal, included in the second category, *internal response* (IR), is the most critical part of the story because it is proposed that story knowledge is basically organized around the goal of a protagonist. The internal response category not only contains the statement of a goal, but it may also include an emotional reaction to the initiating event and thoughts or plans about how to achieve the goal. The primary function of this category is to motivate the protagonist to carry out a set of overt actions, defined as the *attempt* (A) category. The protagonist's attempt is representative of an internal plan of action that is externalized for the purpose of achieving the goal. The attempt then results in the *consequence* (C), signifying whether or not the protagonist attained the goal. The final category, *reaction* (R), can include one of several types of information: the character's emotional and

TABLE 9.1
Categories and Types of Causal Relations Occurring in a Simple Story

| 1. SETTING | Introduction of the protagonist; contains information about the social, physical, or temporal context in which the story events occur. |

Allow

↓

EPISODE

| 2. INITIATING EVENT | An action, an internal event, or a physical event that serves to initiate the story line or cause the protagonist to respond emotionally and to formulate a goal. |

Cause

↓

| 3. INTERNAL RESPONSE | An emotional reaction and a goal, often incorporating the thought of the protagonist that causes him or her to initiate action. |

Cause

↓

| 4. ATTEMPT | An overt action or series of actions, carried out in the service of attaining a goal. |

Cause
or
Enable

↓

| 5. CONSEQUENCE | An event, action, or end state, marking the attainment or nonattainment of the protagonist's goal. |

Cause

↓

| 6. REACTION | An internal response expressing the protagonist's feelings about the outcome of his or her actions or the occurrence of broader, general consequences resulting from the goal attainment or nonattainment of the protagonist. |

Example of a Well-Formed Story

Setting	1. Once there was a big grey fish named Albert. 2. He lived in a big icy pond near the edge of a forest.
Initiating event	3. One day, Albert was swimming around the pond. 4. Then he spotted a big juicy worm on the top of the water.
Internal response	5. Albert knew how delicious worms tasted. 6. He wanted to eat that one for his dinner.
Attempt	7. So he swam very close to the worm. 8. Then he bit into him.
Consequence	9. Suddenly, Albert was pulled through the water into a boat. 10. He had been caught by a fisherman.
Reaction	11. Albert felt sad. 12. He wished he had been more careful.

cognitive responses to the goal attainment, the events that occur as a direct result of having attained a goal, or the reaction frequently can include a moral summarizing what the character may have leanred from achieving a particular goal, or admonishing the reader about the futility of attaining the goal under consideration.

In all of the recent descriptions of story structures, it is evident that each category in an episode could directly cause the occurrence of the subsequent category. One exception to a direct causal chain concerns the relationship between the attempt and consequence. It has been proposed (Mandler & Johnson, 1977; Stein & Glenn, 1979) that the protagonist's actions can directly cause the consequence to occur. However, in some stories, the attempt may merely "enable" the occurrence of the consequence. For example, in a story used by both Mandler and Johnson (1977) and Stein and Glenn (1979), the protagonist, Epaminondas, agrees to carry a cake to his grandmother's house (an internal response goal). He wraps it in a leaf (attempt), puts it under his arm (attempt), carries it to his grandmother's (attempt), and when he arrives (consequence), the cake is all crumbled (consequence). Here, the acts of wrapping the cake in a leaf and carrying the cake underneath the arm may have physically resulted in the cake crumbling.

In other stories, however, the relationship may be less direct. The attempt may set up the necessary preconditions, but not directly cause the consequence. As an illustration, consider a fox who wanted to catch a chicken for supper (internal response goal). The fox went to a henhouse (attempt), set a trap for the chicken (attempt), and then waited for the chicken to fall into the trap (attempt). Independent of what happened at the end of the story, the fox's attempt did not directly *cause* the consequence; rather, it established the preconditions for the occurrence of the consequence. Although there are variations in the relations linking the attempt and consequence, the organization of story events is, for the most part, assumed to be causally constrained. As a result of the causal chaining, certain types of information must be included in a story and must occur in a temporal sequence that corresponds to the real-time order of events.

It should be emphasized that this description of story structure refers to the reader's or listener's story knowledge and not to the structure of stories that exist in texts. This point is important because the structure of texts may not correspond to the proposed internal organization of story knowledge. For example, internal responses and reactions are often deleted from the text structure of an episode and must be inferred. At other times, the text begins with the character's internal response and may not include an initiating event. We assume, however, that although these categories are omitted from the text structure, they are inferred and are included in the underlying representation of the story in memory.

From the previous description of story schema, it is evident that many assumptions are being made about the expectations comprehenders have acquired about the causal and temporal organization of stories. Both Mandler and Johnson (1977) and Stein and Glenn (1979) have offered a set of specific predictions concerning the comprehension of texts that conform to or violate a comprehender's knowledge of stories.

One hypothesis concerns the way in which a subject would spontaneously generate or spontaneously organize a story given all the necessary components, with the exception of the correct temporal sequence. If subjects have acquired a story schema as described in the grammars, then the order of events in a story should directly correspond to the canonical sequence described in the grammars. All subjects should attempt to follow a real-time order in their construction of a good story.

Stein and Nezworski (1978) have offered support for this hypothesis when adult memory for disorganized stories was examined. In their study, adults heard stories containing a random order of events, originally taken from a story conforming to the canonical structure proposed in the grammars. Subjects were given one of two sets of directions: either they were asked to recall the disorganized text in an order conforming to their idea of a good story, or they were asked to recall the text in the exact order as they heard the story (e.g., in the disorganized order). Adults who attempted to make a good story, while recalling the text, ordered their statements in almost an exact correspondence with the predicted canonical sequence. Thus, following the real-time order of event sequences was a primary consideration for adults telling their version of a "good" story.

Those adults who were asked to maintain the exact order of randomly ordered stories could not do so. Instead, they recalled a sequence of events that corresponded more to the canonical order described in the grammar than to the randomly ordered text sequence actually heard. These results suggest strong support for the hypothesis that prior knowledge of story structure greatly influences memory for stories, even under conditions where a deliberate attempt is made to retain a "verbatim" account of incoming information.

Our next question concerned the development of schematic knowledge. If young elementary school children were asked to perform on a similar task, would they order their stories in a similar fashion to the adults tested by Stein and Nezworski (1978)? What we are asking is whether elementary school children have acquired enough knowledge about stories to have developed a set of expectations conforming to the descriptions provided in the recent grammars.

From several recent studies (Day, Stein, & Trabasso, 1979; Mandler & Johnson, 1977; Stein & Glenn, 1979), we know that even children as young as 4 years of age have little difficulty recalling stories in the exact order of the text sequence, provided that the sequence corresponds to the canonical form outlined in the grammars. These data contradict Piaget's (1923/1960) statements that preoperational children do not have the skill or capacity to make use of causal relationships or to maintain the correct temporal order of text information. In fact, in an effort to understand why Piaget made these statements about the discourse skills of young children, Stein and Trabasso (1981) reanalyzed Piaget's (1923/1960) data and found very few ordering errors in his subjects' recall of folktales! Thus, we know that seven year olds have sufficient skill and knowledge of story structures to be able to recall a sequence of causally related events in the correct temporal order.

The question of concern, however, was whether young elementary school children could use their knowledge of temporal and causal constraints among story events to construct or generate their own stories. Performance on generation tasks requires a somewhat different type of knowledge than performance on recall tasks. During construction or generation tasks, children are not given an organized structure of events. They must create the structure. The use of generation tasks provides an excellent mechanism for investigating whether children have developed a stable and fully elaborated concept of a story. Young children could easily understand that some stories must have temporal and causal relations connecting the events, but that not all stories have to incorporate this feature.

In order to determine whether elementary school children had acquired the necessary knowledge and ordering skills to *construct* story sequences, we carried out two different experiments. In the first one, children were given 12 single events in a randomized order. If these events were properly rearranged, a story conforming to the canonical order would emerge. Children from the second and sixth grades were asked to rearrange the events so that the emerging sequence corresponded to their notion of a good story.

In our second experiment, children were given the setting components of a story, which included the introduction of a progatonist and a description of the physical location in which the protagonist lived. Children were then asked to generate a complete story about the protagonist, making sure that the resulting sequence conformed to their notion of a ''good'' story.

Our expectations concerning the results of the studies were as follows: If children have acquired expectations about the structures of stories as described in the grammars, then the order of events in the stories constructed and generated should conform to the sequence of a canonically organized story; if, however, children's concepts of a story are braoder than originally proposed (e.g., where their belief is that not all story sequences *have* to include temporal and/or causal links among events), then we should not expect all sequences to conform to the canonical version of a story.

It should be noted that in the description of a story schema, both Johnson and Mandler (1980) and Stein (1979) argue that there are certain types of events in the story that may be inverted. The primary type of inversion that is permissible is one that interchanges the order of the character's overt attempt with the character's previous goal statement. For example, if the canonical form of a story is:

Albert wanted to eat the worm for dinner	(IR)
so he swam very close to the worm	(A)
and then bit into him.	(A)

Then, an acceptable order would also be:

So he swam very close to the worm	(A)
and then bit into him because	(A)
he wanted to eat the worm for dinner.	(IR)

Stein (1979) also suggests a second permissible inversion: a reordering of the consequence and reaction. She states, however, that the inversion of these two categories will occur most often when the reaction category contains information relating to the internal state of a protagonist rather than to the further implications of achieving the character's goal. Thus, if children are presented with the following statements,

Suddenly, Albert was pulled through the water into a boat.	(C)
He had been caught by a fisherman.	(C)
Albert felt sad.	(R)
He wished he had been more careful.	(R)

it would be permissible to reorder the story in the following fashion:

Albert felt very sad.	(R)
He wished he had been more careful because	(R)
he had been pulled through the water into a boat	(C)
and had been caught by a fisherman.	(C)

If, however, the story ends in the following fashion,

Suddenly, Albert was pulled through the water into a boat.	(C)
He had been caught by a fisherman.	(C)
The fisherman wrapped Albert up	(R)
and had an excellent dinner that evening.	(R)

it would not be permissible to reorder the occurrence of the consequence and reaction categories.

Comparing the frequency of temporal inversions in a story construction and generation, we would expect more inversions to occur in the stories *generated* by children rather than in those reconstructed by children. The primary reason for our hypothesis is that in the story reconstruction tasks, children are constrained by the type of individual events given to them. Although *temporal* markers were included in one version of the story sequences children received, the markers were not of the type that would facilitate cause–effect inversions usually signaled by a *because* marker. Although children could possibly infer the correct temporal marker if they inverted the sentences given to them, this task may be more difficult than ordering the events in the proposed canonical sequence. In the tasks where children had to tell their own stories, inversion should occur more readily because children could add rhetorical connectors whenever they thought it was appropriate.

EXPERIMENT I

Methods

SUBJECTS

Twenty second graders and 20 sixth graders participated in this study. All children attended an upper middle-class school in St. Louis County, Missouri. The age range in second grade was from 7.1 to 8.3, while the age range for sixth graders was from 10.11 to 12.4. All children were reading at grade level or above at the time of this experiment.

MATERIALS

Three different stories were constructed: the Albert story, the Melvin story, and the fox story. Two versions were constructed for each story. Both versions contained the six basic categories and intercategory relationships required in a one-episode simple story. In one version of each story, there were no temporal connectives or markers included in any of the single statements, and there were no pronominal references used in the beginning of each statement. All verbs used were in the past tense. Thus, any cues, other than the semantic content of individual events, were removed. Table 9.2 contains the version of the Albert story where all rhetorical and beginning pronominal references were removed. This version is referred to as the *markers deleted* version.

In the second version of each story, the sequence of events occurred in the standard fashion, similar to the stories in a basal reading textbook. The second half of Table 9.1 contains a version of the *standard* Albert story where both rhetorical markers and beginning pronominal references were included. Each story version was typed in capital letters on blank white sheets. The sheets were then cut into 12 strips so that each story statement was on an individual strip of

TABLE 9.2
An Example of a Story Sequence with the Temporal Markers and Beginning Pronominal References Deleted

Albert was a big grey fish.
Albert lived in a huge icy pond.
Albert was swimming around the pond.
Albert spotted a big juicy worm on top of the water.
Albert knew how delicious worms tasted.
Albert wanted to have a worm for dinner.
Albert swam very close to the worm.
Albert bit into the worm.
Albert was pulled through the water into a boat.
Albert was caught by a fisherman.
Albert felt very sad.
Albert wished he had been more careful.

paper. There were 12 single events per story version and therefore 12 strips to each version.

DESIGN AND PROCEDURE

Children in each age group were divided randomly into two groups of 10 each. The first group of children participated in the markers deleted condition. These children received stories with all rhetorical and beginning pronominal information deleted. The second group of children participated in the standard story condition. These children received the standard stories with all rhetorical and pronominal information present.

Each child was tested individually and was asked to construct sequences for three stories. The order of story presentation was randomized within each group. Each child was presented with 12 lines from a story that were randomly distributed on a piece of white cardboard. The experimenter read each line to the child, and then had the child *read back* each line to insure that there were no comprehension difficulties. Afterward, the child was asked to order the items so that the sequence conformed to the child's concept of a good story. After the child ordered the events, the experimenter recorded the order. The experimenter and child then reread the sequence, after which the experimenter gave the child a chance to change the order of any events the child thought were inappropriate. Because there were so few changes in the event order (1%), the second order of events was used to determine the child's temporal sequencing strategy.

Results

The first analysis carried out on the data concerned the order in which children sequenced the events in their stories. To determine how closely the constructed sequences corresponded to the proposed canonical order, a Kendall's Tau rank order correlation was computed for each subject. The results from both conditions are presented in Table 9.3. As the data indicate, the mean correlation in each condition shows a higher correspondence between the subject's order and the canonical sequence than would be expected by chance. Thus children do exhibit knowledge of story sequences similar to that proposed in the grammars.

The results from an analysis of variance on the Tau scores, however, showed significant development and story condition differences. In both story conditions, sixth graders constructed sequences that more closely resembled the canonical form of a story than did second graders ($F_{(1,38)} = 18.11$, $p < .01$). Thus, although, at first glance, second graders have some knowledge of story structure, their knowledge appears to be less complete. However, the addition of temporal markers significantly increased the probability of both second and sixth graders reconstructing canonically organized sequences ($F_{(1,38)} = 12.11$, $p < .05$). In order to explore more fully the developmental and story condition differences influencing reconstruction accuracy, an analysis was carried out on the type of inversions occurring in the story sequences.

In all conditions, two predominant types of inversions occurred: (a) alternative orderings of internal response statements; and (b) alternative orderings of reaction statements. Children placed the internal response statements in two different locations in the sequence: either before the initiating event or after the attempt statements. The more frequent inversion of the internal response was with the initiating event. This type of inversion occurred in over 50% of all stories, whereas the attempt–internal response inversion occurred in only 15% of all stories.

The way in which the stories were written, however, may have caused the type of internal response inversions found in children's reconstructions. For example, in the standard version of the Melvin story, the most frequent ordering of events was:

Melvin lived in a big red barn.	(S)
Melvin became very hungry.	(IR)
Melvin wanted to eat just a little bit of cereal.	(IR)

TABLE 9.3
Mean Kendall's Tau Correlation for Sequence Ordering in the
Standard Story and Markers Deleted Conditions

	Grade	
	2	4
Standard	.68	.94
Markers deleted	.47	.80

> *Melvin found a big box of Rice Crispies underneath some hay.*   (IE)
> *Melvin saw a small hole in the cereal box.*   (IE)

In this sequence of events, it is highly likely that children inferred that Melvin's hunger and desire for cereal *caused* him to seek out some food. In this case, the ordering of events should *not* be considered an inversion. Rather, the ambiguity of meaning contained in the individual story statements could give rise to more than one ordering corresponding to a real-time order of events.

Comparing the frequency of the internal response–initiating event inversion errors in the standard and markers deleted story condition, where the proposed canonical order in the Melvin story read,

> *Melvin found a big box of Rice Crispies underneath some hay.*   (IE)
> *Melvin saw a small hole in the cereal box.*   (IE)
> *Melvin became very hungry.*   (IR)
> *Melvin wanted to eat a little bit of cereal.*   (IR)

80% of all subjects inverted at least *one* internal response statement with one initiating event. In the standard condition, where the four lines read,

> *One day, Melvin found a big box of Rice Crispies underneath some hay.* (IE)
> *Then Melvin saw a hole in the cereal box.*   (IE)
> *Melvin became very hungry.*   (IR)
> *He wanted to eat just a little bit of cereal.*   (IR)

the number of internal response–initiating event inversions dropped to 30%. Thus, the presence of markers (beginning pronominal references) and definite articles clearly constrained the sequencing of events so that the resulting order corresponded more closely to the canonical order.

In an examination of the internal response–attempt inversions, the frequency of reorderings did not vary as a function of the story condition. The fact that these inversions occurred infrequently (15%), and the fact that internal responses were usually placed after *both* attempt statements in the story, may indicate that these reorderings are true inversions where the child is inferring a *because* relation to link the attempt with the internal response.

The consequence–reaction inversions occurred in approximately 40% of all story reconstructions and did not vary as a function of the story sequence. Most inversions resembled cause–effect reversals where the children inferred the appropriate causal connection between two events. The most common inversion in the Melvin story was:

> *Melvin had eaten every bit of the Rice Crispies.*   (C)
> *Melvin felt very sad.*   (R)
> *Melvin had become very fat.*   (C)
> *Melvin knew he shouldn't have done that.*   (R)

Similar types of inversions occurred in the other two stories, with the most frequent inversion being one of an emotional state with an action or event statement. Thus, it appears that the majority of inversions, even under constrained conditions, are similar to those predicted by Johnson and Mandler (1980) and Stein (1979).

An examination of inversions in the markers deleted condition, however, indicates a greater variation in reorderings than would be predicted by either of the above investigators. After analyzing these additional inversions, the reason for the greater variation became apparent. Most of these were reorderings of information *within* a category, where the absence of temporal markers and other cohesive devices lessened the certainty by which the exact temporal and causal constraings could be inferred. As an example, take the statements in the setting category of the Melvin story. In the standard version of this story, the setting statements are *not* temporally related to one another. However, with the addition of temporal markers and a specific syntactic form signifying the introduction of a protagonist, the order of the two sentences becomes extremely constrained so that no subjects inverted the following statements:

> *Once upon a time there was a skinny little mouse named Melvin.*
> *Melvin lived in a big red barn.*

However, when the temporal markers and cohesive devices were deleted, so that subjects were presented with the statements,

> *Melvin was a skinny little mouse.*
> *Melvin lived in a big red barn.*

there was nothing to prevent subjects from inverting these statements. In fact, many subjects did reverse the order of setting statements. Similar types of inversions occurred in the reaction category, with emotional states being interchanged with cognitions (e.g., *Melvin felt sad; Melvin knew he shouldn't have done that*). Thus, the greater increase in inversion errors in the markers deleted condition could be accounted for by the lack of specific event information pertaining to a definite temporal or causal ordering os tatements.

As we mentioned earlier, even when temporal markers, pronominal references, and definite articles are included in single statements, there are still many instances where the information in the statement is not specific enough to ensure that it will be sequenced in the particular order chosen by the experimenter. Many of the alternative orderings were judged by us to be good sequences, reflecting the real-time order of events.

Many of the inversions found in the second-grade data, however, could not be identified as alternative real-time orders. These inversions were indicative of errors in logical reconstruction. In some of the protocols, there were strings of three, four, or five events that were clearly put together with a coherent theme in mind. Then, the remainder of statements were just tacked on in almost any order. Thus, some of the second graders were not capable of completing the entire task. It should be noted, however, that there was great individual variation in the second-grade performance, with some Tau scores being as low as .15 or .20 while others were as high as .80 and .85.

There are several reasons why the second graders might have experienced difficulty with this task. First, the memory demands involved in constructing such a sequence may be too great for some children. Some second graders may not be able to attend to all the various cues that are necessary to construct a full canonical sequence. Under conditions where working memory is taxed. young children may operate upon a smaller number of units in the given sequence and infer the appropriate logical relations only within the smaller set of events. The resulting sequence would contain many more inversions, even though most of the events were arranged into some type of temporal–causal relationship.

An excellent example of this type of grouping strategy can be found in the protocol of one 7-year-old who chose to make two fairly well structured episodes out of the 12 events. The sequence read:

Melvin was a skinny little mouse.	(S)
Melvin lived in a big red barn.	(S)
Melvin saw the small hole in the cereal box.	(IE)
Melvin wanted to eat just a little bit of cereal.	(IR)
Melvin found the big box of Rice Crispies underneath some hay.	(IE)
Melvin ate up every bit of the Rice Crispies.	(C)
Melvin became very hungry.	(IR)
Melvin slipped through the small hole in the box.	(A)
Melvin filled up his bowl with cereal.	(A)
Melvin grew very fat.	(C)
Melvin knew he had eaten too much.	(R)
Melvin felt very sad.	(R)

In this story, Melvin eats the Rice Crispies *twice*. Each episode is almost fully intact. This type of strategy accounted for 5–10% of the sequence orders found in the second-grade data.

The other strategy frequently used was to initially attend to the logical features inherent in the event relationship and then to somewhat randomly sequence the remaining events. For example, the following second-grade protocol has some elements of a logical sequence, but also many of the events are randomly placed:

Melvin lived in a big red barn.	(S)
Melvin was a skinny little mouse.	(S)
Melvin became very hungry.	(IR)

Melvin found a big box of cereal.   (IE)
Melvin knew he had eaten too much.   (R)
Melvin wanted to eat just a little big of cereal.   (IR)
Melvin filled up his bowl with cereal.   (A)
Melvin slipped throug the small hole in the box.   (A)
Melvin saw a small hole in the box.   (IE)
Melvin felt very sad.   (R)
Melvin grew very fat.   (C)
Melvin ate up every bit of the Rice Crispies.   (C)

From an examination of the second-grade protocols, it is evident that these children have some idea about the importance of logical relationships in ordering story events. However, it is still unclear as to the exact locus of their difficulties. Are memory difficulties the primary source of their inversion errors or are the difficulties more indicative of a knowledge they have about structure? It could be that young elementary school children have not developed enough of a specific set of expectations about stories so that they would order *all* events in the prescribed canonical sequence.

In order to test this notion, Experiment II was conducted. In this study, children were asked to tell their own version of a good story. Even very young children (Botvin & Sutton-Smith, 1977; Pitcher & Prelinger, 1963) have been heard to tell their own stories, drawing on their repertoire of important or imaginary everyday happenings. By allowing children to freely structure all of the output, we can begin to decipher their concept of a story, not only in terms of the expectations they have acquired about the temporal order of events in a story, but also in regard to the type of information that should occur in a story episode, and how this category information should be ordered.

EXPERIMENT II

Method

SUBJECTS

The subjects participating in this study were 54 children from each of three grades: kindergarten, third, and sixth grades. Half of the children in each grade level were from an upper middle-class school in St. Louis County, Missouri, and half were from an upper middle-class school in Pittsburgh, Pennsylvania. The mean ages at each grade level were 5.4, 8.6, and 11.5, respectively.

MATERIALS

Three stems were constructed so that the setting category of information was incorporated into each stem. Two types of information were included: the protagonist introduction and a description of the social or physical context that should influence the remainder of the story. The three stems were:

ALICE

Once there was a girl named Alice
who lived in a house near the ocean.

FOX

Once there was a big grey fox
who lived in a cave near the forest.

ALAN

Once there was a boy named Alan
who had many different toys.

PROCEDURE

Each of the 18 children at a grade level were tested individually. When the children felt comfortable with the experimenter, they were then told that they would be given the very beginning of a story. Their task was to take the beginning and construct a full-blown story that would have everything in it that a good story should. Thus, their task was to construct a story from the stems that would match their definition of a good story. Each child was given three stems, in a randomized order, and asked to complete a good story for each stem.

Results

The first analysis concerned the frequency with which children told stories that contained the basic episodic motive–resolution sequence described in the grammars. The results show that at the kindergarten level, 50% of the children told at least two out of three stories with a basic episodic structure; at third grade, 72% of the children's stories met this criterion; and at sixth grade, 78% of all stories were episodically organized. Although there appears to be a developmental progression in the number of stories that were episodically structured, the differences between grade levels were not found to be significant.

The major conclusion to be drawn from these data, however, is that elementary school children have a concept of a story that is more broadly based than the descriptions in the grammars would permit. Some children tell stories that do not contain all of the components of an episode or a problem-solving sequence. The nonepisodic stories could be classified into three major categories:

1. *A descriptive sequence story,* in which states, traits and actions of a pro-tagonist are included, with no temporal constraints on the sequence of events produced. These sequences were more like elaborated setting state-ments rather than episodic sequences.
2. *An action sequence story,* corresponding to Schank and Abelson's (1977) notion of a script. Here, the stories contained the habitual everyday actions of a protagonist, temporally arranged in order of occurrence, usually from the beginning of a day to the end. Despite the temporality, there were not necessarily any direct causal connections between the events, and there was not a discernible motive–resolution sequence with a beginning and an end.
3. *A reactive sequence story,* where there was a beginning and an end, with the events causally related to each other. In this type of story sequence, however, the protagonist never developed a goal or a plan because of external circumstances. The protagonist's well-being was totally dependent on environmental circumstances or actions of other people. Thus the core of a story, the goal or plan, was deleted.

Although it is evident that some children did not generate episodically struc-tured sequences as stories, the majority of children at each grade level did tell stories that could be examined with respect to the temporal relations among events and the type of information that is always included in a story. Also, even those stories not containing an episodic structure (the action and reactive se-quences) could still be subjected to a temporal ordering analysis to examine whether or not real-time order was followed.

In order to determine the types of ordering strategies used, we first examined all of the episodically structured stories as to the proportion of events that were inverted in all of the story sequences. These data were collapsed across grade level because there were no developmental differences in frequency of inver-sions. The mean proportion of inversions occurring in all stories was 6%. Thus, when children as young as five tell their own stories, they do so in an order corresponding to real-time order. Contrary to Piaget (1923/1960) or Fraisse (1963), young children have little difficulty adhering to a logical sequence of events.

Of all the inversions made, 90% were inversions between statements from different categories. Almost all of the inversions (94%) were both tem-orally and causally constrained rather than just temporally constrained. For example, the two inverted sentences could be linked by a *cause* relationship rather than just a *then* relationship (e.g., *He went into the forest* after *he found some berries*). Additionally, the majority of the inversions were spontaneously marked. The probability of marking the inversion, however, increased significantly as a function of age. Kindergarten children marked 73% of their inversions, whereas third graders marked 90% of theirs, and sixth graders marked 98% of theirs. So, although there were no developmental differences in the number of inversions made during storytelling, the incidence of *marking* these inversions changed as a function of age.

When the pattern of inversions was analyzed, 69% of all inversions were attempt-goal inversions, supporting the hypotheses offered by Johnson and Mandler (1980) and Stein (1979). Reaction–consequence inversions accounted for 12% of the reorderings. A few of the inversions were goal–initiating event reorderings; however, this type of inversion accounted for at most 4% of all intercategory inversions—nowhere near the frequency found in the reconstruction tasks.

A fourth but not very frequent type of inversion was found at the end of some stories—a consequence–setting was included at the end of an episode. This type of inversion occurred primarily when the protagonist *did not* sttain the desired goal. If a negative ending occurred, the storyteller would often include a *reason* for the goal failure, often referring to a physical or mental state of the protagonist as the reason for goal failure. For example, if the fox were pursuing a rabbit and missed catching the rabbit, children would often state:

> But the rabbit got away because the fox just wasn't clever enough.

For the class of nonepisodically structured stories, an analysis was carried out on those sequences that were judged to have temporal (an action sequence) or both temporal and causal relations (a reactive sequence) connecting the story events. The incidence of temporal inversions in these types of stories was even lower than the number of inversions occurring in episodically structured sequences. Only 1% of all lines were inverted, with most of the inversions being of a similar type to the consequence–setting inversions in episodic stories. For example, in generating an action sequence story where the primary events concerned the normal stereotypical everyday patterns of a protagonist, sometimes children would say:

> Alan played with his trucks every day because he really liked them.
> So he would get out all of his toys, then he would line them up.
> (etc.)

In this story, the inversion included an action with an internal affective state, where the affective state was given as an explanation for the action. Other than this type of inversion, the remainder of the sequences followed the real-time order of events.

The second type of analysis carried out on the generation data focused on determining whether children included in their stories the specific types of category information proposed in the grammars. From the description of an episode, it is evident that not only does the sequence of events follow a real-time order, but also that certain types of information should always be included in a story. The normal episodic sequence should be:

Setting

Initiating event

Internal response

Attempt

Consequence

Reaction

Three exceptions to this strict sequence have been proposed. Stein and Glenn (1979) and Stein (1979) have argued that the basic components of a story sequence are (*a*) events from which the planful nature of the protagonist's actions can be inferred; (*b*) the overt action carried out in the service of the goal; and (*c*) the outcome, pertaining to whether or not the goal has been achieved. If the structure of an episode is reviewed, it becomes evident that not all five episodic categories (the setting is not considered part of the episode) are necessary to convey this basic information. Specifically, there are times when either the initiating event, the internal response, or the reaction categories can be deleted while the story sequence maintains its basic cohesive structure.

Johnson and Mandler (1980) attempted to specify those conditions under which a particular category can be deleted. These investigators argue that initiating events (beginnings) can be deleted under two conditions:

1. The initiating event may be deleted in the first episode of a story, when the protagonist's internal response is not linked to any observable specific external event. They cite Propp (1958), who gives examples of stories beginning with the perceptions of a "lack" state, whereupon the protagonist sets out to achieve a desired goal.
2. The initiating event may be deleted when the content of such a category would be the perception or appraisal of the protagonist concerning events that have occurred in previous episodes.

The explanation for these deletions is based primarily on principles of predictability and inferability. What is being suggested here is that in many stories the reader could easily predict a plausible motive from the remainder of the story events so that a coherent representation of a story could be constructed.

Similar arguments underlie the permissibility of deleting the internal response and the reaction categories. Both Johnson and Mandler (1980) and Stein (1979) argue that internal responses can be deleted if an intiating event is present in an episode. On the surface, allowing the deletion of the internal response is somewhat paradoxical because the *goal* that is included in the internal response is hypothesized to be one of the more important pieces of information in a story. The number and type of goals motivated by an initiating event, however, are quite limited (Heider, 1958). The nature of human motivation and human interaction makes the goals quite clear if access is given to the event that *motivated* the goal and the action that followed the goal.

Grounds for the deletion of the reaction are similar to those proposed for the deletion of an internal response. However, the permissibility of deleting the reaction information is constrained by other factors in addition to the inferability of this information. Johnson and Mandler (1980) argue that the reaction can only be deleted if another episode follows the one where no reaction was included. Thus, if a child were telling a one-episode story, according to Johnson and Mandler (1980), the reaction category (equivalent to their Ending) would have to be included. However, if a two-eipsode story were being told, the reaction could be omitted from the first episode, but not from the second. Table 9.4 summarizes the types of permissible subsequent category responses that may follow each episodic category. Table 9.5 contains the data illustrating the type of information that followed each one of the episodic categories.

The responses following the setting category were predominantly initiating event statements. Over three-fourths of the kindergarten and third grade stories and 91% of the sixth-grade stories included initiating events. Although there was an increase in the inclusion of initiating events as a function of age, the differences were not significant ($z < 1.96$; $p > .05$). The data suggest that although it might be permissible to delete the initiating event in telling a story, the great majority of children do *not* exclude this information.

TABLE 9.4
Predictions about the Types of Permissible Story Categories that May Occur after Each Specific Category in a Story Sequence

Stimulus category	Responses
1. Setting	Initiating event
	Internal response
2. Initiating event	Internal response
	Attempt
3. Internal response	Attempt
4. Attempt	Consequence
5. Consequence	Reaction
	Initiating event (second episode)
	Internal response (second episode)

TABLE 9.5
Probability of Particular Category Responses to Each Stimulus Category in Stories Generated by Children

Stimulus category	Category responses	Age group		
		K	3	5
Setting	Initiating event	.78	.77	.91
	Internal response	.22	.23	.08
Initiating event	Internal response	.56	.73	.53
	Attempt	.44	.25	.40
	Consequence	.00	.02	.07
Internal response	Attempt[a]	.68	.85	.88
	Consequence	.32	.16	.12
Attempt	No Subsequent category	.10	.03	.04
	Consequence	.90	.97	.96
Consequence	No Subsequent category[a]	.30	.15	.08
	Reaction	.43	.60	.62
	Initiating event	.15	.10	.10
	Internal response	.12	.15	.20

[a] Denotes that K proportion differed from at least one of the other age groups, $p < .05$ by the binomial test.

Our analysis of the semantic content of stories suggests that children most often use the initiating event as a thematic anchor point that then serves to initiate the goal. The stories where the initiating event was not included almost always concerned the fox stem, where many children stated that the fox was going to catch something to eat. The preponderance of this theme for the fox stem made us aware that foxes are strongly associated with hunting and capturing both animals and humans. Because many children told stories reminiscent of *Little Red Riding Hood* or the *Three Little Pigs,* we suspect that the fox was closely associated with the wolf character who appears in many children's stories.

Information generated after an initiating event was of two types: internal response and attempt information. It is clear from the data that children more often delete internal response information than initiating event statements. Internal responses, especially goals, are likely to be more inferable than initiating events simply because the goal of the protagonist can be inferred from almost any event in the story sequence (see Nezworski, Stein & Trabasso, 1979; or Stein & Trabasso, 1981, for an illustration of this phenomenon). The data are strikingly similar to the recall data from several studies (Mandler & Johnson, 1977; Stein, 1979; Stein & Glenn, 1979), where the internal response information is frequently deleted in recall even though this information is presented in the original text.

The subsequent responses to the internal response category are interesting because they include the first set of developmental differences in the generation data. An average of 86% of the third- and sixth-grade stories always included an attempt after an internal response statement. However, only 68% of the kindergarten children's stories included this category of response.

Initially, it may appear that another deletion rule for younger children is necessary. However, from a closer examination of the data, we think an additional rule is unnecessary. If the absolute frequency of including an attempt is calculated for kindergarten children, 80% of all their stories contain attempt formation (this figure includes stories with the following sequences: (a) IE–IR–AT, (b) IE–AT, (c) IR–AT). Secondly, our examination of stories where the attempt was deleted showed that some of these stories had prolonged *plans*, where the protagonist was mapping out just what he was going to do. Much of this information normally appears in the attempt category. It seemed that some kindergarten children were planning out loud, and once they finished the plan they saw no cause to reiterate the same events in the attempt category. Some of the kindergarten children, however, simply deleted the attempt, implying that they either could not generate an appropriate attempt or that the attempt could easily be inferred.

The overwhelming majority of events occurring after the attempt category could be reliably classified as consequence statements. There were no developmental differences in the frequency with which these statements were included in an episode.

Statements occurring after the consequence could be classified primarily in the reaction category; however, the overall probability of including a reaction at the end of an episode increased significantly as a function of age. Kindergarten children were almost as likely to delete a reaction as they were to include it in their stories. This was true for one-episode stories as well as for multiple-episode stories. Older children were more likely to include the reaction category. However, even with the significant increase of the inclusion of reaction information, nearly 40% of the children in the third and sixth grades did not include this information in their stories. This finding suggests that the reaction can be deleted from one-episode stories whether or not a second episode follows.

GENERAL DISCUSSION AND CONCLUSIONS

Children's Sequencing Skills on Reconstruction and Generation Tasks

The results from these studies illustrated how the current story grammars can be used as a powerful analytic technique to assess the type and degree of story knowledge that has been acquired by young children in elementary school. It was our intention to examine whether children as young as 5 have acquired a concept of a story that is reflected in the current grammatical descriptions. Our first task required that children make good stories from randomly ordered arrays of events, which, when organized properly, would correspond to a canonically structured story. Our results showed that both second and sixth graders' sequences conformed more to the canonical order than would be expected by chance. There were differences in performance, however, due to both the type of materials presented and the age of the children. When children were presented with 12 story events that contained no temporal markers, no beginning pronominal references, and no definite articles, they constructed sequences that corresponded less closely with the canonical order than when presented with events that contained all of this information.

These results were attributed to the fact that a single event, without the cohesive markers included, can serve more than one categorical function in a story. A given action can sometimes be classified either as an initiating event, as an attempt, or sometimes as a consequence, depending upon other events in the story. Many of the inversions in the children's ordering of events were considered to be good alternative real-time orders of events. The data showed the importance of including rhetorical markers in a text during reading to lessen the ambiguity of the position of an event in a story sequence.

Developmental differences in the ability to construct canonical sequences, however, could not be ignored. Even when story events contained cohesive markers, sixth-grade children constructed story sequences that conformed more to the canonical order than did second graders. Several reasons for these differences were considered, many of which were thrown out. For example, the possibility that children do not have the cognitive skills to order events in a logical sequence was not considered to be a viable explanation. We know from recall studies that when children hear stories presented in a canonical order, even 4-year-olds retell the story in almost a perfect canonical form (Day, Stein & Trabasso, 1979).

The more telling proof that children have these logical skills comes from studies where children are given stories that *violate* a canonical form and are asked to recall the noncanonical form exactly as they had heard it. Data from our laboratory (Day, Stein & Trabasso, 1979; Stein & Glenn, 1978) and from other investigators (Brown, 1976; Mandler, 1978; McClure, Mason & Barnitz, 1980) have indicated that children cannot recall or reconstruct noncanonical stories with a high degree of accuracy. Instead, what they do is transform the noncanonical input so that it corresponds almost identically to a canonically organized story. Younger children have been shown to be even more dependent on the canonical form and, therefore, less able than adults to remember poorly formed stories relative to well-formed stories (Day, Stein & Trabasso, 1979; Mandler, 1978; Mandler & DeForest, 1979).

A second explanation was considered. It was proposed that ordering a 12-line sequence of story events might overtax the working memory of young elementary school children. In order to perform this task successfully, children must continually monitor the type of relations that may link each event to a number of other events. The systematic search necessary for success may be too difficult for very young children to sustain. The error data from the reconstruction task offered support for this hypothesis. Second-grade children would often logically order part of their sequence and then randomly order the remaining events, almost as if the children had grown tired and could not organize the remainder of the event sequence. Additionally, second graders sometimes ordered the 12 events into smaller shunks, constructing two full episodes from the 12 lines rather than one episode, suggesting that second graders may have been able to use only one line in each category before proceeding on to the next category in an episode.

Alternatively, second-grade children may not know as much as older children about the possible order and placement of some events in the sequence. The failure to order some of the events may have been caused more by a lack of real-world knowledge about the specific theme and content rather than by the failure to use a more systematic scanning strategy during reconstruction.

The data from the present set of experiments is not conclusive enough to eliminate either an "immature" strategy hypothesis or a lack of relevant real-world knowledge hypothesis. It should be noted, however, that knowledge of the normal or usual preconditions and events occurring in story sequences significantly increases as a function of development (Stein & Trabasso, 1981). The addition of critical real-world knowledge about the probability of event occurrence may rapidly facilitate young children's skills at constructing canonically organized sequences. If this were the case, immature scanning strategies would be a function of the amount of knowledge children had acquired about an event sequence.

An interesting finding in both the reconstruction and generation studies was that children do make systematic inversions in event locations where the type of inversions almost always corresponded to the permissible temporal inversions set forth by Johnson and Mandler (1980) and Stein (1979). A major question concerns the function of these inversions given that they *do* occur in a generated or reconstructed story. In many literary stories and films, inversions serve the purpose of an explanatory device when the author has consciously misled the reader at the beginning of a story. Many authors will allow a reader to expect one set of events when, in reality, a second set of events occurs. Then the author must explain why these actions occurred instead of the expected actions. Sometimes the ending of a story occurs first in an episode, encouraging the reader to participate in the problem-solving process to figure out exactly how the outcome occurred.

It would illustrate fairly sophisticated storytelling strategies if this type of planfulness were evident in children, but there is a more likely reason for the inversions. Story generation is a demanding task, often requiring children to integrate information in a novel way. Because the planning process is quite "effortful," children are often not aware of the ambiguity in what they have generated until they actually have a chance to review what they have said. They then realize that their story lacks "explanatory power" and insert inversions so that their tale is more comprehensible.

The differences between this strategy and one employed by more mature authors are those of knowledge and planfulness. The function of children's inversions appears to be explanatory in nature; children in the elementary years do not often attempt to deceive their audience. (At least this element appears to be absent during the oral generation of stories.) As children reach the age of 10 or 11, however, they may become much more aware of the structure of stories (Stein & Trabasso, 1981) and more sensitive to the effects of different text variations on the listener. In time and with experience with texts, children may learn to plan stories with structures that differ somewhat from the canonical form.

Expectations about Story Categories and Story Structure

In addition to examining children's ordering strategies in the construction and generation of story texts, we examined their knowledge about the higher order structures occurring in stories. By asking children to generate their own "good" stories, we could determine whether or not children perceived all stories to be episodically structured and, if so, what types of information they perceived to be necessary to include in the structure of an episode.

Our data showed that the majority of children in kindergarten through fifth grade generated stories with episodic structures, indicating validity for the descriptions in the grammar. However, the results also showed that "stories" were generated that were not episodically based, that did not contain all of the necessary features of a canonical story. These data suggest that children have a concept of a story that is more broadly based than the description offered in the grammars. If this were the case, children should not include as many features in their definition of a story as compared to the grammatical description. Thus, many more types of texts should be labeled as stories than originally proposed.

Data from our laboratory (Stein & Trabasso, 1981) support this contention. When second-grade children were asked to decide whether or not different passages could be defined as stories, children judged nonepisodically structured sequences to be considered stories. Thus, the results from our generation task were not simply due to a production deficiency in children's generation abilities, where children become overloaded by the memory demands of a task. Second-grade children actually believed these nonepisodically structured sequences to be stories.

Despite the fact that children's concepts of a story are more broadly based, most generated stories were episodically bound. Thus, we evaluated their stories as to the types of category information that were included and thought essential to the concept of a story. Overall, children exhibited a good working knowledge of the types of story categories described in the grammars. Certain types of information, however, were more frequently included than other types of information. Children most frequently included initiating events, attempts, and consequences in their stories, while deleting internal responses and reactions. These generation data correspond almost identically to the pattern of results found in the story recall data (Mandler & Johnson, 1977; Stein, 1979; Stein & Glenn, 1979), suggesting that there are permissible deletions of particular categories both in recall and generation.

Developmental differences did occur in some types of the categorical information included in an episode. Older children were more likely to include attempts and reactions in their stories. The question here is what these differences reflect. In almost all tasks we found that older children have more knowledge of stories—as evidenced in the more elaborated nature of their productions, the ease with which they construct sequences, and the way they manipulate the structure of a text.

While the source of these differences remains elusive, three possibilities exist. Younger children may not have an elaborated concept of a story and, therefore, may not need to include all of the categories outlined in the grammars. This hypothesis can account for some of the developmental differences in generation, especially concerning the necessity of including a reaction or ending category in a story. Telling whether or not a protagonist achieved his or her goal may be enough. Including a moral or broader consequences may only become part of the story concept as children become more aware of the different uses and functions of storytelling. As children learn that stories can be used to teach others the importance of pursuing certain goals, endings may become more important, for this category contains the evaluative part of the narrative.

On the other hand, the developmental differences found in the generation task may simply be due to differences in content knowledge about a particular story theme. Older children may have access to more information concerning plausible attempts, reactions, and so on. The increase in the amount of thematic knowledge may make the storytelling task less difficult, enabling older children to produce a more elaborated story.

A third possibility is that younger children assume that the knowledge of their audience is synonymous with their own knowledge. In this case, when children covertly understood something or make a critical inference, they assume that their audience has done the same. Under these conditions, the storytellers can delete much more information than if they do not make such assumptions.

The source of the developmental differences will probably include some combination of these three explanations. It is not clear from the present data which ones will account for the majority of the variance. It is evident, however, that future work in this area should be directed towards explaining the locus of the differences in understanding.

REFERENCES

Black, J. B., & Bower, G. H. Story understanding as problem solving. *Poetics,* 1980, *9,* 223–250.

Botvin, G. J., & Sutton-Smith, B. The development of structural complexity in children's fantasy narratives. *Developmental Psychology,* 1977, *13,* 377–388.

Brown, A. L. The construction of temporal succession by preoperational children. In A. D. Pick (Ed.), *Minnesota symposium on child psychology* (Vol. 10). Minneapolis: University of Minnesota Press, 1976.

Day, J. Stein, N. L., & Trabasso, T. *A study of inferential comprehension: The use of a story schema to remember pictures.* Paper presented at the meetings of the Society for Research in Child Development, San Francisco, 1979.

Fraisse, P. *The psychology of time.* New York: Harper & Row, 1963.

Heider, F. Consciousness, the perceptual world, and communications with others. In R. Tagiuri & L. Petrullo (Eds.), *Person perception and interpersonal behavior.* Stanford: Stanford University Press, 1958.

Johnson, N. S., & Mandler, J. M. A tale of two structures: Underlying and surface forms in stories. *Poetics,* 1980, *9,* 51–86.

Mandler, J. M. A code in the node: The use of story schema in retrieval. *Discourse Processes,* 1978, *1,* 14–35.

Mandler, J. M., & DeForest, M. Is there more than one way to recall a story? *Child Development,* 1979, *50,* 886–889.

Mandler, J. M., & Johnson, N. S. Rememberance of things parsed: Story structure and recall. *Cognitive Psychology,* 1977, *9,* 111–151.

McClure, E., Mason, J., & Barnitz, G. Story structure and age effects on children's ability to sequence stories. *Discourse Processes,* 1979, *2,* 213–249.

Nezworski, M. T., Stein, N. L., & Trabasso, T. *Story structure vérsus content effects on children's recall of evaluative inferences.* (Tech. Rep. No. 129). Urbana, Ill.: University of Illinois, Center for the Study of Reading, June 1979. (ERIC Document Reproduction Service No. ED 172 187).

Piaget, J. *The language and thought of the child.* London: Routledge & Kegan Paul, 1960. (Originally published, 1923).

Pitcher, E. G., & Prelinger, E. *Children tell stories.* New York: International Universities Press, 1963.

Propp, V. *Morphology of the folktale* (Vol. 10). Bloomington, Ind.: Indiana University Research Center in Anthropology, Folklore, and Linguistics, 1958.

Rumelhart, D. E. Notes on a schema for stories. In D. G. Bobrow & A. Collins (Eds.), *Representation and understanding.* New York: Academic Press, 1975.

Rumelhart, D. E. Understanding and summarizing brief stories. In D. LaBerge & J. Samuels (Eds.), *Basic processes in reading: Perception and comprehension.* Hillsdale, N.J.: Erlbaum, 1977.

Stein, N. L. The comprehension and appreciation of stories: A developmental analysis. In S. Madeja (Ed.), *The arts, cognition, and basic skills.* St. Louis: Cemrel, 1978.

Stein, N. L. How children understand stories. In L. Katz (Ed.), *Current topics in early childhood education* (Vol. 2). Norwood, N.J.: Ablex, 1979.

Stein, N. L., & Glenn, C. G. *The role of temporal organization in story comprehension.* Unpublished manuscript, 1978.

Stein, N. L., & Glenn, C. G. An analysis of story comprehension in elementary school children. In R. O. Freedle (Ed.), *New directions in discourse processing* (Vol. 2) in the series, *Advances in discourse processes.* Norwood, N.J.: Ablex, 1979.

Stein, N. L., & Nezworski, M. T. The effect of organization and instructional set on story memory. *Discourse Processes,* 1978, *1,* 177–193.

Stein, N. L., & Trabasso, T. What's in a story: Critical issues in story comprehension. In R. Glaser (Ed.), *Advances in the psychology of instruction.* Hillsdale, N.J.: Erlbaum, 1981.

Thorndyke, P. W. Cognitive structures in comprehension and memory of narrative discourse. *Cognitive Psychology,* 1977, *9,* 77–110.

Thorndyke, P. W., & Yekovitch, F. R. A critique of schemata as a theory of human story memory. *Poetics,* 1980, *9,* 23–50.

Subject Index